LOW WATER

A Further 'Final' Fishy Tale

Dedication

This book is dedicated to my Dad, Frederick William Normandale, 1922-2016

During the war, Dad served on Merchant ships in Atlantic convoys then onboard armed trawlers in the Mediterranean with the Royal Naval Patrol Service. Based in Malta, he saw action at the North African and Italian landings. After the war he returned home to fish in steam trawlers, herring drifters, ring-netters, keelboats and cobles.

He was a loving Father, Fisherman, Teacher, Example, a constant source of encouragement and an unfailing supporter throughout my fishing career.

Absent friends!!

* * *

This is another volume I never thought I'd write. Having spent my working days at sea and recording the way of life, I realised that though I was now ashore, there were still tales to tell and memories of my later days of tall ship sailing to share.

LOW WATER

A Further 'Final' Fishy Tale

FRED NORMANDALE

ISBN 978-0-9568558-2-4

Cover design by Clare Brayshaw

Cover photograph:
Front cover: Danny Normandale, Sean Crowe, Iain McLean
Back cover: Colin Woodhead, Fred Normandale, Dave Mercer
Spine: Fred Normandale

Prepared and printed by:

York Publishing Services Ltd
64 Hallfield Road
Layerthorpe
York YO31 7ZQ
Tel: 01904 431213

Website: www.yps-publishing.co.uk

CONTENTS

ACKNOWLEDGMENTS

I'm indebted to Jilly Manser, my sister, Jan Mercer, Dave Winspear, Arthur Godfrey and Colin Woodhead for their dedicated and meticulous proof reading. Also thanks to all at YPS, especially Dave and Christopher Mercer and Clare Brayshaw for producing another quality volume.

Fred Normandale, January 2021

BY THE SAME AUTHOR

FIRST OF THE FLOOD

SLACK WATER

THE TIDE TURNS

EBBING TIDE

Chapter 1

Good Luck

The south-westerly wind was gusting a screaming seventy knots. Though there were no heavy seas in the bay, the water was white and spindrift was being hurled high into the air with each blast. How did mariners manage in these conditions in the days of sail, before engines were invented? Sometimes they didn't.

Hunched against the gale, I scanned the harbour pointlessly, knowing my search was in vain.

Over on the south side of our little port, the inverted canvas cone on the Vincent Pier, indicating a southerly gale, was swinging and spinning violently on its mast. The dozen or so remaining boats in the fleet were spread singly at the fish market and North Wharf. All were well-fendered and double-roped. It wasn't long ago the craft in Scarborough harbour had to tier-up four abreast, such were the number of inshore trawlers. The only vessel missing from the fleet today was my son's boat, *Scoresby* with her five-man crew.

I hadn't really expected to see her, but half hoped she'd turned up on the recent tide. It was now more than two days since I'd heard any news. Perhaps her radio aerial had been damaged in the storm. Maybe the telex machine, from which I frequently received printed messages, was faulty. Danny kept in touch whenever possible and I was concerned, as I'd heard nothing.

I'd already asked the recently arrived Skippers if they'd heard anything of *Scoresby* but the answer was uniformly negative. For the first time in all the years I'd been going to sea, it dawned on me how worrying it was for those onshore when their loved ones were at sea in poor weather. I'd been in severe gales many times, and wasn't usually too concerned, but of course my family at home weren't to know that.

Making my way up the steps to the Alliance Fish Agency, of which I was a partner, I entered the office. Terry, the manager was at his desk in the adjacent room, reading his newspaper. "Hiya Freddy" he said briefly, then went back to his paper.

I rang Aberdeen Coastguard, asking if they'd heard anything from *Scoresby;* last known position 'due east of Shetland' two days ago. Receiving another negative, this time from the shore station, I asked the operator if the Coastguard would broadcast a message to all shipping in the Northern North Sea, requesting vessels to keep a look out for fishing vessel *Scores*by.

I knew Danny intended to fish the Cormorant oil field, to the east of Shetland, but didn't know if he was still fishing or was transiting to a port. The boat wasn't in harbour anywhere or Danny would have been in touch.

It was Saturday, so having drawn a blank around the harbour with my enquiries and with no fishermen around the piers to chat to, I wandered up the hill to the Leeds Arms. I knew that sooner or later, news of some sort, good or bad would filter through. I'd done everything possible. The wind was easing now, as forecast, but the storm had been violent and prolonged. It had covered most of the North Sea, but maybe hadn't been as bad four hundred miles to the north.

This was a full 48-hr passage for most fishing vessels. I hadn't really expected *Scoresby* to be in Scarborough, but in the time lapsed, since I'd last received news, she could have just about made the distance, though it would have been a head punch, and not plausible or sensible.

We'd bought this 20.89 metre, wooden vessel, built in 1980 as *Margaret Jane* FR 297, during the previous year from Whitby owners, who'd renamed her after the famous whaling family that had sailed from this old port. Though we'd spent quite a lot of money renovating her, *Scoresby* had been worked hard over the years and had seen her best days.

Scoresby in Scarborough – Fred Normandale

I walked through the small doorway of the almost empty bar to be greeted by Mick and Shirley. They'd only recently become the pub's landlord and landlady, having previously been customers and were now wonderful assets to the community. Both from fishing families, Mick's Dad, Walt had fished with me on my first owned vessel, *Courage* many years ago. Shirl's Mum, also Shirley, could remember me being born. Now she occasionally babysat for my grandchildren.

The previous hosts, Simon and Hilary, who'd taken over from the inimitable, legendary 'Les' had also been great custodians of the old establishment, but Simon, tragically, had been killed in a motorcycle accident. On his death Hilary had vacated the pub immediately leaving a vacuum, which the present incumbents had filled well.

"You look a bit preoccupied," Shirl' said. "What's up?"

I was part way through my explanation when the public phone, mounted on the end of the bar, rang. Picking up the receiver, Mick said, "Hello," then listening to the caller, looked my way and said, "yes Pete, 'e's 'ere. E's just come through t' door. Ah'll pass yer over to 'im." Then in my direction said, "it's fo' you, Fred."

"'Ullo", I said, to the unknown caller.

"Fred, it's Pete Exley. I'm on *Brent Charlie*. I was in our radio shack just now when I heard a message on the 2182 frequency, asking for any sightings of *Scoresby*. I knew that was Danny's boat, so my ears pricked up."

Pete was a Scarborough man and was Superintendent of the production rig *Brent Charlie* to the east of Shetland. He and his petite wife Wendy were regular visitors to the pub when he was at home. Pete went on to say that on hearing the message he'd gone onto the VHF radio and transmitted on Channel 16, raising *Scoresby* immediately.

"He's ok," Pete said. "He's still fishing, but will be heading for Peterhead shortly for Monday's market. He'll ring you from there. The boat's telex machine is bust and his 'big set' radio isn't transmitting."

If Pete had been stood next to me, I'd have kissed him. How fantastic was that? Four hundred miles away, this man had heard the message I'd requested the Coastguard to transmit, and he'd responded. Not only responded but, knowing where I'd be on Saturday lunchtime had taken the trouble to contact and reassure me that all was well. This was extremely humbling and brought a lump to my throat.

"Thanks Pete. That's great news. Ah'm really grateful fo' the info. That's a great load off me mind. Ah promise t' fill yer full o' lager when yer next 'ome."

I'd be delighted to buy drink for Pete, though filling him up was a tall order, he was quite corpulent. We chatted briefly, but he was a busy man with an extremely responsible job and he quickly rang off, promising to see me in 'L.A.' soon. This exotic sounding promise was only an abbreviation for the Leeds Arms but sounded great to the uninitiated.

A weight had been lifted from my shoulders immediately and I rang Dotty at home to let her know the good news, though she hadn't been too perturbed. This wasn't a new experience for her.

"I've learned to switch off," she said. "I'd have gone mad years ago if I'd worried every time you were at sea in bad weather. I only worry when you and Danny are out in your cars."

Promising I wouldn't be late, I replaced the receiver.

I suppose my wife had a point about our driving. I'd collected a few points for speeding over the years, though not quite accumulating enough for a ban. Danny was much worse. He'd been a dreadful boy-racer when younger.

His first car, a Ford Escort 1100cc, had been personalised with stickers, various strobe lights and 'go faster' stripes: an obvious target for the local constabulary. He was a deckhand aboard the *Allegiance* with Bluey, my former crewman and now business partner in this vessel. She was built at Cochrane's Yard, Goole in 1987.

One morning early, when the vessel had been taken to Grimsby for slipping, painting and underwater maintenance, Danny had driven to the Humber port to meet her in and bring the crew home to Scarborough. He'd delivered the last member of the crew to his home on the north side of town and his return journey was around the Marine Drive. This headland road linked Scarborough's two bays.

With no other traffic on the road he'd put his foot down and the car had quickly gained speed. What he (and many others before him) hadn't taken into consideration was the adverse camber of the bend at the north easternmost section, near the Coffee Pot Rock.

Out of control, his car had mounted the pavement and with hardly a jolt of resistance had hit and ploughed through the three-bar, cast-iron railings, plunging twenty feet into the sea. Fortunately, the car had landed the right way up and it was high water. Though early morning, it was daylight and his flight had been observed. The only other motorist on the road, heading in the opposite direction, had seen the unplanned launch and drawing up at the broken railings, stopped to assist.

The man rushed to grab the lifebuoy with rope attached, housed against the wall on the opposite side of the road. He then flagged down a Council truck with several employees onboard, as it appeared around the bend, travelling at a more sedate pace than the previous vehicle, which was now sinking.

In the car, Danny, who'd been wearing a seat belt, remained conscious. With the car now semi-submerged and quickly filling, the external pressure was preventing the door from opening, but he'd had the presence of mind to wind down the window, filling the car and equalising the pressure. A good swimmer and having done basic diving training, he barged the door open with his shoulder and surfaced.

There was a light, northerly swell in the water, creating wash against the barnacle-encrusted sea wall, but the lifebuoy, floating close to hand, was in easy reach. The group of men hauled Danny up the sea wall with little effort, and soon he was standing, sodden and shoeless on the pavement. His only injury, a scuffed wrist; grazed as he was hauled, unceremoniously over the curved, wave-reflecting top of the hundred-year old construction.

I was fishing aboard *Emulator* at the time and we'd recently installed an analogue mobile phone. I answered the ringing to hear Dotty say, "Fred, Danny's gone through the railings on the Marine Drive in his car."

It seemed like an eternity before she added, "but he's alright. He's in the shower just now. The man who rescued him has just brought him home." She added, "the lifeboat maroons have just gone off as I'm speaking to you. I wonder if they're going to rescue Danny."

"They're a bit late, if they are," I replied, quickly coming to terms with recent events.

Years later, my mother, ever the sceptic, revealed that at the time Danny went into the sea, she heard footsteps coming downstairs and leaving the house. Soon after, she heard the door open again and feet on the stairs, ascending. She called out, "who's there?" and looked upstairs, but there was no one to be seen.

My parents lived in our previous house, further down the cobble-stoned hill. During the family discussion relating to Danny's old bedroom, Dotty said her sister, Margaret and also her mother, Doris always felt a presence, when sleeping in this room.

Mum had never mentioned her experience relating to Danny until that day.

CHAPTER 2

A CLOSE SHAVE

It was just after daylight, early in January and I'd not been out of bed long when the phone rang. Lifting the handset, I heard the distinct, broad Scottish voice of Hazel McLean on the line. She sounded distraught.

"Fred, the boat's doon but I dinna ken aboot ma 'loon'." (boy)

I was stunned and lost for words. Her son Iain was Skipper and my partner in the 22.5 metre vessel *Galatea,* which we'd bought from Bogg (Holdings) Ltd in Bridlington a couple of years earlier. She was one of three steel vessels built in Bideford. The others were *Langdale* and *Majestic*. Iain had been doing well in the vessel, catching a mixture of fish and prawns. I assured Hazel I'd find some information as soon as possible and get back to her immediately. I hung up and again found myself calling Aberdeen Coastguard.

The operator was immediately cautious when I asked if there was any news of the crew of *Galatea* and asked what my interest in the matter was.

Speaking in a clear voice I replied, "I'm co-owner of the vessel. I've just had a call from the Skipper's Mother and she's been told her son's boat has sunk. Can you give me any information that I can relay back to her?"

The Officer was a little more responsive, saying there were several boats in the area of the loss, which was thirty-five miles east of Peterhead, but this was still an ongoing situation. He said when there was further information, he'd get back to me.

Though I'd left my number with him, this line of enquiry didn't sound very promising. Official channels were notorious for keeping a lid on things and I could be hanging on for a message that wasn't forthcoming. Who else could I ring? The boat's agents may have some news. I rang the Fraserburgh Inshore Fish company office and my call was answered immediately by Alan Mutch, the company's manager.

Alan was aware of the situation and was trying to contact any of the fishing vessels working close to where the incident had occurred. He said he'd let me know immediately he had further information. This was a better response and I knew I'd get news from this source first.

Switching the kettle on, I paced the kitchen, my mind in turmoil. Poor Hazel, how must she be feeling? Time was standing still. The kettle, though singing was taking an interminable time to boil. Eventually I brewed a strong, black coffee but couldn't drink it. The mug stood untouched on the worktop.

The phone rang and before it could ring a second time the receiver was in my hand. "Hello," was my immediate, single word response.

It was Alan again. "Fred, they've got 'em all. *Audacious* has picked 'em up frae a liferaft an' they're on their wae tae Peterhead."

"Phew," I exclaimed, my relief palpable. "That's fantastic news Alan, thank yer so much! Ah'm really grateful, Ah'll let Hazel know straight away."

Without replacing the receiver, I pressed the twin buttons on the phone holder then dialled the McLean's number, which I knew off by heart.

This phone was also answered immediately. I found it difficult to speak I was so choked. "He's alright Hazel. They've all been picked up from their life-raft," I blurted. "They're aboard *Audacious*, on their way t' Peterhead. They'll be there in about four hours."

The words of reply from Hazel were difficult to comprehend, but her relief and joy was obvious, and something only a mother could know.

I'd known George McLean, Iain's Dad, since I was a schoolboy and had sailed with him and the crew of the Scottish drifter, *Hazael III*, fishing for herring among the migrating shoals. What an amazing experience it had been for a young lad, sailing in the early evening to return next morning with a catch of the little silver fish. I'd sailed many times on different drifters and had been dreadfully seasick on the early occasions.

I recalled when George had asked me to go to the florists, up in the town centre to send flowers by Interflora to Hazel, back home in Gardenstown on the birth of their first child, Joyce.

Iain was the youngest of their four children, following Jane and Callum and was now, years later a Skipper and my business partner. Today he'd almost lost his life.

A couple of days later, when things had settled down, Iain rang to tell me, first-hand what had happened.

Galatea had been trawling before a big, lazy swell following a recent southerly gale, in an area notorious for sticky mud. This type of ground was ideal for catching prawns.

It was Iain's turn for a nap below and one of his crew, John was on watch in the wheelhouse. The net had stuck in the mud when the boat had dropped on the back of a swell. Now stopped and with the wire trawl warps restraining the vessel, *Galatea* began to ship water over her stern. The boat was fitted with a watertight shelter-deck, which was put in place to increase the stability of what we were later to discover, was a poorly designed vessel. Steel doors were fitted at the after end of the construction on both sides of the main-deck, for access to the stern of the boat. These doors should have been closed in poor weather to maintain the watertight integrity of the shelter, but had been left open for the crew to access the winch for'ard, while the trawl was in the water.

Now, the waves breaking over the boat's stern were also washing over the eighteen-inch sill, flooding into the aluminium structure. The shelter, designed to add buoyancy and keep water out, was now having the reverse effect. In seconds the weight of water built up, making the stern of the boat heavier and lower, allowing even more sea to flow in. The water inside the shelter-deck, slopping about uncontrollably, caused *Galatea* to lose stability and the boat quickly began to list, from which there was no way back.

The watchman in the wheelhouse had eased the throttle back to slow as soon as he'd realised the net was stuck. The crew below, on hearing the change in engine tone had left their bunks, intending to make their way on deck to haul the trawl.

Galatea fishing – Fred Normandale

Iain immediately realised something wasn't right: that this wasn't just a normal 'come fast and retrieve'. The vessel was listing, vibrating and he could hear water washing onto the deck above the cabin. Dressed only in underwear, he and the other crewmembers quickly went up the tilting ladders to the deck level, where they met the watch-keeper coming down from the bridge. John had just managed to send off a hurried 'Mayday' on the VHF working frequency to other boats close by. *Galatea* was awash around the stern and heeling over.

The 'free surface effect' of water moving uncontrolled inside the shelter meant the situation was already irretrievable. Even small amounts of free surface water can have a catastrophic effect on vessels, as has been discovered with the loss of many car ferries, which, by the very nature of their job, cannot have watertight compartments.

I recalled the stability lessons I'd learned at college, where I'd spent three months gaining a Second Hand Special, Skipper's certificate for small fishing vessels. The practical course was unbelievable. An egg cup full of water would prevent a large orange box from floating level in a tank of water, when previously the box was perfectly balanced.

Galatea's crew of five had somehow managed to get onto the top of the shelter deck, despite the increasing list, and Iain, having thrown over the nearest life-raft, began to haul on the painter rope to inflate the craft, not knowing this line was 120 feet in length. He was exhausted before the thin rope was fully extended and someone snatched it from him to complete the job, allowing the raft to inflate.

The crew struggled to remain on board as *Galatea* listed further on to her side, each man waiting to get into the now inflated, orange coloured raft, but the canopy, as it expanded had become stuck under the horizontal landing pole, which was secured on top of the wheelhouse. The freezing men had a real struggle to release the trapped raft, damaging the tubes in the process, before they were finally able to get inside the flimsy craft.

The second raft had inflated unaided when the automatic hydrostatic release was triggered as the boat capsized. Though floating free, this potential lifesaver was upside down. Somehow the desperate survivors, despite the deep swell, managed to paddle their damaged craft to the drifting second raft, then turned this flimsy rubber boat the right way up. Eventually all hands, bitterly cold, were able to transfer to this little craft without loss of life.

Several boats had heard the Mayday, but all had their nets down and would take up to half an hour to haul and retrieve their gear before steaming to the site of the sinking. Fortunately, the Skipper of *Audacious*, the nearest vessel, three miles away, had the presence of mind to release his trawl by letting the wire warp run out from his winch, freeing his vessel of the drag, allowing him to head immediately towards the site of the loss. The Skipper hoped to recover the many thousands of pounds worth of equipment later, when time allowed.

The crew of *Galatea* were shivering in the raft, unaware their rescuers were heading at full speed in their direction. *Audacious*, with men standing on the shelter-deck, keeping a sharp look out, was heading to the rescue, though the Skipper didn't know if there'd be anyone to save.

The rescue was a complete success, and the hypothermic, but otherwise unhurt crew were landed safely into Peterhead. The Skipper of *Audacious* returned to the site and was able, with much difficulty, to grapple and reattach his missing fishing gear.

Before the purchase of *Galatea,* Iain had fished with his father-in-law onboard *Vision*. She was a sistership of *Galatea*. She'd originally been called *Majestic*. This vessel had capsized when listing to starboard with a large haul of fish on board. Tragically, one of her crew had been lost when *Vision* had foundered.

Galatea was lost on 5/1/1999

CHAPTER 3

STS *LORD NELSON*

Surprisingly, I'd been invited to join the local Rotary Club, which I thought a most extraordinary happening. Me! In Rotary!

Despite thinking they'd got the wrong candidate, I'd accepted the invitation and attended the Monday meetings, which were interesting and usually involved guest speakers on a variety of subjects. These talks were limited to twenty minutes and even then, one or two of the older members dozed off.

After a couple of months of membership, President Howard announced that the Club was sponsoring a teenage lad to sail on the Sail Training Ship, *Lord Nelson*, making the passage from Kings Lynn to Newcastle, and did any of the members wish to accompany young James. Anyone wishing to sail would be required to fund their own voyage.

I'd seen this wonderful, three-masted barque in Amsterdam a few years previous, but never thought I'd get the opportunity to sail on her, so was extremely keen to do this trip. Little did I know that this simple four-day passage in the North Sea was to change my life for ever.

Along with two other Rotary members, Richard and Alan, our teenage charge was delivered by car to the dock in Kings Lynn. I was able to make the journey with Dotty, who subsequently drove home alone.

While standing on the quayside, I looked up in awe at the numerous squared yards, and miles of rigging. My reverie was broken when I was hailed from the main deck by a stocky, boiler-suited, wild-looking man with curly, ginger hair and matching beard. In a lovely Suffolk accent, the smiling, twinkly-eyed sailor called out, "hullo there bhoys. Welcome t' *Lord Nelson*. Pass yer bags darn an' come aboard."

I gratefully followed his instructions, passing over our kit, and was about to lead the way, stepping onto the ship's side, intending to jump down to the deck when the cheery crewman quickly called, "you'll ha' t' use the gangway t' come aboard, ol' bhoy."

This was an early safety lesson and was initially quite alien to me, having spent my life to date clambering over fishing boats and up and down ladders. I wasn't used to gangways and it didn't make sense, but as Cyril, the boiler-suited Bosun explained simply, "there can on'y be one set o' rules fo' everyone ol' bhoy."

Other people were joining the ship and once onboard we were all directed below, for'ard to the lower mess, where three, fore and aft tables were situated. This was the dining area where we were to be signed on as 'voyage crew' by the Medical Purser, Jane, sitting at the starboard table. I was to discover that this really cheery, attractive lass from Halifax, West Yorkshire was a hospital theatre nurse in real life. Short, blond hair, button nose and twinkling eyes, Jane was energetic and very efficient.

There was a pair of single bunks on each side of the lower mess, outboard of, and above the tables. I later discovered these were known as 'holes in the wall' and were usually used by the Bosun's mates, Cook's assistant and one of the four watch-leaders.

After signing on, we were each given a sticky nametag for ease of identification. Next, those newcomers requiring sea gear were directed to the port side of the mess where oilskins and sea-boots were being dispensed by the two volunteer Bosun's mates. I'd brought the oilskin suit and short boots I'd previously used on *Undaunted* before I'd finished fishing.

We were issued with a broad, white nylon belt that fastened back on itself through a large buckle, retained in place with a wide

Velcro strip. A three-foot lanyard was attached to the belt, with a stainless-steel spring-clip spliced in the outer end. This was to be used to clip on to thin wires around the deck when we were at sea, if required. The same clip was used on the safety wires when climbing out round the 'futtock shrouds' to gain access to the platforms on the masts and also to clip to safety wires when out on the yards.

The voyage crew had been divided into four watches, for'ard port, for'ard starboard, aft port and aft starboard. Each group had a 'watch-leader' who'd sailed on the ship previously. Some were more experienced than others. Fortunately for us, our watch-leader, Wilton Jones, was an elderly, tall ship enthusiast, whose love of the Jubilee Sailing Trust was clearly evident. Bespectacled with his shoddy, faded grey boiler suit and battered, denim yachtie cap, he very much had the appearance of an old seafarer.

In real life Wilton was a Housemaster in a boys' boarding school in Doncaster, but spent all his holiday time onboard the ship. His knowledge of the vessel was total and he didn't suffer fools, including those members of the permanent crew who didn't shape up to his expectations.

Wilton introduced me to my buddy, Roger, then took us to our designated berth. Roger was a big, red-faced, ginger- haired lad from Birmingham who spoke with a heavy regional accent. Our berth was mid-ships on the port side, one of four cabins on each side. The cabins had two bunks, upper and lower, each with a small drawer and locker for personal effects. Roger, who wore a built-up shoe to compensate for a shorter leg, took the lower berth. Though not needed, there were anchor points fastened into the deck to secure wheelchairs.

Privacy amounted to a pair of full-length, heavy, green plaid curtains, screening the little cabin from the fore and aft alleyway. These drapes could be drawn and pinned back during the day but, as we were to discover, when pulled closed and with the ship rolling, the curtains appeared to swing both to port and starboard, though in reality, remained vertical while the ship moved.

Leaving my buddy to unpack, I went back up the companionway to the main deck. Tea and coffee were available in the upper mess where the permanent crew usually ate. Grabbing a brew, I now had time to look round the ship's deck, familiarising myself with the layout and meeting new shipmates. A few late arrivals had turned up and were being directed below to be signed on.

Back below, I explored more, discovering that for'ard from the mess-deck was the fo'c'sle. This area accommodated the remaining voyage crew. Tubular metal framed, utility-type beds, tiered three high, were on both sides of the ship, usually housing females on the port side. Each bed had a lee-cloth, which could be fastened at the top of each bunk, fore and aft to prevent incumbents falling out of bed when the ship rolled.

At the other end of the ship, aft side of the curtained berths, through a soundproof door, I was delighted to discover a small, but well laid out bar. This cosy little place had a counter, optics and well-stocked fridges. The glasses were secured in racks on the port corner, aft. The remaining space was taken up with cushioned seating against the starboard side, below which, I learned, were lockers for additional wines and spirit storage. Four small tables, made from aluminium beer kegs fitted with wooden tops, were very serviceable. The bulwarks were adorned with plaques and trophies *Lord Nelson* had been presented with by other vessels and ports over the years.

Beyond the bar, through another door, towards the stern, was the private, permanent crews' accommodation, where each member had their own, small cabin. The Captain's larger, personal berth was on the main deck near the stern.

At 1600 hours the ship's speakers sounded to summon all hands back to the lower mess. Everyone found a seat round the three tables in readiness for introductions to the permanent crew and to be given a safety briefing.

The Captain, John Fisher, introduced his permanent crew of ten. First Mate, Second Mate, Bosun, Engineer, Cook, Medical Purser, two volunteer Bosun's mates and a volunteer Cook's assistant. The Cook, Martin got the loudest cheer when he stepped forward to say hello. This was a reaction that I found happened every time the Cook was introduced.

"You haven't tasted the food yet," Martin retorted, grinning and getting a laugh from the audience.

Emergency signals and fire alarms were demonstrated and a brief outline of the proposed voyage ahead given. Marco, the Engineer gave a talk about the ship's plumbing and especially the 'heads' (toilets). The filter system was prone to blockages and was the bane of the Engineer's life. He pleaded with the new crew not to put anything into the toilet system that had not gone through their own body systems first, apart from flimsy toilet paper.

We were given a brief description of the vessel, which I found helpful. Knowing little of sailing ships, I felt quite out of my comfort zone, but wasn't alone in this respect. At least I had some general nautical knowledge, which gave me a slight advantage over many of the other newcomers.

As we were not due to sail until the following morning, most of the voyage crew and some of the permanent hands congregated in the bar, where an enjoyable evening passed quickly. Everyone was mixing and telling salty sea-yarns, (swinging the lamp) and trying to impress their new shipmates with their sea experiences. This evolved into shanty singing, interspersed with joke telling, which I got involved in. People from all walks of life were bonding together.

During a brief lull in the evening I said, "here's a nautical question for you all. Captain Cook made three voyages to the Pacific. On which one was he killed?"

Some said, "second."

"Is it a trick question?" a lady asked.

My next question was, "who can name three fish beginning and ending with the letter K".

No one could get even one answer, despite much thought.

"Number one is killer shark," I said, then quickly, before anyone could speak said, "the next is king-sized haddock," but when I said, "the last one is Kilmarnock," I was faced with blank stares until I said, "it's a plaice in Scotland." This brought a large, universal groan.

The following morning after breakfast, we took part in the first of two emergency evacuations from below. Wheelchair users were not allowed to use the stair-lifts, but were safely hauled up the companionways to deck level by block and tackle and strong arms. All the voyage crew then gathered at the four designated muster stations, appropriate to their watch to don lifejackets stored in fixed, white, fibreglass boxes. The speed of this evolution was timed by the Mate.

Next in the busy schedule was 'hands aloft', called over the speaker. Those wishing to climb the masts gathered on the main deck for instruction and guidance. This is what I'd come for. I was looking forward to climbing the rigging.

Cyril gave clear, concise instructions and would be positioned at the 'course yard', just below the 'fighting top'[1] (the first platform) to guide those who would struggle to achieve this level. A Bosun's mate was kneeling on the platform, looking over the edge to advise the climbers where to place their hands.

Soon it was my turn, and I was rushing up the wooden rat-bars, holding the stainless steel, middle shroud when the Bosun's voice boomed down at me.

"Slaw dar'n a bit matey. It ain't a bleedin' race."

I certainly slowed down when I reached the 'futtock shrouds'. The access to the fighting top becomes an overhang, and climbers have to lean outwards to gain their goal, first clipping on to a tight stainless-steel safety-wire. The wire would prevent a potential plummet back to the deck or over the side. Splash! or splat! as the landing was described by the Bosun's mates.

It was an interesting exercise as I climbed and leaned outwards, but discovered that the edge of the platform was a good handhold and above this, a stanchion and a large rigging screw (bottle-screw) were good handholds to get me to the level. I was breathing heavily despite being reasonably fit, and my heart was racing when I shuffled round the front of the railings to stand on the slatted platform.

From this height the view of the town and surrounding flat countryside was spectacular. I wondered what the scene would

---

1   From the days when marines would shoot down on the decks of the enemy. *Lord Nelson's* 'fighting top' was about 30 feet from the deck.

be like from the next, higher and smaller platform. This was the 'cross-trees'.[2]

Eventually there were a dozen members of the voyage crew on the fore mast and a similar number on the main mast. It was very cosy with everyone in close proximity. Numerous people were waving across the void from the main mast, some with cameras (attached to their persons) were snapping shipmates on the fore mast.

When we were back on deck, appointed hands were designated to harbour stations. I was on the stern platform, an overhanging section from the stern, edged with two-bar, white rails, where I helped haul in the springs and stern lines. Once on board, the four, heavy, eight-stranded, plaited ropes were coiled on the platform, then lashed to the railings.

Lord Nelson, with pilot onboard and under engines, cruised down the Great Ouse river, heading for The Wash, then continued north east under power through the buoyed channel, out to the open sea.

These wreck-strewn waters were shallow and discoloured with silt from this river and the huge Humber estuary. I'd fished in this region, from the Wash to the Humber entrance, many times over the years with both trawl and pots.

Trawling with *Courage, Independence* and *Emulator,* I'd avoided the wrecks like the plague. When I began potting in *Undaunted*, I researched the scores of broken ships keenly, knowing they were rich lobster habitat. These wrecks were in shallow water, so had been dispersed to prevent them being a hazard to shipping.

No soon had the pilot stepped aboard the cutter, leaving the ship at the end of the entrance channel than we commenced the second evacuation drill, again gathering at our relevant stations fore and aft, wearing lifejackets. This exercise was also timed and the result entered in the ship's log. Following this statutory requirement, it was time for bracing practice.

---

2   When ships had wooden masts, the builders would find the tallest of trees, but the masts were so high that more than one tree was needed. The pair would be fastened together, hence, 'cross-trees'.

The two forward watches manned the foremast port and starboard braces, the other watches took the mainmast. Bracing, or hauling the yards from square to port or starboard enabled a ship to sail 'across' the wind. This was heavy, manual work for those hauling the big yards round, though much easier for the 'slackers', on the other side. For the first time, it occurred to me this was the nautical origin of the word, 'slacker'.

Until Cyril instructed us to look aloft to watch the effect of our labours, few of us realised the principle of this evolution. The braces for the foremast were midships and the mainmast braces were aft. When I looked aloft it immediately became obvious. The yards could only be hauled round through blocks leading to the mast behind.

We soon realised there was a skill in getting the yards to come around together. Each one was a different weight with varying lengths and diameters of rope to haul on. Now we would take pride in bracing uniformly.

When the yards had been braced to port, to starboard and back to port again, instructions coming from the bridge, it was announced it was time for Smoko! Having been in the Merchant Navy in my teens, I was aware this was the traditional name for a tea break and time for a smoke for those who indulged. This welcome interlude was taken mid-morning and mid-afternoon. Pulling on the braces was warm work.

Cookie had made and sliced fruitcake and there were plenty of biscuits. These would accompany the unlimited supply of hot water from catering sized thermos flasks for self-service tea and coffee. This welcome snack was brought from the galley by Jilly, the volunteer Cook's assistant (Cook's ass) and her mess team, who placed the food and drink on a fixed, steel box structure on the starboard side, near the main mast. I was later to discover this, and an opposite box held the ship's fuelling points. These were the bunker boxes.

The half hour rest period passed quickly and was followed by an extremely interesting and informative sail setting talk below; the Second Mate naming the various sails and the order in which they were set. Under supervision and the unblinking eyes of watch-leader Wilton, we were soon to put this knowledge into practice.

The four cross yards on both the fore and main masts from the top down were the royal, t'gallant, tops'l and course. I thought it very strange that the tops'l was the second one up. The Officer pointed out that the two lower sails, were stowed on top of their yards, secured with 'gaskets', (short strops) while the upper sails were roller furled inside the hollow, aluminium yards. These were deployed through letterbox type slots, handled from deck-level, by crew hauling on endless furling lines.

Three triangular jibs flew from the foremast to the bowsprit; the inner jib, then again confusingly, the outer jib, beyond which, the furthest forward was the flying jib. From both the main and mizzen masts triangular, fore and aft staysails could be set, these rolled around spools. These sails were great for steadying the rolling of the ship when across the wind, though very little forward drive was gained from the stay s'ls.

Aft from the mizzen was a heavy boom from which the spanker flew and from a smaller boom above, an upper spanker. These sails performed best with the wind astern. Both were secured vertically to the mizzen mast with gaskets when stowed. I'd never remember all this!

Now at sea, a call came over the speaker, asking for hands wishing to go aloft to 'toss off' the gaskets. I was up for this challenge. Along with several others, I volunteered to climb the for'ard shrouds onto the 'fighting top'. From the platform it was a short climb then a step out on the portside tops'l yard. I didn't leave the rigging until I was clipped on to the stainless-steel safety wire, running the length of the yard.

I could feel my legs shaking with the wobble of the footrope and was clinging on to the front of the yard and furled sail with white knuckles. It didn't help that we had to shuffle out, dipping our heads under tight buntlines and stepping round vertical stirrups that held the footrope to the yard.

As each person, in turn, manned the yard, the call, "stepping on," was shouted, notifying those already standing on the moving footrope. At the back of my mind I knew I wasn't in real danger, but was definitely out of my comfort zone and didn't want to fall off the yard, to be seen dangling in space.

Once in position, we released the gaskets securing the sail onto the yard. When we were all ready, on a count of three, we pushed the rolled-up tops'l off the yard and I grabbed the metal rail the sail was fastened to. This feeling of insecurity aloft was a sensation I'd encounter many times before eventually feeling comfortable, though I'd never admit it.

The canvas didn't drop far, as the buntlines were tight, now retaining the sail under the yard. These buntlines led to the deck, fastened on belaying pins and were released to deploy the sail.

* * *

Years later, early one evening, I'd been sent aloft to the port side of the main tops'l yard. The bights of the sail clew were flogging badly in the wind and I was to put a sea stow in end of the sail to secure them. *Nelly* was head to wind, and in the strong breeze she was lifting her head to the swell. My short safety tether was clipped on to the safety wire and I shuffled out along the yard, ducking under the tight buntlines as I went, as far as the shortening footrope would allow. Next I stepped on to the 'Flemish Horse', the additional short bight of footrope, allowing me access to the extreme end of the yard.

I was attempting to fold the pleats of loose sail with both hands, putting my chest on the folds when the ship lurched, and I was propelled backwards. I grabbed the back jackstay, but the momentum had projected me off the yard, my legs shooting forwards with the safety tether taut. Reaching the end of the swing, the pendulum effect brought me backwards, and amazingly, I was able to stand upright again on the outer footrope.

"Phew!" I thought. At least no one had seen me. I was quite shaken, but after a couple of minutes rest my composure returned, and I hurriedly hitched the clewline around the yard.

I was pleased to shuffle back along the yard, avoiding the buntlines again and with relief, made my way back to the deck. I was greeted by a couple of elderly ladies who'd been on lookout duty on the bridge, and had seen my incident.

"Did you mean to do that Fred? It was very clever."

"Shh, Mum's the word, Ladies," I said, winking, smiling and putting a finger to my lips. I'd almost got away with it.

* * *

With a fresh breeze from the south-west, we continued motoring downwind to the north-east, then altered course due north. We braced the yards to starboard then with the engines stopped, began to put our sail-setting evolutions into practice under the direction of the Mates and scrutiny of our watch-leader.

Starting with the tops'ls, within an hour we were under full sail, heeling wonderfully to the wind and making about six knots.

Manning the yards – unknown
Note the fighting top and crosstrees

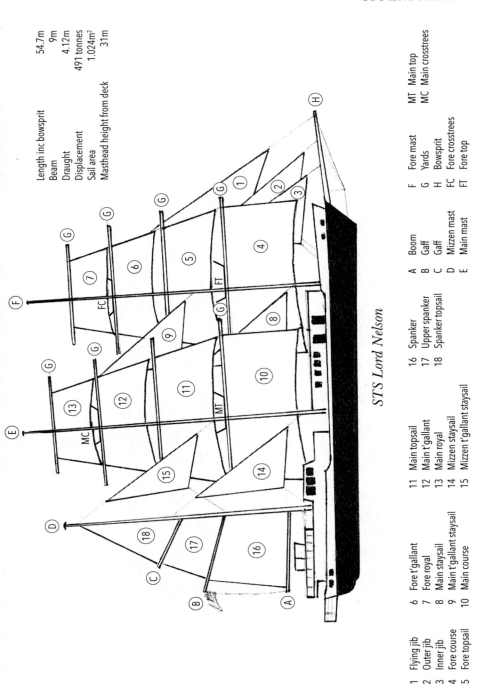

STS Lord Nelson

Length inc bowsprit — 54.7m
Beam — 9m
Draught — 4.12m
Displacement — 491 tonnes
Sail area — 1.024m²
Masthead height from deck — 31m

1	Flying jib	6	Fore t'gallant	11	Main topsail	16	Spanker
2	Outer jib	7	Fore royal	12	Main t'gallant	17	Upper spanker
3	Inner jib	8	Main staysail	13	Main royal	18	Spanker topsail
4	Fore course	9	Main t'gallant staysail	14	Mizzen staysail		
5	Fore topsail	10	Main course	15	Mizzen t'gallant staysail		

A	Boom	F	Fore mast	MT	Main top
B	Gaff	G	Yards	MC	Main crosstrees
C	Gaff	H	Bowsprit		
D	Mizzen mast	FC	Fore crosstrees		
E	Main mast	FT	Fore top		

25

Sailing north, I later recognised the Amethyst gas field, in the position of the now defunct, Dowsing Light Vessel. It was from here to the south that I'd worked my pots in *Undaunted*. The rig was 65 miles from Scarborough.

Further north still, before nightfall we'd see the Rough Gas Field, a triple unit with accommodation platforms, looking like an elongated monster. This installation was 40 miles from home. 2.5 hours in *Undaunted*, 5 hours in *Emulator*.

We soon got into the ship's routine and were standing watches. Roger and I were called at 2330hrs and quickly dressed in warm clothes and oilskins ready to meet Wilton by the mainmast, ten minutes before midnight.

I was aware from past experience in the Merchant Navy that it was good practise for the oncoming watch to turn up a few minutes early. The watch-leader quickly explained this to our watch-mates.

It was like a blast from the past, standing on the wing of the bridge, keeping lookout in the black night. I was a seventeen-year old, ordinary seaman when I'd last been a lookout. Our duty was to report lights on our side of the ship to the Duty Officer, navigating inside the chartroom. I was well aware he could see all the surrounding shipping on the bridge radar, but this was part of the voyage experience.

All the watch would take a turn at steering *Lord Nelson*, or doing a 'trick at the wheel' in M.N. speak. We were allowed frequent breaks throughout the watch for tea and coffee in the upper mess.

I was one of eight, voyage crew on watch, supervised by our watch-leader. Our ninth member, had been on galley duty during the day, so was exempt from watchkeeping.

There were two dog-watches, 4-6 and 6-8, leading to the evening 8-12. Next, the night watch 12-4 was followed by the dawn watch 4-8. Each morning the 4-8 watch would call the ship's company as required, bringing the ship alive for the day. There were two more four-hour watches during the day, then dog-watches again. These short durations ensured the watches were rotated daily.

Next day it was my turn for galley duty. I was called at 06.45 and along with one person from each of the other watches, reported to the upper mess. After grabbing a quick coffee, Jilly briefed us on our duties, hygiene and the pitfalls of preparing food. No one was to enter the domain of the cook, the hot galley.

We ate a quick breakfast, along with the on-going watch, then served the voyage crew in the lower mess at 08.00. These meals came down via a small box lift, directly from the galley.

Following the meal, we'd feed the crockery, cutlery and the Cook's utensils through the dishwasher/steriliser. This was a great machine, set on gimbals, allowing the washer to work in all but the worst of weather. It could churn a full tray of soiled crockery through every minute. The secret was to have someone stacking the trays quickly at the sink, where the heaviest contaminants were removed. The other couple of messmen emptied and stowed the clean items as they came out, red hot from the machine.

Next we joined our watches to hear a report of the Captain's morning briefing from the bridge, attended on our behalf by Wilton. He'd inform us of the distance covered in the past 24 hours and prospects for later in the voyage, which could be subject to change, then the programme for the day.

I returned to the upper mess for an hour of cleaning lockers, wiping deckheads and sweeping the deck, then it was Smoko. We escaped from the mess to the deck for a half hour break, returning to prep' vegetables for lunch and dinner. The morning passed quickly.

Our voyage was only four days duration so there was no opportunity to call in to Scarborough or Whitby. Our only port of call would be Seaham Harbour. This little port was close enough to the Tyne to ensure our arrival into Newcastle on time, the following afternoon.

Seaham Harbour, a few miles south of Sunderland, was a lovely little town, though now very quiet. The port was built for shipping coal from the Durham coalfields to the Thames. Historically there would have been a never-ending stream of colliers plying their trade from here. I could remember the latter part of this coal trade from my teens. The ships would sail south, passing about three miles off Scarborough, loaded to their marks with coal, then return north again, a few days later, light ship. Some of these vessels had telescopic masts, allowing them to pass under the Thames bridges and steam further up the river with their cargoes.

That evening we served a tasty dinner to all on board and were quickly finished, thanks to willing hands helping with the washing up, then it was shower time.

About a dozen from the ship, including half the permanent crew went ashore for a fun filled evening of jokes and banter in the local pub. This must have been the busiest night the landlord had encountered for some years, and at closing time he was very keen to lock the door, keeping us a little longer.

There were a few hangovers next morning when we let the ropes go to sail the few miles north. Fortunately, the weather was fine, with a fair breeze. We set most of the sails for a gentle passage to the Tyne, arriving off the entrance about noon where we handed sail and picked up the pilot.

Entering the river, we were soon passing North Shields to starboard. I'd been here several times over the years. The first time I entered the Tyne in 1968 aboard the Scarborough trawler *Evelyn, LH 23* there were four little tugs berthed in pairs at the quayside, on hand to assist larger ships in the busy river. Now the pier was empty.

'The Gut', the protective little harbour keeping fishing boats out of the tidal stream was next to starboard. This haven was half filled with small local trawlers of many colours. These craft would be mostly fishing for langoustines on the muddy inshore grounds. A couple of men repairing a damaged net on the quayside both gave a friendly wave as we motored by.

In years past there was a thriving fleet of steam trawlers fishing the North Sea from this Tyne port and in early Summer the old harbour was filled with Scottish drifters. Now Shields was a shadow of its former glory.

We motored the ten miles up the famous river, once lined with ship building yards, but now showing much dereliction. The view from the tops'l yard was fantastic. It was great fun being part of the team standing on the footropes, chests on the yard, as we put a harbour stow in the sail, under Bosun Cyril's supervision.

Lord Nelson was soon tied up alongside the pier in Newcastle and Dotty was on the quayside waiting, having driven north to collect me. It was the end of what had been the most amazing experience.

I was heading for the gangway to bring Dotty on board to give her a tour of the ship when Cyril tapped me on the shoulder.

"We like you, bhoy. Yer seem t' know what yer doin' aboard of 'ere. If yer want t' come back, yer can be a Bosun's mate nex' time yer sail."

Little did I know this had been the first of what was to be more than ninety voyages, over the next twenty years of fantastic, life changing sailing.

CHAPTER 4

SALTY NUTS

Back home it was another busy weekend in the Leeds Arms, with lots of cheery banter among the customers. Mick, the landlord had gone for a walk on to the seafront for a sandwich and a breath of fresh air, leaving Shirley and barmaid Jilly behind the counter, serving and chatting with customers.

"Can I 'ave a packet o' peanuts, please Shirl," I asked, offering the correct coinage.

"Ah'm sorry Fred", she replied. "We 'aven't got any till ah can get t' wholesalers after t' weekend. We 'ave plenty o' crisps."

"Nah it doesn't matter," I replied. "Ah'll go t' 'Scattercash's shop over t' road. 'E'll 'ave peanuts in stock."

Stepping down the few steps to leave the pub, I crossed the little street, colloquially known as City Square and entered the grocer/off licence. The proprietor, Richard, whose lack of philanthropy invited his nickname, was a portly, Dickensian looking character sporting large, lamb-chop sideburns. He was the only son in a family of four children from a branch of the Mainprize fishing family, but he'd flatly refused to go to sea, despite significant coercion from his parents. He'd spent his career in grocery retailing.

Richard and his long-suffering wife Ann, had a thriving business when the Scarborough fleet was at its height. He delivered the vessels' supplies onboard each weekend, ready for the boats'

Sunday sailings. Recently this trade, reflecting the fishing industry, had dried up completely. His shop was now the sole grocers' remaining in the 'Bottom End' where, pre supermarket days, there had been more than half a dozen little family businesses.

My conversation with the proprietor of the corner shop was brief and returning with the bag of peanuts, placed these on the counter. Shirley kindly poured my purchase into a couple of small glass dishes, placing these on the bar for communal consumption. I took a small handful, projecting them into my mouth. These nuts were much saltier than those sold in the pub.

"Can I make a complaint, Landlady?" I said loudly, so the majority within the bar could hear. "These nuts are too salty."

"Yer've jus' brought 'em yerself," she replied, equally loudly and indignantly. "I've just poured 'em out for yer. You'll be wanting me to suck the salt off yer nuts next."

The pub fell silent and a look of horror came over Shirley's countenance. She put her hand to her mouth, realising what she'd said, and that everyone had deliberately misconstrued her words.

Several hands went into the air and cries of "yes please," were heard round the bar.

"And me."

"Can ah be included as well," called an old fisherman in the corner, adding to the landlady's embarrassment.

A few minutes later, when the topic had dried up and normality restored, Mick came back through the door, calling out, "what's been going on up 'ere while ah've been away? I'd only been gone from t' pub fo' ten minutes when ah met a customer who'd just left.

He said, "you'd better get back up there quick. Your Missus is offering to suck salt off yer customers nuts."

Shirley, extremely embarrassed, quickly changed the subject saying, "did you 'ear about me Mother this morning?"

She went on to tell everyone that her Mum had been standing on the seafront earlier in the day with her little shopping trolley on wheels, waiting for her daughter. They were planning to head

31

into town together. While waiting, a catering delivery van had pulled up; the driver asking for directions.

Mother had just finished giving the driver instructions and he'd pulled out into the extremely busy traffic when young Shirley arrived on the scene.

Curious to know about the driver's enquiry, the daughter had said, "what did the van man want, Mum?"

"E wanted t' know where t' Coffee Pot was," replied Mother.

"And what did yer tell 'im?" asked Shirl'.

"Ah sent 'im round towards t' North Bay. Everybody knows where t' Coffee Pot is. It's that big rock, 'alf way round t' Marine Drive."

"Yer silly bugger. 'E's looking for t' Coffee Pot Café. Why would a van driver want t' deliver vegetables an' frozen chips to a rock, a 'undred yards offshore?"

"Well 'e never said 'e wanted a café. 'Ow was ah t' know?" Mother replied defensively. "'E'll find out soon enough."

The pair began walking along Sandside towards the town, Mother trundling her distinctive little trolley in front. Ten minutes later, an extremely irate van driver drove past, horn honking loudly and a fist shaking from the open window, hurling abuse in their direction.

"Well 'e knows it's not round there now," Mother said.

CHAPTER 5

BACK IN COURT

We were going to court again. It seemed we'd never be able to avoid the pitfalls of the increasing and ever-changing fishing regulations.

The two Skippers, Bluey in *Allegiance* and Mally in *Independence* had been pair trawling, along with two Whitby pair teams. They'd all been visited by a Royal Navy Fisheries Inspection vessel, with a DEFRA (Department for Environment Food and Rural Affairs) Inspector on board. These people, doing the dirty work of the European Commission at the sharp end, were a special breed, devoid of feelings for the suffering they were inflicting by their actions. The current Senior Inspector, portly, with several chins, and bad body odour, was particularly vindictive.

The UK fleet was contracting annually, but the regulations and policing still got tougher. It was clear to anyone who 'wanted' to see, (and this ruled out most UK politicians) that without a reversal of the downward spiral of quota opportunities, the Yorkshire Coast fishing industry as we know it, would be finished in the not too distant future.

The current offence of all six Skippers was that the percentage of cod retained on board was in excess of that allowed under the EU regulations. Since when did fish swim in percentages? As part owner of the two Scarborough boats, I was also summoned to appear. The case was to be heard in the Magistrates Court in Whitby.

The owners of two of the Whitby boats had hired a firm of solicitors from North Shields, the other pair engaged Andrew Jacksons, maritime lawyers from Hull. With my two partners consent, I opted to act on our behalf. If nothing else, we'd save the cost of the legal fees.

The UK interpretation of the regulations stated that after the first twenty-four hours, vessels using netting with a mesh of between 110mm and 119mm had to conform to the catch composition rules, retaining only 20% cod on board. The French, among other nations, viewed this rule with much more pragmatism and their catch percentage was an annual calculation at the end of the calendar year. This was much more sensible and prevented the pointless discarding of good quality fish when they were caught in large numbers.

In preparation for our case, I took photographs of boats landing their catches in port with their 'landing poles' elevated. I snapped the depth from the top of the boats' shelter-decks down to their fish room floor. This was the extent the boxes of fish would have to be hauled up, to be then discarded overboard into the sea. The problem was that the landing gear could not be topped out at sea, as this was far too dangerous when the boats were rolling. I wanted to prove this was a law that couldn't be safely complied with.

The day of the case arrived and the little courtroom, for what was to be one of the last cases heard in the Whitby Court House, was quite full. All the Skippers, owners and representatives were present in the front of the court, and at the side was a large posse of DEFRA personnel, all attending to see the results of their many hours of paperwork and police-style, taped interviews. At least our two boats were back at sea. Both vessels had good crewmen standing in as Skippers, while Bluey and Mally were in court.

As all the cases were of the same nature, the three presiding Magistrates opted to hear all the cases together. The Clerk of the Court read out the charges and asked each defendant how they pleaded. All said, guilty, because technically, they were.

These pleas brought satisfied smirks from the inspectorate on the left of the room, and a fierce glare from me in their direction.

The prosecution opened its case with the usual propaganda, saying the European Commission was legislating to save declining fish stocks. He omitted to say that the Commission's ludicrous laws were forcing fishermen to kill and dump more fish than would otherwise be necessary. It meant the boats were spending longer at sea, scouring diverse areas for the correct balance of species, in a mixed fishery.

The Government lawyer churned out the wonderful regulations the EU had implemented to conserve fish stocks, obviously quoting verbatim from the work of ICES, the impartial? body of scientists, based in Copenhagen. This august group were contracted by the EU to supply research and informed data. In effect they gave answers to questions phrased by the EU Commission, though not necessarily the information they would wish to advise the fishing industry, had they been totally impartial.

In turn, the two defence lawyers mitigated for their Whitby clients, expressing the difficulties faced by fishermen due to the severity of the all-encompassing rules, and the inability of fishermen to be constantly aware of the changing regulations.

Andrew Oliver, the lawyer from Hull, pointed out to the Bench that all the DEFRA officials were sent on lengthy courses to learn and absorb the complex regulations. Fishermen, not the most academic of people, are expected to know these rules.

At this point I was permitted to speak on our behalf. I presented the photographs to the Bench that I'd taken on board *Allegiance* and *Independence* when they'd landed previous catches. I endeavoured to explain how it was impossible to discharge fish from below once it had been processed and boxed. I said that in years past the industry had been bedevilled with illegal landings, but all fishermen were now honest men, trying to make a living in an impossible environment. I said the fleet was massively reduced due to European laws, and that the overused 'unlevel playing field' analogy, was exactly that.

The Bench were about to retire to consider their judgement when I whispered to Andrew Oliver, "can you ask the Magistrates not to give us a 'conditional discharge' or the bastards will never leave us alone till they get us back in court."

"I can't do that," he replied. "It's up to them what penalties they wish to levy," but then, thoughtfully added, "but maybe you could get away with asking them?"

He attracted the attention of the Clerk of the Court, who approached the desk.

"Mr Normandale wishes to address the Bench," he said, putting me on the spot.

The Clerk whispered to the Magistrates, all of whom appeared to have shown interest in my mitigation. The trio directed their gaze in my direction and the Chairman, a well-groomed, middle-aged chap, looked over his glasses and smiled encouragingly.

I cleared my throat, and in my best voice said, "Please Sir, whatever you decide in judgement, we'd be most grateful if you'd consider 'not' giving us a conditional discharge'? We all know we'll be hounded endlessly by DEFRA if we're given a conditional discharge. We'll be summoned to court again before long, and today's verdict will have to be taken into consideration in any subsequent case."

The Chairman looked to his associates in turn, then stared sagely over his glasses again. Smiling, he said, "we hear what you say, Mr Normandale."

We all stood as the Bench retired to consider their verdict, leaving us free to discuss the possible outcome. The maximum fine for these offences was £50,000, though for an early guilty plea, this was usually reduced. I recalled the words of a Magistrates Clerk friend, years ago, when Bluey and I, along with a relief Skipper were in court for a different, cod related offence.

He said, "look for about ten percent of the maximum," but then we were given three helpings of that. Today we could potentially be levied four sets of fines, as I was part owner of both vessels, and there were two Skippers involved.

Time dragged endlessly as we waited for the decision, but eventually a bell rang and the Clerk called out, "all rise." The three pillars of society took their places, then the spectators sat. We all stood in line, awaiting sentence.

There was a stony silence as the Chairman of the Bench gathered his words in readiness for delivery. "Gentlemen," he said, addressing the row of men before him. "We have paid attention to your early guilty pleas, and also your well-argued mitigation. Under the circumstances," he paused, as if for effect, then slowly said, "each one of you is given an unconditional discharge. All parties are to meet their own costs." The Chairman then smiled benevolently and said, "you are all free to go."

"Wow!" I said, just audibly. "We've won. We've beat the buggers."

Andrew Oliver, at my side turned and shook my hand. "Well done," he said. "I certainly didn't expect that. You've missed your vocation. You should have been a lawyer."

"Well," I replied, "I 'ave t' say, ah didn't expect that either. Our track record in t' courts isn't that good. Last time we were 'up before the beak', we got well an' truly shafted."

As we filed out of the court, I couldn't resist looking across at the enemy, still seated at the side, and now it was my turn to smirk. The odious headman's face was crimson. He looked incandescent with rage. I couldn't resist giving him a beaming smile.

As the door to the chamber closed behind us, we gathered in the entrance and knowing I'd be heard inside, couldn't resist throwing clenched fists in the air and shouting, "Yes!"

There were many victorious smiles as we left the building, but then a Whitby voice said, "will yer be givin' us a contribution towards our legal costs? You 'avn't 'got any."

For the first time that day, I was briefly lost for words, but quickly found some appropriate expletives.

It was late afternoon when we drove back to Scarborough and, feeling jubilant I went straight to the Alliance office to inform our fish-salesman.

"We won," I said, as I entered his office. "We beat 'em."

Terry looked up from the sports page and was delighted to hear my news.

"Hey! That's great. Well done! You'll be able to tell the crews. The boats will be in the harbour in an hour or so. They've done alright for one day's fishing. We're about to go home."

I was standing on the quayside with my fellow defendants when *Independence* came around the pier end and into view. *Allegiance* would be a couple of miles behind. Of the two, the older boat was the faster.

We weren't alone. The posse of Fisheries Officers who'd been in the courtroom were also waiting for the boats. They could hardly wait for the ropes to be made fast before a pair made their way down the ladders, intent on inspecting the boat's logbook. The senior of the two then asked the Skipper to sign to affirm the accuracy of the document. Both immediately returned to the quayside, counting the boxes and checked the species in each, as the catch came ashore. They checked some of the weights in the boxes, but nothing was untoward.

At my suggestion, Bluey went down the ladder into *Independence's* wheelhouse and called *Allegiance* on the VHF radio, giving instructions to his relief Skipper. A couple of minutes later, his vessel came around the corner into view. The bogeymen prepared for the next boarding, but were in for a long wait.

Once more the inspectors were down the ladder quickly, requesting the voyage logbook be brought up to date. The Skipper complied with the instruction but then, instead of landing the catch he joined the crew and they began to overhaul the trawl, mending holes and small splits that had previously been cobbled together to save time. They took time out from this work when the Cook brought mugs of tea on deck.

The DEFRA men were incensed. They'd intended to stamp their authority on the fishermen, but were already out of office hours and were now hanging about doing nothing, while the fishermen were gainfully employed.

The hour of killing time went much faster for the crew than for the observers, but eventually the men relented and very slowly, landed the day's catch, allowing the maritime police to complete their mundane task, then go home.

The undeclared war went on for weeks, and the boats were also boarded at sea regularly, inspectors taking their time with their work, delaying fishing. This was harassment in a manner that wouldn't be tolerated by other nations vessels. Foreign politicians would have intervened on their fishermen's behalf, but no more prosecutions were pursued against our vessels. A precedent had been set.

Eventually the Government introduced additional regulations, giving their inspectorate sweeping new powers. Of their own volition the fisheries police could now impose fixed penalty fines and loss of fishing days at sea for set offences. The inspectors were now judge, jury and executioners. The saving grace was, fishermen still had recourse to the courts if they chose not to accept the DEFRA sentence.

I vowed I'd always take my chance with the courts. Some years later, we were again to face catch composition offences when Iain's replacement boat, *Rebecca* was boarded off the Tyne. We chose the court.

The North Shields Magistrates wouldn't accept the precedent set in the Whitby Court with reference to the catch percentage situation, but must have had sympathy for our case, as we were only fined £1500. It could have been much worse.

CHAPTER 6

BACK ON *NELLY*

Later in the year I boarded a plane in Manchester, flying to join *Lord Nelson* in Lisbon. I was sailing as Bosun's mate, one of the two volunteer deck crew on board, making the passage to Las Palmas in the Canary Islands.

I'd received the location of the ship in the post from the Jubilee Sailing Trust office in Southampton, and on arrival in Portugal, gave the directions to a taxi driver. I'd have no problem spotting the ship; her white masts and yards standing tall. I found her berthed well up river in this ancient city, on the north bank of the Tagus.

For centuries, every Spring the Portuguese Banks' Schooners, their decks stacked high with up to seventy 'dories' gathered here in this big river, before crossing the Atlantic to fish for cod off Newfoundland, the Grand Banks and Davis Straits. Once on location, the dories would be swung out overboard and each little sailing craft, with one man aboard, would be rowed away from the mother ship. Once clear, the fisherman would lay a length of line with a couple of hundred hooks attached, baited with pieces of herring. If the fishing was good, the little vessels would return to the mother ship loaded to the gunwales with huge cod. These would be pitch-forked on to the deck to be gutted, headed, split then stowed below, preserved in salt.

The little dories were launched every morning at daylight, returning before dark or when filled. The schooners would fish all Summer, returning home filled with salted cod each Autumn.

Many of these fishermen had never spent a Summer at home from their teens to retirement.

The cod stocks in these northern latitudes were phenomenal. There is evidence that the Portuguese had discovered the New World, decades before Columbus's voyage, and he'd gained knowledge of this land from fishermen. The fishing vessels had only to sail due west, keeping an approximate latitude to reach their destination.

* * *

I'd found the ship, but was quite nervous about joining her as a Bosun's mate. I was used to the sea and had seamanship skills, but the miles of rope in the rigging were complex. I'd picked up some knowledge on my previous four-day voyage, and could identify braces and buntlines and knew the order of the square sails from bottom to top, but was worried I wouldn't be up to the job in a hurry, or in the dark if I had to advise the voyage crew.

I was welcomed on arrival and chatted to some of the crew over a cuppa in the upper mess, telling them I'd sailed before and had been Skipper of a fishing vessel for most of my working life, but was worried about the BM role.

The present Bosun, Piers, known to many as Piles, a tall, thin, swarthy chap with long, black, scruffy hair, was very reassuring. "Don't worry, Mr Fish, yer've plenty of sea time under yer belt. Yer miles ahead of most o' the Bosun's mates we get."

This was great encouragement from someone who'd worked on most types of sailing vessels from an early age, and who knew the ropes comprehensively.

He'd called me Mr Fish. For the next twenty years, I'd be known on *Lord Nelson* and later on the new ship, *Tenacious* as 'Fred the Fish'.

Marco, the Chief Engineer was another tall, cheerful, long-haired member of the permanent crew. Although a North London lad, his father was Italian; his facial features reflecting this. He and

Piles had a great rapport and bounced humour off each other constantly, when not working. I knew immediately I was going to enjoy their company. I later discovered Marco and I had both sailed with the obscurely named, Bolton Steamship Company, albeit many years apart.

The voyage crew were not due to join the ship until the following day so Marco asked if I wanted to go ashore with half a dozen of the crew for something to eat and a few drinks.

I was quite pleased at the invitation, which gave me a feeling of inclusion, even though I was the new boy. This was something that would never change and every newcomer was made welcome.

It was already late, so getting a quick shower, I changed and, leaving most of my bag unpacked, the clean bed linen still in a pile on the mattress, I met up with the shore party in the ship's bar. Two or three drinks later, I left the ship with my new shipmates.

The first stop, and second and third were little street cubicles, selling port type drinks, which though small, were very tasty, went down easily and I suspected, were strong.

"We're heading for the Chicken Bar," Marco informed me. "It's the place we usually go when we're in Lisbon." The others in the group seemed to be aware of this plan already.

I kept up with the crew in the busy narrow streets, following the Engineer's lead, knowing that I'd never find them again if I lost touch. A couple of sharp turns, then a steep hill and we were there. The waiters greeted Marco like an old friend and directed us up the stairs. We sat at a plain table with a white, paper covering, overlooking the narrow, sloping street outside.

Several bottles of red wine appeared on the table and this was liberally distributed among the gang. Further bottles followed.

Trays piled with chicken and chips arrived and were shared among the diners. As each tray was emptied, another took its place. No wonder Marco liked this place. His appetite was considerable. The main course was followed by another tray containing a selection of desserts; then of course, the waiter brought a bottle of schnapps, giving everyone a shot. These were downed in one.

By the time we left the Chicken Bar I felt bloated and my head was swimming. Pleading tiredness after a long day's travel, I chose to bail out, getting a taxi back to the ship, leaving the crew to continue their night ashore.

Arriving back on the ship, head scrambled, I quickly realised my bed was still unmade, but in my confused state, I only managed to fit the sheet and pillowcases and hadn't a clue how to get the quilt into the cover. I climbed into the bed wrapping both around me. I'd never make that mistake again. I'd always make my bed soon after arriving on the ship.

The voyage crew joined the following afternoon and along with Nigel, my opposite number, I began dispensing oilskin jackets, trousers, short sea boots and waist belts to the new arrivals. Nigel was a short, stocky Welshman who'd been a Bosun's mate for several years and had completed about seventy voyages. He certainly knew the ropes and was a great font of knowledge and was full of helpful advice.

The forty, voyage crew, paying for the privilege of working and sailing on a tall ship were a real mix of society. Of course, some people stood out for various reasons, and these were the names I'd remember first.

Joshua, a whiskery, tussle-haired gentleman in his sixties, confined to a wheelchair, was a lawyer and called himself 'Ironside' after the American TV attorney.

There were several youngsters in their late teens or early twenties and numerous young at heart, adventurous older folk. Notably missing, for obvious reasons, were the generation with jobs and young families. One or two had recently found 'empty nest' syndrome, and were looking for a challenge, while still young. By the end of the voyage I'd know everyone's name.

When all hands had arrived, there was the usual meeting in the lower mess, where the permanent crew were introduced to the voyage crew by Captain Fisher. Now I was part of the permanent crew. Sometimes, if there wasn't a full complement on board, the ship would carry a volunteer Second Engineer. This would change eventually to two permanent Engineers.

Following introductions, came the safety briefings, then it was time for 'hands aloft'. Now I'd be on the platform assisting and encouraging the voyage crew. This became one of my favourite tasks. The challenge for able-bodied and less able was such, that I'd seen tears of joy and been privileged to share joyous hugs with happy achievers. In a world where health and safety ruled, and people were told "you can't do this, and you can't do that," it was wonderful to see so much positivity and 'can do' spirit. This was inspirational.

On a future voyage, with the yards square, I was to see two blind men, each with a Bosun's mate in support, ascend to the top of the foremast, one from each side of the ship then shake hands across the fore end of the mast. What a heart-warming occasion. Cheers and applause rang around the ship.

* * *

The voyage south was superb with fresh, fair winds and in one twenty-four-hour period, *Nelly* managed over two hundred miles. I didn't realise at the time what a spectacular achievement this was. The ship was on the port tack, heeling to starboard, which was great for me, as I was in a starboard bunk and couldn't fall out. Those on the port side were using lee cloths to hold themselves in their bunks. Having sailed in trawlers all my working life, I'd never used a lee cloth. I just wedged myself in the bunk with feet and elbows.

A couple of days short of our destination the wind eased and the sun shone all day long in a clear, blue sky. The Captain announced there was the possibility of seeing a 'green flash' as the sun set. Before this, the only green flash I'd heard of, was on a pair of squash shoes, but I was there at the ship's rail with half the sun's diameter already set. For the first (and last) time in my life, as the upper limb of the sun dropped from view, there was a distinct, split-second green flash.

* * *

Next morning, to my surprise, Marco streamed a fishing line over the stern on the starboard side, out of the ship's wake. I found the makings of another line in a tackle box, paying this from the other quarter. The lines had treble hooks on catgut and were dragged on the surface. We did catch some small tuna, though could only use the lines when we were not working. We'd hitch the fishing lines to the handrails, and did still catch the occasional fish, but at speed the hooks would pull out from the fish's mouth. This problem was resolved by attaching bungee cord to the line and the ship's stern rail. The spring in the bungee would absorb a fish's snatch. We caught more fish. 'Fred the Fish' began to live up to his name. I'd be sure to bring new tackle whenever I joined the ship in future.

Any fish caught were delivered to the galley, where the cook, on this occasion Fiona, was in command. Fiona, a large, jovial, mischievous lady, red of face with long, straggly hair was constantly laughing. Laying in my bunk, early mornings, I'd know it was time to get up when I heard Fiona laughing above my head in the galley.

One evening at dinnertime, I was queueing with other permanent crew in the entrance to the upper mess awaiting our meal. As I reached the stack of plates and trays that Fi was dispensing from, I noticed a small blob of cream on the surface of the worktop; a drip from a trifle. Putting my fore finger in the white blob, I thought it would be amusing to pop a little spot on the Cook's nose. I regretted this immediately when Fi wasn't amused, quickly realising it wasn't a good idea to wind the Cook up when she was at her busiest.

I regretted the badly timed joke even more an hour later when, down in the bar, with my back to the companionway, I didn't hear Fiona tiptoeing down the stairs, large bowl in hand. The contents, a huge dollop of trifle, was inverted over my head, coating hair, head and shoulders. Fi and the entire crowd in the bar were laughing at my condition. The Cook, no longer annoyed, had tears running down her face.

Not only was I coated in trifle, I had the mess to clean up, and the dish to wash. A valuable lesson learned. Don't mess with Fiona when she's busy.

* * *

We'd made such good time on our passage south that the Captain decided we'd head for Los Cristianos at the south end of the island of Tenerife, where, on arrival we dropped anchor off the little harbour. 'Hands to swim' was announced over the speakers. This was going to be fun. The crew had obviously done this evolution many times before, and in no time the small rubber DOTI[3] boat was in the water and manned. A lifebuoy was streamed overboard and a gate in the ship's side opened then fastened back.

A hinged platform was lowered to horizontal, then a long, aluminium ladder, reaching into the water, was bolted into position adjacent to the open gate.

In no time, the crew were jumping from the platform into the water. A couple of the permanent crew unhitched the main tack-line, the thick rope spliced into the corner of the course sail, which held the sail down and in position, when set. At present the big sail was stowed on the yard and the tack line now dangled overboard in the water. Like pirates boarding a ship, each of the crew held the tack-line, then swung out over the water, letting go and dropping from a height into the sea. This was a great experience and one I enjoyed watching immensely.

"Don't I get to go in?" Ironside said to Dave the Mate, as he watched the hijinks from his wheelchair. "I swim in the pool at home."

Dave was also the ship's Safety Officer. He thought for a while then said, "we'll let you in if you wear a lifejacket."

"Agreed" said the now grinning Joshua. "Do you want me to sign anything?" Taken below by his buddy, ten minutes later the doughty lawyer was back on deck in a pair brightly coloured baggy, swimming shorts.

BM Nigel was despatched to bring a lifejacket from the cleaning locker. Half a dozen old blue and grey, paint stained jackets were stored there for crew maintenance when working over the side.

There was still the problem of getting the fearless swimmer into the water. The Mate had intended to lower him in a helistrop

---

3   *Approved to 'Department of Trade and Industry' standards.

from the stainless-steel davit at the platform. This davit was usually deployed to raise and lower physically handicapped voyage crew in and out of the DOTI boat and to the ship, while in their wheelchairs.

"Don't bother with that," Joshua said. "Lower me from my chair onto the platform and give me a shove."

The Mate shrugged, grinned and said, "OK." He waved to the safety boat, signalling the driver to come closer, made sure the area below was clear, then nodded to the group assisting Josh.

What a character. He was a big man and, dropping eight or nine feet, entered the water sideways. He hardly went under due to the buoyancy of the floatation device and surfaced spluttering, and laughing loudly.

Josh swam about for a while, then was hauled back on board by a bunch of his shipmates in the helistrop, on the end of a block and tackle on the davit. The grinning lawyer was lowered into his chair to a round of applause, then was taken to the deck shower by his buddy.

I felt compelled to go into the water and, climbing to the life-raft platform above the deck, I asked for the tack-line. Fifteen feet above the water, I made sure my legs were clear of the bight of rope leading back to the deck, then swung out. It was essential to let go once over the water, or the trajectory would bring me back inboard and possible disaster.

High above the water, I let go of the rope and dropped, entering the water feet first, unlike a later adventurer, a Japanese girl, who landed on her back. I went very deep, and was gasping for air on reaching the surface.

An hour later, the anchor and DOTI boat recovered, we were heading for Santa Cruz de Tenerife and the end of the voyage.

Tied alongside in port, and following a couple of drinks in the ship's bar with Bosun Piles and BM Nigel, it was time for the crew party. Almost the whole compliment filled a pre-booked shore side restaurant for a last night celebration. The voyage had been fantastic and everyone wanted to party. This was always a fun night, when folks let their hair down after their sailing experience, and before they went their separate ways. It was a great evening, and was a fitting end to what had been a terrific voyage.

It's extraordinary that ten days earlier, most of these people had never met and now they were the best of friends, despite the difference in ages and coming from varied backgrounds. They were shipmates.

Many would return for another voyage. Some would stay in touch and remain firm friends. The Jubilee Sailing Trust certainly changed lives. It was changing mine.

I returned from the Canaries to Manchester airport and after humping my heavy sea bag from the baggage reclaim area to the train, I felt weary. The bag seemed heavier than when I'd departed. The tough voyage must have sapped my strength. At least that's what I thought, till I arrived home and opened my bag.

A large, ancient, heavy bottle-screw, wrapped in bagging, was stashed in the middle of my gear. No question of who the bloody culprits were, but I couldn't help but laugh. What a great wheeze.

In return I wrote a bogus letter to the pair, saying what bastards they were, and that I'd been asked by airport security if I'd packed my own bag. I'd said, "yes" then had been asked why I had a large, useless metal object in my luggage.

I also wrote that I'd been delayed boarding, which in turn delayed the flight. I said I was the last one to board the plane and they'd been waiting ages. I'd been booed by all the other passengers when I boarded.

The pranksters must have believed the letter's contents because for some time after, whenever I joined the ship, I was questioned about the supposed airport incident.

* * *

Having had such a good time on the ship, I was now totally hooked on tall ships and the Jubilee Sailing Trust. I immediately obtained the following year's brochure. Scanning the programme, I found a particularly interesting prospect: a voyage around the Western

Isles. This was to take place the following May, and was from Oban, returning to the same port a week later. I asked my Dad, who was 77, if he also fancied this voyage, that I'd treat him to the experience. I explained that there were plenty of people older than him sailing, and who were nowhere near as fit as he was.

"You book it an' ah'll go," he said, with his usual Yorkshire enthusiasm!

CHAPTER 7

TROUBLES ON *SCORESBY*

It had been a poor Autumn so far and today was no exception. It seemed there was a constant, endless stream of low-pressure areas sweeping across the Atlantic, all passing into the North Sea. There were hardly two fine days, back to back.

I'd only been in bed a few minutes when the phone rang. I hated getting phone calls during the night. Since I'd been Operations Manager of Scarborough's Lifeboat these past few years, this usually meant taking a call from the Coastguard, requesting the launch of the lifeboat. This protocol was necessary as the RNLI was not a Government body.

Following my sanctioning of the launch, I'd set off pagers via my mobile phone, summoning crew and designating either the inshore, 'ILB', the all-weather 'ALB', or both, then make my way to the boathouse. It was amazing that despite living close, being the first to get the news, then calling the crew, I was never first to the boathouse. A couple of the keener ones must have had clothes arranged, ready to leap into from their bed!

On the Coxswain's arrival at the boathouse, I'd discuss the launch request and potential time duration, then remain in the station following the launch, listening to the radio traffic. Along with a few of the shore team, we'd hear the communications between our boat, the Coastguard, and occasionally the vessel requiring assistance. It was a pre-requisite that the Ops' Manager would remain on station until the boat was back from her service and re-housed.

On this occasion I was totally taken aback. The call wasn't from the Coastguard but from *Scoresby*. It was a ship to shore, satellite call from a very worried Billy, on board the boat. Where was Danny? I leapt out of bed.

"Fred, it's Billy. Danny's unconscious in the alleyway. 'E's been knocked out by a 'eavy sweep chain on t' afterdeck. We're across t' sector line in Norwegian waters. What shall ah do?"

He quickly went on to tell me that their net had become stuck fast on an obstruction in heavy weather. The wind, a screaming southerly, was blowing storm force ten. Two men had manned the winch and begun hauling back on the wires. While the net was still fastened to the bottom, waves were dropping aboard the stern of the boat in big lumps, swamping the deck. Eventually, by pulling on one end and slacking on the other, in a seesawing motion, the net had jumped free of the unknown obstruction.

The trawl may have been freed, but had come to the surface in a tangled knot of net, heavy chain and wire, entwined together. This mess was hanging over the stern of the boat in a huge ball, and *Scoresby* was bouncing violently.

With nothing further to do in the wheelhouse, the Skipper, Danny had donned oilskins and sea-boots and gone onto the pitching after-deck to assist in untangling the heap.

No sooner was he out of the door and onto the deck when the ship dropped into a deep trough between two swells and a heavy chain, previously taut around the transom stern, had jumped inboard, striking Danny on the head and laying him out cold, with a possible fractured skull. He'd been washing around on the deck, unconscious, from where the crew had dragged him, pulling him out of the water, into the galley passage.

"Gi' me yer position, Billy," I said, heart racing. "Ah'll call t' Coastguard for advice an' get back t' yer."

I garbled the news to Dotty, then immediately rang Aberdeen Coastguard, requesting to speak to the Senior Duty Officer. I explained to the operator that I was the Ops' Manager of the Scarborough Lifeboat Station, but needed some assistance for my own vessel, in trouble over in Norwegian Waters.

The Senior Officer was quickly on the line and I elaborated on the brief words I'd given to the operator. I said my son was unconscious onboard *Scoresby*, giving her position, and asking if he was able to get helicopter assistance from his counterpart in Norway.

The man said he'd never had a situation like this before, but would do what he could. The Officer was true to his word and rang back ten minutes later saying he'd contacted the emergency services in Bergen, and they would launch a helicopter for the casualty.

With grateful thanks and relief, I was able to contact *Scoresby*, assuring Billy there'd be a helicopter on its way shortly, and asked how things were with them.

"Danny's semi-conscious now Fred," he said, "an' we've been able t' scramble the 'eap o' tangled trawl aboard. It's in a big mess. We're jus' dodgin' 'ead t' wind, waitin' for instructions."

I suggested he make his way as best he could towards Bergen and to listen out for the helicopter on the emergency VHF Channel, 16.

"Keep me posted," I requested, as he signed off.

Two hours later I received another call from Billy. The helicopter had been and gone again, the pilot saying the weather was so bad that under the circumstances, they couldn't chance a lift off, and the boat with casualty, should make their way to Bergen as best they could. The good news was that Danny was now conscious, but not surprisingly, had a violent headache. It was a long way to Bergen, and in the current conditions would be a slow passage.

It was late on the following day when *Scoresby* finally arrived into port, tying up at the quayside. Waiting on the pier was a local man who, asking for Danny, gave him a quantity of Norwegian currency then delivered him to the local hospital.

It was no surprise that the merchant was waiting for the boat's arrival. Earlier in the day I'd rung Kurt Christiansen in Grimsby, a friend since my earliest days of fishing. I explained the situation, asking if he knew anyone in Bergen who could help. Kurt had known Danny since he was a boy and said, "I think I can help, Fred. I'll see what I can do and come back to you."

Half an hour later the Grimsby agent rang back saying, "you're not gonna believe this, but!" He went on to relate how he'd rung an associate in Norway and the recipient of the call had been up in the mountains, skiing.

"Leave it with me Kurt. I will attend to the matter for you," had been the response to the request from my Grimsby friend. From his position, high in the mountains the man had, on learning the E.T.A. of *Scoresby*, arranged for a member of his staff to meet the vessel on arrival.

On the completion of these calls and arrangements, I paused to think how fantastic modern communications had become in recent years. Messages had been sent from the boat to me, to Aberdeen, to Norway, to Grimsby and finally to a man up a mountain. Incredible!

Sadly, the hospital services were not as good as the communications network. The doctor had looked at Danny's blood matted scalp injury and remarked, "we can do nothing with this now. The wound is old. You should have come here yesterday."

Danny had gone to a hairdresser with the idea of having the hair from around the injury shaved to expose the wound. With amazing good fortune, he'd stumbled upon a Canadian lady hairdresser who'd been a nurse, and who not only shaved the damaged region, but carefully put a soothing balm on the injury then dressed the wound.

The vessel stayed in Bergen for two more days until the headaches had subsided and the Skipper felt well enough to sail the boat back across the North Sea to Scotland for a well-earned, few days off.

* * *

One Tuesday morning, only a few weeks later, I received another phone call from *Scoresby*, but this time from Danny. "Dad, ah've fucked up. We 'ave a screw-full. There's a bight o' bellies stuck in t' nozzle."

He went on to say some slack netting had come up under the boat and had been sucked into the propeller. "We're bein' towed in t' Peterhead an' should be in about six o'clock tonight. Ah've rung a local diving company 'ere but they want three 'undred an' fifty quid t' clear it. Bloody robbers. It's not a big job. If I 'ad any diving gear aboard, ah'd do it meself. What d' ya think? Shall I pay 'em? Ah' want t' land the fish we 'ave aboard an' get out again."

This was an exorbitant charge. The usual charge in Scarborough was sixty to a hundred pounds, depending on the difficulty of the job. "A'll ring Clarky and see if he's doin' anythin'. Ah'll call yer back."

Tommy Clark was my diving buddy. He was a self-employed joiner, but could be relied upon to clear propellers for beer money when anyone was 'fanned up'.

"Hiya Tommy, d' ya fancy a trip t' Peterhead t' clear *Scoresby*'s prop?" I asked, as if a four-hundred-mile journey each way was something we'd do regularly. "Danny 'as a screw-full, an' 'e can only get pro-divers costing silly money. We can be there tonight an' back tomorrow afternoon. It'll be worth a good day's pay for yer."

He took little persuading and we were on the road before noon with diving kit and a change of clothes in the back of the car.

The road north is a good run, once out of Yorkshire, and it's one I've done many times, (and collected more than one speeding ticket along the way). Though long, this was an easy journey in good company. I'd informed Danny we were coming north, and asked him to book a twin room for us in a local hotel.

On arriving in Peterhead, a town of mostly grey buildings, we pulled up on the quayside next to *Scoresby*. The engine was running in neutral, generating power, and all normal signs of occupation were evident, but *Marie Celeste* like, there were no crew to be seen. I tried ringing Danny's mobile phone, but the signal was so poor that I couldn't get through.

"We might as well do the job now, while were 'ere," Tommy said and, pulling his bag from the back of the car, began to kit up. I climbed into my wetsuit and prepared my diving gear in readiness, though wouldn't go into the water unless Tommy needed back up.

Descending the ladder to the boat, I found a sharp, serrated-edged knife stowed on the deck, handy for net mending and put the blade in a bucket: lowering this to the waterline for the diver to reach, when required.

Five minutes later, Tommy, fully kitted up, heavy cylinders on his back, mouthpiece in place and hand on facemask, characteristically jumped the ten feet from pier to water near the stern of the boat, entering with a big splash and a cloud of bubbles. He sank deep into the harbour water, but didn't resurface immediately, instead swam directly under the boat to assess the situation.

Surfacing minutes later, he took out the mouthpiece and gasping, called out, "it's not too bad. There's quite a bit o' net in, but it's twisted tight and will cut out easy with a sharp knife. I'll 'ave t' make a mess o' the trawl."

I assured him that damaging the net wasn't important and that a patch of netting would easily (if not quickly) repair the slashed section. There'd be plenty of time to rectify the damage on the way back to the fishing grounds.

Ten minutes of energetic sawing and heaps of bubbles brought the job to a satisfactory conclusion. Tommy replaced the knife in the bucket and with his fins now hanging on each wrist, climbed the ladder back to the quayside, mission accomplished. The job was done, but there was still no sign of the missing crew.

We decided to head for our accommodation at the Palace Hotel, where we could get showered and changed, and where Tommy could get rid of the taste of harbour water.

It was still early in the evening so, now cleaned up and changed, we went downstairs to the bar for a beer. Entering the brightly lit room, with a large circular bar, I was surprised to see only one customer, perched on a tall, high-backed bar stool. We stood near him as we ordered our drinks.

"All right matey?" I asked, not wanting to be pushy, but not wanting to ignore the stranger.

The man looked in my direction with glazed eyes and spoke with slurred, incomprehension.

"Aye, OK, Ah know what yer mean," I reply, then looked towards Tommy.

"'E's well pissed," I whispered. "Don't make eye contact."

Our drinks arrived and clinking our glasses, I said, "cheers, Tommy, and well done," while deliberately ignoring the drunken man. But we wouldn't be able to ignore him for much longer.

"D' yer remember that drunk in t' Mishnish in Tobermory?" Tommy whispered, smirking.

I couldn't help but laugh as he reminded me of the tale.

We'd been on a diving trip in the Sound of Mull and were staying in a dive lodge behind the imposing Western Isles Hotel, which commands magnificent views of Tobermory Bay, Calf Island and the Sound.

Having had a couple of great wreck dives during the day, then eaten a feast of diver-caught scallops for dinner, we'd descended en masse down the steps to the waterfront and the famous Mishnish pub. The dozen or more divers had managed to gather sufficient stools and chairs close to the fixed wall seating, and by pulling a couple of tables together we'd gathered cosily around, ready for a pleasant, convivial evening. An ashtray full of money in the centre of the table was the 'kitty'.

Tommy and I, ready for refills, made a list of the round and, taking a couple of notes from the ashtray had gone to the bar to get drinks. I squeezed between customers to get close to the bar and gained the cheery barman's attention. Standing next to me, a rotund, unshaven local man wearing a woolly hat, bristled and glared when he heard my voice.

I read from the list, and as the glasses were placed on the bar, Tommy passed them back to Alana, who'd come to assist, and was efficiently delivering the drinks to our tables.

The order complete, I was waiting for the change from the bartender when the adjacent Scotsman said, "Hey mon! Yer woman's awa wi ma dram."

Tommy must have accidentally taken the man's drink, passing it to Alana.

The barman was still standing close behind the counter so quickly and cheerily, I said, "and a whisky fo' this gentleman please," waving the flat of my hand in the Scot's direction.

Tommy was hovering at my shoulder, watching the encounter with interest.

My new acquaintance said, "it was a feckin' double."

"Can yer make that a double please, barman," I called out pleasantly.

The drink was duly placed before the man, and I proffered the additional coins, thanking the man behind the counter.

With the new double whisky in hand, the drunk muttered, "feckin' English."

Feeling a little mischievous, I turned and quite seriously said to the man, "hey! Excuse me, ah'm not English! Ah'm from Yorkshire!"

A look of total confusion came over the man's countenance and he muttered, "Well ah suppose they're nae sae bad."

Tommy, glass to mouth, nearly choked as he sprayed beer back into his glass.

"Yer cheeky bastard," he chuckled when we were out of earshot. "'Ow did yer get away wi that?"

* * *

Seconds later a loud bang brought our attention from the Mishnish, back to the hotel bar in Peterhead. The man who'd been at our side was now on the floor. He'd leaned backwards in the large chair, glass still in hand, and fallen flat on his back, unconscious. The glass had shattered on the floor close by. The long bar mat he'd grabbed, attempting to stop his fall, was draped across his chest. We looked at each other, then made a move to help.

"Och! He'll be a'right," called the barman from a few feet away, now heading in our direction. He's had a dram or twa too mony. Ah'll see tae him."

We took the barman at his word and, quickly supping up, left the hotel bar.

It was getting dark now, so we walked back towards the harbour, calling into another bar, en route, still looking for the missing crew. There was music playing in the background and a few hardened drinkers talking loudly at the bar. As we approached the counter, two of the men began throwing punches at each other. We made a swift one hundred and eighty degree turn and left the premises.

There was still no contact on the phone. "One more try," I suggested, "then, if we don't find 'em, we'll go an' eat."

We headed for the nearest pub to where *Scoresby* was berthed, but found no familiar faces. A man was sitting at a table with his back to us. We passed by, approaching the bar. Ordering a pint each, we stood surveying the surroundings and the many photographs of fishing boats around the room.

The door swung open loudly and a big, brawny, red-faced man strode into the room. In seconds he was at the table of the seated man and immediately grabbed the poor unsuspecting fellow in a headlock. The brute began smashing his victim's forehead on the table, shouting, "what ha' yer been doin'wi' mah wife, ya bastard? Ye'll ne'er go near her agin, cos ah'm gonna feckin' kill yer."

Startled, Tommy said, "Fuckin''ell, Nommy! What sort o' place 'ave yer brought me t'? It's like cowboy land."

The bartender, hearing Tommy's exclamation, leaned over grinning, saying,

"Hey Jimmy! If yer think thas is rough, yer need tae be here on a weekend, yer ken! This is jus' a quiet nacht in the Blue Toon. (The locals nickname for Peterhead)

We eventually found the crew of *Scoresby*, or at least they found us. They'd been in the Creel Bar, a short walk away. Danny explained that none of the crew had any money, but the Landlady had given them all credit until their catch was sold and the crew paid.

* * *

A few days later, out of the blue, I received a phone call from a journalist, intending to write a series of articles about various 'night workers' and their jobs for the Daily Telegraph magazine. The young lady was looking to pen a story about fishermen and their way of life.

I explained that I no longer went to sea, but could give her the background story if it would help.

The journalist said, "yes please," and arranged to come to Scarborough from London the following weekend. She said, "I'll be bringing a camera along."

"I can't guarantee there'll be any boats in," I added, but was told it didn't matter. I was confused and remained so until the following week.

The attractive young lady turned up at the house the following Saturday, driving an estate car, the rear of which was stacked with photographic equipment, some of which she began to unload.

"Do you have any of the old-fashioned oilskins, still?" the tall blond asked.

Fortunately, I had. There was a yellow oilskin and a pair of full-length sea-boots, stowed in the garage.

Twenty minutes later I was standing on a large, blue sheet, mounted on a frame, forming a backdrop, in front of the fireplace, clad in heavy weather gear; a most incongruous situation.

The article, when published, quoted me complaining about Spanish fishermen plundering the Grand Banks, off eastern Canada. The column was seen by many friends and acquaintances, so of course, I was the butt of jokes for being a shore Skipper and dry land sailor.

Subsequently the same article appeared in Virgin Train magazines, then Virgin Airlines, following which, I received several letters, two of which were very amusing and are reproduced below. Both were hand written.

The first, sealed in a small brown envelope, the rear of which, in black print said, 'On His Majesty's Service'. This envelope must have been at least 50 years old. The missive read;

Dear Skipper

To tell you the truth I was almost at the point of cancelling my account for the Daily Telegraph. I'm sure you will agree that it has of late become rather wishy washy and may soon be reduced to one more pinko rag.

What a delight to see your cadaverous Anglo Saxon face peering at me over my breakfast egg. You sir are an example to the whole sad state of this nation.

A two-hundred mile exclusion zone? My foot. Were I a younger man, with stout fellows like you alongside me we should make it two thousand miles or I'm a Dutchman. Mind you, we shall all be Dutchmen if this damned Common Market nonsense goes much further.

I saw my daughter at the weekend and have given her instructions to produce a gansey for you on her knitting machine featuring a large cod swimming across a red maple leaf. I showed her your article and she thought a skull and crossed bones might be more to your liking. Ha Ha good show. What do you think?

Anyway time is pretty much my own now I have retired and I would be very pleased to join your crew next time you are steaming down to Dago fishing grounds.

I shant need any pay and I have my own small piece. (gun?) probably not much use at any range but handy enough if we have to board. So let's be knowing, asap. I do not want to be trekking up north on spec'.

Meanwhile Frederick I raise my hat to you.

Yours sincerely Lt Col Reggie Walmer

PS Any chance you could pick me up at a port on the south coast. And by the way, I do swim but if I go overboard don't worry, I'm not a lingerer and my colostomy bag will probably pull me down anyway.

The GPO have given me an approximation of your address. I hope there will be no delay.

The second letter, addressed to me via The Harbour Master, Scarborough said,

Dear Mr Normandale

I saw your picture in the Telegraph magazine and I thought you looked great in your rainwear. I've got a lovely rubber mackintosh that would suit you down to the ground. I would love to see you in it.

I hope you don't mind me writing to you but I thought it was an advert and I was going to send for a catalogue, secretly hoping there would be more pictures of you. Then I realised it was not an advert and that you are a real person. I had to dash off for a cold shower. But in my rubber wear of course.

I hope you will write back telling me what you boys get up to in those long nights below deck.

Is Dottie into rubber too? Do you ever come up to London? I could put you both up and have some great new oil that does not damage rubber.

Send me a long letter and undraped photos.

Bye Toni Mileowski.

I didn't write back but was tempted!

CHAPTER 8

MAINTENANCE ON *NELLY*

I'd made several voyages on *Nelly* now and had decided to drive to Southampton while the ship was in port, to assist with maintenance. I left home at 05.00 and making good time, had arrived about 09.45, parking close to the ship. By the gangway I found Carolyn, the current Medical Purser, who gave me bunk number 21. This was one of the coveted holes in the wall on the starboard side. I threw my bag in the bunk. There was work going on in various places around the ship, so I went looking for the Bosun, to enquire where I could be best employed.

There seemed to be activity in the cleaning locker on the port side, aft. This was the deck storage cupboard under the bridge, containing deck brushes, buckets and detergents. Further back, a myriad of other useful equipment was stowed away. Though only accessible on hands and knees, this locker was deep, almost crossing the width of the deckhouse.

Crouching, I looked through the pinned-back door, nodding to the Bosun, who was in discussion with a small, dark-haired, lady, clad in overalls, who was intent on inspecting the locker floor.

The pair were discussing a leak that had been dripping from the cleaning locker into the accommodation below, probably near to the entrance, which was frequently wet.

Having spent my career on fishing vessels with wooden decks, which occasionally leaked, this was something I had experience of. Bobbing under the low door sill, I took out a pocketknife and began inserting the blade into any likely seam where caulking could have become loose. After two or three failed attempts, my efforts came to the attention of the lady, who it transpired was the Mate, and whom I'd never met before. This was Barbara Campbell, who I was soon to realise, was a force to be reckoned with.

Directing her ire in my direction, the Mate said, "Who are you? What do you think you're doing? Get out! This is nothing to do with you."

Ouch! I thought, smarting and beating a hasty retreat backwards to the deck. I didn't deserve that. I was only trying to help.

Making my way to the upper mess, I brewed a mug of tea then walked aft down the starboard side, sitting on a coil of rope on the stern platform, licking my wounds and feeling sorry for myself.

Soon after, Barbara appeared on the platform. "I think I owe you an apology. I didn't know who you were. I'd heard of 'Fred the Fish', but didn't know you were he."

"It's ok", I replied, still smarting from the unwarranted bollocking. "I was on'y tryin' t' help."

I calmed down, and soon after was allocated a job, cementing inside a fresh water tank.

Over the next few days Barbara and I became better acquainted and would, subsequently sail together many times over the coming years. She was a firm favourite of the crew and though short in stature, the bright-eyed, competent, formidable lady was the most energetic person I'd ever met. It was said if you wanted to find Barbara on the ship, stand still, she would soon be passing. Put out your foot and you'd stop her.

There wasn't a part of the masts and rigging that Barbara didn't know, and as Mate, the lady would spend a great deal of time climbing aloft, inspecting standing rigging, running gear and sails.

Barbara was married to husband Chris, who was a Marine Engineer with Calmac Ferries, when they met.

Soon after my visit to the ship, Barbara left the Jubilee Sailing Trust to sail as Master in the brig, *Stavros S Niarchos*, belonging to the Sail Training Association, where she served for a couple of years. Meanwhile I continued sailing with the JST.

Barbara returned to the Jubilee Sailing Trust as Master, and hadn't slowed down any. The new Captain arrived on board in Southampton at the commencement of a maintenance period. Always popular, the other permanent crew had been mulling over ideas to welcome the 'dynamo' back to the ship.

Knowing that at her home in Dunoon, husband Chris kept their strip of lawn in immaculate, manicured condition, the decision was made to 'turf' her cabin. The thinking was, this would ensure the new Captain would feel at home.

The rolls of grass arrived in the morning and were immediately fitted in the cabin by the Engineer and Bosun, while Barbara was whizzing all over the ship. A 'keep off the grass' sign was also painted and positioned strategically.

The cabin door was then closed, as this was adjacent to the ship's office. The crew then waited for the discovery. They waited and waited, but the Captain didn't go near her quarters.

It was immediately before dinner when everyone in earshot heard the call, "Marrrccoo!!!"

The Captain arrived in the upper mess to a huge round of applause, and a shout of, "welcome back" and was handed a glass of wine.

At this point, the Bosun had to admit his failure. Steve had been dispatched to find a couple of lambs to graze on the grass. "I found the sheep," he said, grinning. "The bloody taxi driver wouldn't let them in his cab!"

* * *

The Trustees of the Jubilee Sailing Trust had decided to build a new ship to compliment *Lord Nelson*. She would be a wooden ship, built with laminate strips, which would give her immense strength. Under direction, volunteers would pay to work on the ship during her construction. Many who sailed on *Lord Nelson*, would later turn up to live on site and to work on the new vessel.

Lord Nelson in Scarborough – Colin Lawson

Completed in 2000, the vessel would be slightly longer and have more beam and draft than *Nelly*. Her name was to be *Tenacious*. I would sail in her many times, but my favourite would always be old *Nelly*.

With her immense cost, the need for two crews and reliefs, plus additional office staff, it would be imperative to keep both ships filled. Sadly, this wouldn't always be the case.

Chapter 9

The Final Dive (i thought)

It was late September and the end of the diving season at home. The Scarborough Sub Aqua Club had enjoyed a great Summer, recovering many artefacts, and this was to be the finale of the year in UK waters. I was one of a dozen keen divers who were going to the Orkney Isles to dive on some of the ships of the German Grand Fleet. These huge battleships and cruisers had been scuttled in Scapa Flow in 1919 following Germany's surrender at the end of the Great War.

A few of us had been to the Islands previously, and had spent several days exploring this unique dive site. I was keen to go again and planned to drive north to Scrabster with Tommy to meet the ferry. We'd been dive buddies frequently, and it was a standing joke that though I'd dived with Tommy many times, I'd never come back with him.

We'd made good time and arrived at a small guesthouse an hour short of our destination in the early evening. With no pub nearby we enjoyed a tasty dinner and turned in. An early start the following morning got us to the ferry. It was only a short crossing of the Pentland Firth, with its massive, boiling tidal flows, passing to starboard, the 'Old Man of Hoy', a unique natural rock stack at the entrance to Scapa Flow.

We docked in the old town of Stromness with its ancient, stone-built houses and flag-stoned, paved streets. This little port had an amazing history. All Arctic expeditions and whalers called here for water, additional boat crews and fresh provisions in early Spring, before sailing north.

The Hudson Bay Company in Northern Canada, established for hundreds of years, recruited many of their permanent staff from among the Orcadians, including John Rae. This famous son of Stromness trekked thousands of miles throughout the northern wastelands, discovering the final part of the long unsolved, North West Passage. He also discovered the remains of some of the men from the missing Franklin expedition, after many organised rescue voyages had failed to find the missing ships, *Terror* and *Erobus*.

Sadly, his achievement was never fully acknowledged, as on his return to London, Rae reported that the last remaining crew members of the ill-fated expedition had resorted to cannibalism. In Victorian England, when British explorers and sailors were all heroes, John Rae's revelations were unacceptable, and he was vilified by London society for making his findings public.

Lady Franklin, who'd petitioned and lobbied the Government to send many expeditions in search of her missing husband's ships, could not accept Rae's findings. Sadly, John Rae was never given true recognition for his life's work, though many arctic explorers of his day were honoured.

It was subsequently discovered that much of the food on the Franklin Expedition was in large tins, but these containers had been sealed with molten lead, causing debilitating weakness and death among the crew from lead poisoning and botulism, causing the eventual collapse of the expedition.

* * *

Most of our group had crossed to Orkney on the same ferry, so it was a small convoy of vehicles, loaded with diving paraphernalia that drove along the old stone pier, seeking the dive boat chartered for the expedition. She was the 50-foot, converted fishing vessel, *Radiant Queen*, a cruiser stern vessel with forward wheelhouse. She was easily found and the kit loaded on to her deck. This done we could now seek out our accommodation, dump the bags in the rooms and, having no further use for them, park the cars close by for the duration of our stay.

Stromness was a small, attractive little place with a narrow main street. Everywhere was in easy walking distance. The Ferry Inn, a low-ceilinged, friendly pub by the harbour was a great place to spend an evening, following an enjoyable fish and chip bar-meal.

Next morning, feeling slightly fuzzy from the previous night's fun, we gathered on the quayside awaiting the Skipper of the dive boat. As ever, tales from the pub were revisited and exaggerated while we waited. It was my forty-ninth birthday.

The Skipper and his crewman hove into view, dead on time and fifteen minutes later the old vessel slipped from her berth, her engine throbbing strongly.

We headed towards the middle of 'The Flow', to the scene of the mass ship suicide that took place on 21st June 1919. Not all the seventy-four warships in Scapa Flow sank on that fateful morning; twenty-two were prevented from sinking by the Royal Navy and of those that did founder, not all remained in this seabed graveyard. In the 1930s quite a few of the sunken vessels were raised in a phenomenal, cutting edge salvage operation by Cox and Danks Shipbreaking Company[4]. The recovered ships were towed away, to be broken up for valuable scrap.

Our group, enthusiastic, were kitting up as the dive-boat made her way towards *Brummer*. This German cruiser was lying on her side in twenty-six metres of water, the site marked with a floating plastic oil-drum, fastened to the wreck.

The biggest ships of the battle fleet had totally capsized when they'd flooded and were upside down. The leviathans were now huge artificial reefs covered in a mass of marine growth. The ships bore no resemblance to sunken vessels, so were of little interest to our party.

Tommy and I jumped from the boat's side, plunging under water with the momentum of the five-foot drop and weight of our gear. We didn't resurface. Though diving buddies usually floated up

---

4   See *The man who bought a navy*, by Gerald Bowman.

and did OK procedures and checks, we made a point of entering the water, turning through one hundred and eighty degrees and continuing downwards, heading towards the shot-rope, a few feet distant.

We grabbed the line, following the rope downwards to the wreck. I always wanted to get down as quickly as possible, knowing my time of immersion was limited, and my wrist computer started when I broke the surface.

The water in Scapa Flow was grey and a little murky, with visibility no more than about fifteen feet. At the bottom of the line we found ourselves somewhere near the foredeck, though with the vast ship on its side, the perspective was strange. The coarse sandy seabed was within sight and dropping down, we disturbed some queenie scallops close to the vertical deck. These creatures flipped up from the seabed, opening and closing their twin shells rapidly to create propulsion, swimming a few feet off the bottom before dropping back down. I'd never seen these creatures swimming and wouldn't have believed they could, had I not seen it for myself. I'd caught many tens of thousands of these tasty morsels when trawling, but thought they'd be too heavy to move. These were only small specimens, a couple of inches in diameter, so I didn't bother collecting any. Fully grown, they'd be twice this size.

Swimming along the bottom we came across a small bed of king scallops, not easily detected. I noticed the little puff of silt as the flat shell, raised to filter the water for food, dropped instantly, on our approach. Unlike queenies, kings had a cupped bottom shell buried below the surface and a flat top shell level with the bottom. These creatures grew to about seven inches diameter, were delicious and very filling.

I dropped half a dozen of the tasty morsels into my goodie bag and Tommy took a similar haul. It was great fun scallop hunting and when we'd dived with the club in the Sound of Mull, we'd had huge feasts of king scallops. I allowed some air to flow into my stab jacket, compensating for the additional weight.

Taking my knife from its scabbard, strapped to my leg, I forced the blade into the gap at the hinge of the shell, slicing open the two halves. Attracting Tommy's attention, I cut the white muscle from the centre of the shell and, taking the regulator from my mouth, popped the piece of meat in, replacing the valve, then laughed, the vibrations audible underwater.

Tommy shrugged and began to swim off. I followed, and we continued our dive. My buddy pointed to a huge, elongated, wide pipe and with great animation, described that I was observing a gun barrel. It was difficult to comprehend that this massive structure was one of the ship's giant guns. Its twin would be buried in the sand.

A six-pound piece of lead that had once been part of a weight belt appeared in my vision, and like a fool, I put the heavy object in my bag. This made my buoyancy extremely negative and I pumped more air in my stab jacket. I was now working harder with my fins and using more air to keep up with Tommy.

We were now at the bridge area of the big ship, but couldn't see a way in. Someone from the Scarborough Club must have found access on a previous expedition because the compass binnacle (minus compass) and incredibly, a piece from a paper navigation chart, now framed, were on display in the clubhouse.

Looking at the computer, I realised we had little bottom time left before decompression was required, so signalled to Tommy with a vertical open hand in the direction we'd come from.

He acknowledged with raised thumb and forefinger and we turned. I followed him back to the surface line, ascending with difficulty, compelled to constantly dump air from my buoyancy aid as the contents expanded with the reducing water pressure. I was monitoring the wrist computer and at three metres, stopped. The decompression indicator said, '0', no decompression required, so I slowly surfaced.

The dive boat was about twenty metres off and someone on deck offered a friendly ok signal, which I returned. Tommy was already half way to the boat. I began to kick after him, head down, occasionally looking up for direction. As I got closer, I realised the ladder to the deck was on the opposite side of the vessel. Instead of making my way slowly around the stern, like a fool, I opted for the shortest distance, swimming under the dive boat.

I headed downwards, no more than a couple of metres towards the thick wooden keel, and being slightly buoyant, grabbed the iron-shod structure, hauling myself under the boat. As I arched my back to surface on the other side, I felt a 'hit' between my shoulder blades and knew instantly I'd got a 'bend'. Decompression sickness was every diver's nightmare, and I was now a victim.

Someone dropped a rope, and in turn I hitched my weight belt, stab jacket and goodie bag to the line. Reaching down, I took off fins, shoving a fist through the straps, then moved my mask up from face to forehead. I ascended the ladder in a state of shock, but everything onboard was strangely normal. I could feel the ache in my back, but there were no visible symptoms and no one was aware I'd got a 'hit'. Compounding my previous mistake, I said nothing.

"What was all that about with the scallop?" Tommy asked, as he handed me a mug of tea.

Though no longer in the humorous frame of mind as when the action had taken place, I said, "yer know we always try t' get new divers to eat a raw scallop as an initiation, after their first dive."

Tommy nodded in acknowledgement.

"Well ah thought they'd be even fresher underwater."

"Silly sod," was his only reply. Tommy gave his scallops to the Skipper, so I handed mine over too. Later the crewman would cook these, though there'd only be one each.

Instead of telling everyone I had a bend, I sat on the deck at the side of the wheelhouse watching as the teams returned in pairs, chatting enthusiastically about their experience. Eventually, with all hands back on board, we headed back for the pier at Stromness. If anyone had said, "are you alright?" I'd have said "no, I think I have a bend," but no one asked.

With *Radiant Queen* back alongside the old quay, the air bottles were taken across the road to be refilled, though I was of little help. The tanks would be recharged ready for the next dive, but I wasn't looking forward to that at all.

Two of the girls, Joyce and Julia had organised a minibus and we were to be transported to Skara Brae. This particular site was a world-famous Neolithic settlement, one of scores of ancient habitats scattered around the Orkneys, some older than the pyramids. This little group of islands must have been at the centre of a civilisation, at the time when pharaohs ruled Egypt.

We changed back into our clothes, leaving diving suits hanging around the deck of our boat. Boarding the twelve-seater bus, we set off the short distance to the famous site, located on the shoreline to the west of the main island.

The ancient settlement was amazing and had I been feeling better, would have been totally absorbed by this phenomenal history. Considering it was five thousand years since the site was inhabited, these people were extremely advanced. Some of the underground houses had now lost their roofs, exposing sections of the little chambers where beds, made from stone slabs were arranged. There were small shelves, which must have held trinkets or ornaments. Archaeological excavations had revealed artefacts that were not native to these shores, meaning that even in these far-off days, overseas trading must have been taking place.

Now short grass covered the entire site, making Skara Brae sanitised, compared with how the place must have been in its heyday. Also, the present climate bore no resemblance to that of this earlier period, which was probably semi tropical.

Heading back to the harbour, we managed a light bite before re-joining the dive boat. I hadn't eaten much or even spoken, hoping someone would notice, asking if I was alright, but no one did.

The second dive was to be on a small trawler that had run ashore, but later dropped back into deeper water. I intended to go to the depth I'd got the bend, then come back to the surface slowly, hoping to cure my problem.

Radiant Queen headed off across the Flow to the dive site and we began kitting up. I wasn't looking forward to this dive and wanted to be on my own to try my decompression plan, so when Tommy and I hit the water, instead of following him, I went off on my own, descending to twenty metres. The wreck seemed well stripped, with nothing special to interest souvenir divers, though had the site shown promise, I wasn't interested. I just wanted to get to the depth I'd been at earlier, then slowly ascend.

The seabed was slightly less than the required depth, so I swam slowly around the bottom for a while. I could see a couple of other divers in the distance, but didn't approach them. They must have found something of interest, as they didn't come my direction. I noticed a couple of feelers protruding from a hole in the ships plating, indicating a lobster. This creature didn't know how lucky he was. Any other time he'd have been in my goodie bag, but I hadn't brought it.

I'd been in the water ten minutes now and began to work my way back up the old wreck to the shallow part; the bows, where bell-hunting divers were in numbers. I pulled myself around for a few more minutes, giving OK signals to divers who were close. "No, I'm not bloody alright," I thought. "Why don't yer ask me when ah'm back on t' boat?" I stopped at three metres for five minutes to decompress, even though I didn't need to, then surfaced. Why hadn't I decompressed this morning?

The boat was standing close by, and I slowly headed towards her on my back, kicking fins with minimal effort till I reached the ladder, boarding as before. Being first back, it was the Skipper who relieved me of my gear and I detached my regulator from the bottle, chucking my loose gear into the bag before heading for the false sanctuary of the wheelhouse side to lie down. I wasn't feeling any better and was now worried I'd compounded my problem. At least the sun was shining and I semi-dozed while the others returned.

The engine revved and I knew we were heading back. I wouldn't forget this birthday in a hurry.

Back on shore, I was in for a shock. Without consulting me, but collectively with the others in the group, Alana had made a booking at a restaurant for a surprise birthday party. Though usually closed on Mondays, the owners had agreed to open for a guaranteed twelve customers, and we could have the place to ourselves. This was a really kind and thoughtful gesture, and any other time I'd have been totally delighted and flattered that these friends had gone to such trouble. I felt awful but would have to go along with the arranged celebrations.

We assembled in the little place in the town's Main Street, almost filling the room. I asked for the wine list, ordering copious amounts of both red and white. This was my treat to thank everyone for their kindness, though never said this at the time.

The three ladies running the establishment were extremely friendly, enjoying and joining in with the banter, which I too found amusing, despite my discomfort. I was quaffing the wine heartily, hoping, stupidly that it might cure my problem.

The menu consisted of quality local produce, scallops, fish, lamb and beef, and the food was magnificent and cooked to perfection. Laughter was resonating round the room, but was capped when Tommy said, "that's a nice bra you're wearing, Julia."

The attractive, slender girl looked down to see the top button on her blouse was undone.

"Thank you," she replied, playing down the comment and re-fastening the button. "It's only an M&S number."

"Mine's nicer," he replied, and unbuttoning his shirt, revealed a low-cut, black and red garment, which looked extremely out of place sitting flat on a very bushy, ginger-haired chest.

"Hey! That's mine," said a very shocked Joyce. "Where did you get that from?"

It transpired that the door of Julia and Joyce's room had been left ajar and Tommy, in passing had spotted the garment on a bed and quickly, 'borrowed' it.

The wine continued to flow and a couple of minutes later, Bince, a big, stubbly bearded, tussle haired, reliable country lad came from the Gents' toilet with underpants outside his trousers, 'Superman' style, creating more laughter.

It wasn't till we left the restaurant, everyone saying a huge, thank you! to the friendly staff, that I realised I was in trouble. Our accommodation was up a steep hill and, under the influence of too much red wine and now with tingling legs, I was making little headway, until Joyce and Julia took an arm each and hauled me up the brae.

Expressing my gratitude to all for my party and for getting me home, I made it into our room, where I finally confided in Tommy that I had a bend.

"Bloody hell," he said, sobering up immediately. "Why didn't yer say summat earlier? What d'ya wanna do?"

"Ah don't know. It's late. Ah don't suppose there'll be anybody around now t' do anythin'. Ah'll leave it till t' mornin'."

I spent the entire sleepless night laying on top of the bed, twitching and tingling then at 0700 next morning dialled 999 on my first ever, mobile phone.

An immediate response asked which service was required and I explained that I needed a doctor, and assistance to access a decompression chamber.

The efficiency of the operator was impressive and I was given the address of Doctor Watts in the town, and I was assured he'd be there when I arrived. Waking Tommy wasn't too difficult. He quickly grasped the situation and uncomplainingly, dressed, then went for the car.

"Bring yer dive computer," he advised. "The doc might be able t' download yer dive profile on his own computer."

It was foggy as we drove the short distance to the surgery, the relevance of which didn't occur to me. Dr Watts arrived minutes later, immediately inviting us through to his quarters. The doctor, who seemed extremely competent said, "you're the sixth bends casualty we've had in just over a week, but we have no decompression chamber on the island, should you need one. You'll have to go to the Hyperbaric Unit in Aberdeen."

Asking my story for his records, Dr Watts was shocked to hear of my stupidity. He gave me a thorough examination then used an implement with blunt and pointed ends, touching my legs in different places, asking which side of the tool he was using. Without comment he picked up his phone and called the coastguard, requesting a helicopter to take a casualty to the decompression unit in Aberdeen, immediately.

The Officer's reply wasn't good news. The chopper couldn't fly in the poor visibility and the forecast was for little change in the near future. Undeterred, Dr Watts made another couple of calls then said he'd arranged for an ambulance to take me to Kirkwall Airport where a small, fixed wing aircraft would take me to Aberdeen Airport.

While waiting for the transport to arrive the GP said, "take my advice, Mr Normandale. Sell your diving gear. You have a spinal bend and could easily now be in a wheelchair. You should make a good recovery, but you've got tissue damage in your back. If you dive again, the damage will not start again where it began previously. The injury will pick up where it left off, and next time the damage could be permanent, and you *will* be in a wheelchair!"

His unforgettable words were still running through my mind when an ambulance arrived with two medics. I thanked the doctor profusely for his dedicated, professional diagnosis and swift arrangements, then, with a lump in my throat, looked into Tommy's disconsolate face and said, "see yer later, matey." I knew I'd see him at some point back in Scarborough.

He turned wordlessly, the concerned look still in place and with a small wave, headed for the car.

I carefully got into the back of the ambulance, sitting on the stretcher. A young, blond, ponytailed female medic in green overalls followed me in, and quite grumpily, insisted I lay down.

This approach seemed a bit excessive, but I didn't argue: just lay on my back, pleased to be going for treatment.

The girl, unspeaking, sat opposite and the vehicle pulled away to drive across the island to the airport at Kirkwall, about 20 minutes travelling. The silence was palpable, almost hostile, as if I was an enemy. Signposts along the road mentioned wonderful, prehistoric sites, but these were hardly registering.

Arriving at the airport, the ambulance pulled alongside a twin-engine aircraft, with pilot and co-pilot waiting to greet the vehicle. With the ambulance doors open, one of the flight crew pointed to the boarding ladder, inviting me to enter. I ascended the steps unsteadily, thinking I was the only passenger, but I was wrong. The unhappy nurse climbed the steps behind me.

We were advised to buckle up while the crew did their routine checks and contacted the control tower. We were soon airborne, but didn't climb very high. The plane quickly levelled out at low altitude, as height and change in barometric pressure could be detrimental to my condition.

I now lay flat on a makeshift bed with a window at eye level to my side. I turned towards the nurse, who was making entries in a notebook. "Are you ok?" I asked, attempting to break the ice.

"I am," was the terse reply.

What was her problem? Had she been called out early? Was it her day off? Was she annoyed at the cost of the incident to the NHS? The answer wasn't forthcoming.

I looked to the window and was surprised to see how low we were flying, as the plane passed over a fishing boat. She must have recently hauled her nets as a cloud of gulls surrounded the vessel, looking for food. This was a little lift for me, recognising a scenario I was familiar with, from such an unusual perspective.

The flight across the Moray Firth was otherwise non-eventful and passed in silence. I'd given up my attempts at talking, and decided there was nothing I could say or do to lighten the atmosphere in the little cabin. It was me who should have been the sad and unhappy one.

The landing was smooth and again an ambulance was waiting for our arrival, though we'd taxied to a distant part of the airport. Aberdeen was a very busy terminal with constant helicopter traffic from the dozens of North Sea oilfields, as well as commercial fixed wing flights and amateur fliers.

I thanked the aircrew, both of whom had left the cockpit to say goodbye, apologising for having caused them work.

"Not a problem," said the pilot, "Hope all goes well for you."

They both gave a cheery wave as I departed.

I said, thank you to the nurse, whose facial expression hadn't cracked since our first encounter, but this was a final, forlorn gesture on my part. At least she could now return to Orkney, not accompanying me further. I had a new driver and nurse to take me to the Hyperbaric Unit at Aberdeen Infirmary.

What a contrast to my previous companion the new nurse was. Small, cheery, dark haired, with a pleasant north eastern accent that I knew well, she was just so friendly. The lady asked how my flight had been, and what mischief I'd been up to, to get the bends?

The traffic heading into the bustling 'Granite City' was heavy, but a blue flashing light got us through quickly. My companion was very reassuring, saying I'd get the best possible treatment at this specialist unit in the hospital.

"It's the finest decompression unit in the country," she stated, confidently.

The hyperbaric base was housed in a separate section, behind the main hospital building, and on entering, discovered I was expected. A nurse quickly registered my details then asked the circumstances of my condition. There was a sucking of teeth as the stupidity of my actions were revealed.

"We sometimes resort to short periods of decompression in the chamber," the registrar said, "but in this case you're going to be in saturation for quite a while. We have two nurses on their way in. They'll be here shortly and will stay with you in the 'pot' throughout your stay."

I'd no idea what to expect. The only decompression chamber I'd ever seen was a coffin-sized, cylinder-shaped unit, on display in a local diving shop window.

The nurse took me through another door into a room the size of a small hanger, containing several huge, cream-painted cylinders, each mounted on supports. There were lots of pipes and valves leading to and from the units, each to a central control panel. This was a very professional looking fit-out.

The nurse saw me looking round, wide-eyed. "This has all been paid for by the oil industry," she said. "They are our main customers and provide nothing but the very best equipment."

I was immediately grateful for their generous input to the hospital, but was impatient to start the treatment. My legs were shaking and back aching.

Two very pretty, young nurses turned up carrying small rucksacks; introducing themselves as Jackie and Elaine.

One of the sweet ladies said we'd be getting twenty four-hour monitoring throughout our period in the chamber.

"Twenty four-hour monitoring," I said to myself. "How long am I going to be in for?" Though didn't care how long. I just wanted to be in the pot.

Jackie pointed in the direction of the chamber superintendent Richard, already at the control panel who, it transpired, was on shore leave at present, but did the very same job when he was on the rigs. Richard would work back to back shifts with another controller. The guy gave me a cheery wave and thumbs up. These men would never leave the panel, other than for essentials. I was in good hands.

I was given a set of green, clinical overalls and shown a changing cubicle. Next, I was given a quick briefing, letting me know what to expect during the compulsory captivity, then I was on my way to the decompression chamber.

It was about this time on the previous day that I'd got the 'hit'. What a bloody fool I'd been. In diving circles, it is now well known that the 'golden hour' is extremely important, and most boats carry an oxygen cylinder for early treatment. If only!

The two nurses were also dressed in green overalls now, and I followed Jackie as she climbed through a circular hole about thirty inches in diameter, waist high at the end of the chamber. Once inside, the young lady assisted me as I entered the aperture. Elaine quickly followed without help. These young ladies were clearly used to working in the chambers.

The heavy door was closed and powerful clamps were secured behind us. Looking round, I found myself in a small toilet compartment. Another, separate airtight door was immediately before me, leading to the capsule's living quarters. It was explained to me that this toilet section could be depressurised separately to enable additional casualties or medical personnel to access the chamber, without having to entirely reduce the pressure.

I traversed this entrance into what was to be my home for as yet, an unspecified period. This part of the tank was about twelve feet in length with a central aisle and two beds at either side. On the left, between the beds was a porthole at mid height. This void had double doors a short distance apart and was a small airlock. All our supplies and requirements would come through this twelve-inch hole. Both doors were usually kept closed but the outer door could be opened and supplies placed inside. The outer door had to be re-secured before we could access the void from our side.

There was a camera on the far end wall, connected to a monitor screen on superintendent Richard's control panel. He was also in contact by intercom. A buzzer indicated a communication, and our controller informed one of the nurses he was commencing pressurisation of the chamber. I had a shock coming. The gas filling our space was helium, and the effect was to make our voices sound like Donald Duck.

I asked Richard, via the radio link, if it was possible to get a message to my wife, to let her know I was alright.

The cheerful chap asked for my home number and said he wasn't supposed to make external calls, but would patch me through on this occasion, though this would be my only call. He would reply to enquiries by landline with updates after this initial communication.

I found the conversation with Dotty totally bizarre. I was attempting to explain to her that I was in a decompression chamber with the bends, and would be there for a while. I went on to say it was only precautionary, and I was pleased to be in there, but it was extremely difficult to be reassuring and calm while talking like a cartoon character. As ever, Dotty was most pragmatic and didn't make a fuss or panic. She'd be aware that the situation was more serious than I'd made it out to be, but would take this latest incident in her stride.

My companions were delightful and as I attempted, in the silly voice, to apologise for their inconvenience, the pair would have none of it.

Jackie, in the same comic tone said, "we're going to be wi' yer for more than forty-eight hours, and that'll be our week's work, plus a wee bit of overtime; it's great. Dinna worry."

Well that at least was both revealing and enlightening. I now knew my 'down time' and was content that these ladies were quite happy to be with me, so didn't feel guilty that I was wasting their time.

The chamber was pressurised down to twenty-nine metres; the maximum depth I'd been before I'd sustained the hit.

It's going to be a long spell in here, I thought, but the nurses were starting work already. They produced a clear, plastic hood with hose attached, placing this over my head.

"Pure oxygen's an excellent treatment fo' the bends, but we canna fill the whole chamber," Elaine said. "This way we can treat yer wi' the gas while still pressurised."

I was given several short periods in this hood, and either psychologically or due to the pressure difference, was feeling slightly better already.

Richard came over the intercom, asking what we'd like from the available menu for lunch; food which was remarkably good, and not as hospital food was reputed to be. It was not only food that came through the lock, but current magazines of choice for the nurses and a daily newspaper.

Normally I'd skip through a newspaper, selecting the best articles, ignoring the less interesting parts, but with so much time available, I read the paper almost cover to cover.

Before the lights were dimmed for the night, we were issued with fresh overalls, and each in turn, climbed into the small section to wash and change. Fresh laundry was passed through twice daily to minimise infections. These were more likely under saturation conditions.

The toilet was pressurised similar to those in aeroplanes and a prominent notice stated, 'do not flush while seated'. I thought of what might happen in this scenario and a shiver went through my body. I'd heard stories from commercial diver friends.

After a good night's sleep, I was feeling happier and following breakfast, found myself pacing the floor up and down to stretch my legs and increase circulation. I was feeling much more positive.

My companions, despite the poor conversational scenario, were really good company. Both were single and twenty-five years old. I was almost twice their age. The pair spoke of parties and dancing and the things I'd long since grown out of, but they were so full of life that they lifted my spirits, and it was a positive atmosphere that the girls created.

The day passed quick enough. I needed no more O2 treatment and had another paper to devour. I walked some more and the girls chatted and read. Being specialist nurses, they'd done many periods in saturation and were quite used to the environment. They were interested in my life and work and listened to some of my stories, which I tried to make amusing.

Another night passed, and more clean linen was due to be passed through the void, but the girls were up to something. They'd been talking to our controller, and I could tell by the mischievous grins on their faces.

The sound of the screw being turned to open the outside airlock galvanised the pair into action and they awaited the delivery with urgent anticipation, shielding my view of the transfer with their backs. The outer door closed and Jackie opened our end. Both grabbed green overalls and passed me the remaining garment, a pink, flowery nightdress. It was a fait accompli. I'd been had! There was no choice but to wear the thing. It would be churlish not to after the wonderful treatment they'd given me.

My reappearance from the toilet chamber after changing into in my little pink number created great hilarity and, looking through the airlock glass got a thumbs up and smile from Richard, who'd viewed the whole episode on his screen.

At lunchtime we got the message from Richard that he was starting the de-saturation process, which would take several hours. Pressure had to be reduced very slowly. "Watch this," Elaine said, reaching for a surgical glove. She put the glove to her lips and inflated the thin blue membrane to the size of the hand it was designed for. Tying a knot in the glove, she placed the 'hand' on a bed. I was perplexed until she said, "watch the glove expand as the pressure drops. That's what the bubbles were doing in yer body."

Sure enough, as the afternoon wore on, the glove grew larger as the atmosphere was reduced. By the time the pressure was equal on both sides of the chamber and the door opened, the glove was the size of a cow's udder. What a clever trick and a graphic experiment.

It was with real tears in my eyes I hugged, kissed and said thank you and goodbye to my recent companions. They'd made such a difference to my life these past few days. I dreaded to think what the experience would have been like, had I had the company of the nurse I'd met following my mishap.

I shook hands with Richard, the ever-present day shift monitor, and said an immense, thank you. He would be going back offshore soon to continue his essential and important work on the rigs.

It was gone six o'clock now and I was dressed in my own clothes, but if I thought I was going home, I was sadly mistaken: not that I could have got a train to connect to Scarborough at this hour. I was considering a hotel for the night and an early start. The doctor examining me seemed satisfied that my situation had improved and I was stable, but he wanted to keep me under observation overnight. The man said I was to be transferred to a ward in the main hospital. At least I could now talk to Dotty properly and to let her know all was well.

Following the examination, I was taken to the main building and up several floors to what seemed to be a male, bronchial ward. Almost all the dozen or so incumbents appeared to be suffering from respiratory complaints. A couple of elderly gentlemen were walking the ward with frames, linked by tube and mask to portable oxygen bottles. What a dreadful place to be, I thought. The long-term prognosis for most of these men was not good. I was to spend the night in this place. At least I was no longer wearing my nightie and was now in pyjamas. The sight of me in a nightie would have made some of these old blokes cough a bit.

I spoke to Dotty, and as ever she was fully up to speed with the situation and not fazed by my self-inflicted condition. She did say that the following was Friday, and we were supposed to be going to a 'roving dinner' with three other couples as part of a Rotary Club event.

Dotty said she'd cancel this on our behalf, but I was most anxious that she didn't.

"I'm ok now," I insisted. "We'll go t' dinner, it'll be ok." I wanted her to go out and relax, and to enjoy the evening after worrying about me over the past few days.

Dotty said Tommy had been on the phone and wanted to know my plans. He was travelling south from Scrabster tomorrow, driving my car and wanted to collect me from the hospital if I was ready. This would be an additional one hundred-plus mile diversion along the Moray Firth from Inverness to Aberdeen. What a star he was.

The night in the ward, with most of the patients coughing, wheezing, shouting and snoring was a nightmare, and I hardly slept, so was pleased when daylight came. They should bring young smokers in here, I thought. It would be a stark lesson of what they could expect in later life. This 'holier than though' thought from me, who'd just committed a cardinal diving sin, and knowing what I should really have done!

The next few hours went slowly but I dressed, ate breakfast, then eventually the busy doctor appeared to discharge me. His parting shot was, "I suggest you give up your diving hobby. You're on borrowed time if you dive again."

I'd already made that choice, and decided I'd never dive again. I'd had many years of fantastic diving and had great memories of wrecks, reefs and underwater adventures. I'd survived, almost unscathed, but now it was time to stop.

At ten o'clock, Tommy entered the ward, grinning. He'd come to collect me. I was free to go home. He'd taken the ferry to the Mainland the previous afternoon and stayed nearby overnight.

"Ow are yer doin'?" he enquired. "Yer lookin' a bit pale. The gang all send best wishes, an' I 'ave t' tell yer, 'you're a stupid twat'! We were all worried about yer."

Together we went to the ward entrance and I was able to thank the Duty Sister at the desk, as we left. I didn't envy her, her position, but all the staff on this ward were doing a fantastic job, and it was very necessary work.

Tommy had driven a long way, so I insisted on taking the first stint at the wheel, despite his protestations. The drive south was pleasant enough. Tommy is always good company. He insisted on taking over the wheel from Edinburgh, then I took over again north of the Tees. During the journey home he gave me an update on the week's diving events and fun. I in turn told him about my two lovely companions, and my extended stay in confinement, including the highlight, my pink nightie!

We arrived back into Scarborough before five o'clock and I pulled up at home. Tommy's van was parked close by. Dotty was waiting on the step, and my poor pal got an undeserved scolding from her, for allowing me to drive.

"But it's 'is own car," he said defensively. "'E can drive it if 'e wants. Ah can't stop 'im."

Dotty was pleased to have me home, but after a big hug said, "you've got to make your mind up, it's diving or me? I don't want this to happen again."

I pretended to hum and ha, asking how long I'd got to decide, but I'd already made the decision to quit diving, and told her so very quickly after my silly joke. I sold my gear to a new member of the diving club a few weeks later.

Early that same evening, Dotty and I took a taxi to the home of Rotary Club member, Colin Woodhead and his wife Pauline. The pair were the hosts and were to produce a tasty main meal. We provided a seafood starter, quickly put together from fridge and freezer earlier. Two other couples brought cheese and port.

We were the last pair to arrive and the waiting company had heard about my diving incident. As we entered the lounge, a little cheer went up as we were directed towards comfortable chairs by the host. No sooner were we sat, than the friendly people began asking after my welfare. Apparently, I was very pale. I also had a nervous tic in one eye, though no one had mentioned this previously.

Colin, tall, thin, bespectacled, moustached and balding was energetic and animated. Along with his brother Stewart, Col ran a family bakery, distributing their produce to many of their own shops, plus local supermarkets. He and Pauline were very kind and were good friends. As well as the main course they'd also provided the dessert, or I should say, choice of three, huge puddings.

David, a retired banker and his wife, Diana were one of the other couples. They'd brought a fine bottle of aged port. David, being a former amateur diver was most interested in my escapade, though Dotty, less so.

The fourth couple, Gilly and Janet, were real entrepreneurs and Gilly, though with little formal education, was one of the shrewdest men I'd ever met. He was also extremely generous, supporting many local charities.

The family of his youth were travellers and toured the fairgrounds in the north east of England. Home had been a single-decker, ex-service bus. He often joked that he settled in Seaton Carew, near Hartlepool because the bus wouldn't go any further. This was in the early sixties and coincided with the new-fangled, prize bingo boom in seaside resorts. Gilly, with Janet, had set up their own business in the town. They'd rented a property, fitted the place out then stocked the shelves with prizes. The pair had never looked back, and now owned two of the largest amusement arcades on Scarborough's sea front, as well as many other properties around Yorkshire and Durham.

Janet had brought a variety of cheeses of sufficient quantity to feed an army. Any one of the four courses would have been sufficient to feed the group, and all had brought wine.

Following a couple of glasses and chatter, Dotty set our seafood platter in the centre of the dinner table and we were all called to dine. I was already feeling weary and not at my best after the experience and long drive, but was determined to see the night through. The company was excellent, as was the food, and the conversation was interesting, at least after I'd retold my story.

The meal went on and on and all was delicious. I told a few old jokes and tried to entertain the folks, but, now full of food and drink, I was deadbeat and it was home time. It had been a hell of a week! We rang for an early taxi.

As we were leaving the room our host said, "no more diving for you then, Fred! You'll be hanging your flippers up now?"

Dotty turned to him, and in a serious voice said, "I told Fred as soon as he got home that he had to decide, it was either diving or me."

"Err! Can I 'ave another think about that one?" I asked, for the benefit of the guests. "'Ow long 'ave I got?" but was quickly shoved out of the door, to the amusement of those present.

My hair at this time was salt and pepper in colour, some grey and some brown, but following this trauma, as the months passed and my hair grew, I noticed it had turned white.

CHAPTER 10

LOSS OF *SCORESBY*

Scoresby was still fishing a long way north and had been landing catches into both Lerwick and Peterhead. One of Danny's favourite areas of operation was the Cormorant Oil Field, where there were several pipelines to be trawled along.

Over the years they'd had some good times and had a few close shaves. There'd been lot of laughter on the old boat, including when Paddy, the ship's Cook had prepared a chicken, placing the bird in a tray in the oven, ready for cooking.

The Cook returned forward, back to gutting and washing fish. Meanwhile, on the after deck, Billy had captured a large gull that had become stranded on the deck, unable to find the distance to take off. Removing the chicken from the oven, Billy replaced this dead bird with the live gull and shut the oven door.

With the recent catch almost processed, Paddy had been dispatched aft to the galley to start preparing dinner. Opening the stove door, with the intention of igniting the gas, the unsuspecting Cook almost had heart failure when the angry bird made its dash for freedom.

* * *

The weather was reasonable for the area with a moderate breeze and a slight swell. Danny was below in his bunk and it was almost hauling time. Billy, the watch-keeper, following standing orders went below to the engine room to engage the bilge pump. Being an old boat and of wooden construction, she was never fully watertight. Seepages accumulated and water drained from the catch into the bilge as fish were sent below and ice melted.

Billy knew instantly there was something wrong when his feet were wet before he'd reached the aluminium plates at the bottom of the ladder. Water was well over the floor and lapping up the sides of the engine. He quickly engaged the bilge pump, which was a forlorn hope. There was something radically wrong somewhere. He dashed back up the ladder and immediately down the adjacent doorway into the cabin, where he raised the alarm, calling the crew urgently.

Danny went down into the engine room to assess the problem, which was found to be a fractured flange on a large bore inlet pipe. The metal piping lead from a seacock to the engine, providing cooling water for the machine. The steel pipe had almost severed, spewing a high volume of water into the engine space.

The problem was that the seacock to this pipe was under the plates, and was now so deep that it was impossible to shut off. Even had this been possible, there was another seacock at the other side of the boat with a similar inlet.

These two pipes joined at a T-junction under the engine, so to stop the surge, both seacocks must be turned off. Hurrying back to the wheelhouse, the Skipper prepared to haul the net.

Scoresby was still trawling along a pipeline and it was essential to get both boat and net away from this multimillion-dollar infrastructure. The boat was steered away from the pipeline, but it would take a while to pull the gear clear of the pipe. The depth was in excess of ninety fathoms and there was more than a quarter of a mile of wire and cable behind the vessel.

As the crew engaged the winch clutches to haul the trawl, Danny put out a 'Pan' message, alerting all shipping in the area that his vessel, *Scoresby* was making water.

With the net clear of the pipeline, hauling was commenced, but it would be a race against time to get the trawl up and onboard before water got to the air intake and the engine stopped, leaving *Scoresby* dead in the water.

As the trawl was coming up, the Skipper was talking to Shetland Coastguard, who dispatched a helicopter from Sumburgh, bringing a powerful pump to lower on to the boat.

The trawl surfaced and was unceremoniously hauled on to the net drum, the fish taken on board, and minutes later the engine, starved of air, stopped. This left the vessel drifting and powerless, but emergency batteries on top of the wheelhouse meant all the boat's radios still worked. Water continued to enter the engine space, but the bulkhead to the fish hold was porous and pressure forced water forward until the fish hold was also filling. It was time to send a 'Mayday'.

This distress call raised many responses, mostly from oil related vessels in the area, all asking for *Scoresby's* position, to compare with their own and to plot a course and distance.

A fast response inflatable craft from an oilrig standby vessel was soon alongside the waterlogged *Scoresby*, taking off three crewmen, leaving Danny and Billy on board. Soon after, a Sea King helicopter was hovering overhead, lowering a pump and hoses on to the shelter-deck.

The two men quickly assembled the suction pipe to the petrol driven unit, lowering this four-inch diameter rubber hose into the fish-hold then, pulling on the attached rope and toggle, started the engine.

A choking cloud of gas quickly cleared and the engine revolutions reduced as water was drawn through the vertical tube into the pump, to be expelled off the shelter-deck, back into the sea. The water level in the hold began to drop; the pump was gaining on the ingress. Optimism returned, but sadly, was short-lived.

Each full box of fish in the hold was covered with a sheet of greaseproof paper, prior to being coated in ice, to protect the fish. These papers were now washing around the hold as the vessel rolled heavily, her stability diminishing. It was inevitable the pump, with no strainer on the hose end, would suck up some of this paper, causing the pump to block and stall.

The level of water began to rise again. There was no back-up pump.

A Lerwick fishing vessel, *Shannon*, Skipper, Ivan Goodlad, an affable and very capable Shetlander, arrived on the scene and soon, despite the now freshening wind and rising swell, had a rope attached to the drifting *Scoresby*. The eighty-foot, red-painted *Shannon* began towing her charge towards Lerwick. Contact would be kept with the towing vessel via a hand-held radio onboard the casualty. It was going to be a race against time, but there was never going to be enough time to save her.

The pair standing on the shelter-deck could only look down into the rising morass of boxes and paper slopping around below and knew the outcome was now inevitable.

Scoresby gave a shudder and Danny spoke into the radio, "Ah think she's goin', Ivan. Yer'd better come an' get us."

The large steel vessel slowed down and immediately began to turn hard to starboard in a tight circle. On board *Scoresby,* the towrope was cast off and dropped into the sea; the slack rope quickly recovered by *Shannon's* crew. Aiming to come alongside the wooden boat's starboard side, the Skipper's skill was absolute and the two vessels clapped together with a resounding crunch, totally closing the gap. It was still a good distance between the rolling vessels tapered upper decks. The pair of pals, standing outboard on the shelter-deck top, holding onto the railings, were poised, waiting for the best opportunity to cross the moving void.

Danny was about to leap, when a sudden thought crossed his mind; the Captain should always be the last to leave a sinking ship. With a quick arm gesture said, "after you," then waited till Billy had made the crossing before hastily following.

Shannon stood by the wallowing *Scoresby* as, in her death throes she rolled to port, showing her red, anti-fouled hull, sounder transducers and keel, then, stern first, was lost from sight forever. Until this point Danny had remained reasonably calm, but with the disappearance of his first ever boat and with only his Skipper's ticket and a photo of his daughters in hand, the only salvaged objects from the old boat, he broke down and wept.

The other three crew men were taken on board *Shannon* from the small craft, and all were delivered safely to Lerwick, where, with grateful thanks they were taken care of by the Fishermen's Mission.

Lots of bills followed the loss of *Scoresby*, mostly from tradesmen worried about outstanding accounts and our ability to pay; knowing there'd be no further income from the vessel. I was surprised to receive a bill for the loss of fish boxes on board, by the Scottish Box Agency and also an account from the Coastguard for the loss of the pump. These, and all other outstanding and subsequent bills were paid, eventually.

This was the second vessel we'd lost in two years, though thankfully, there'd been no loss of life.

Scoresby sank on 8/6/2000 in position 60 degrees 52' N. 00 degrees 32' E.

CHAPTER 11

NANCY'S FUNERAL

Nancy Hines, the formidable, retired school teacher had not been feeling well for some time. She'd tried various medications but eventually, following a visit to the doctor's surgery then to the hospital, announced, quite matter-of-factly, that she had terminal cancer, but had no intention of seeking treatment.

Small, plump with a red, weathered, round face and short, straight greying hair, the bespectacled lady's family had originally moved to Scarborough from East Anglia. They'd settled in the town, like many others throughout the generations, whose families had followed the migrating herring. Nancy's father had been a herring merchant, buying and selling the huge catches that drifters brought in to the harbour daily in late Summer. I could recall seeing barrels and boxes with the 'Hines' stencil, when I was a lad.

Teaching and living in Hull, Nancy returned to Scarborough each weekend to visit her ageing mother, who lived across the street. We would often find sticks of chalk posted through the letterbox for our young children.

As her mother grew older and became more infirm, Nancy gave up her job to become her mother's carer. This was a task she would undertake for a number of years until her Mother's eventual death at a great age.

A keen yachtswoman and an enthusiastic traveller, a lover of museums, stately homes, gardens and art galleries, this lady was no shrinking violet. Nancy had good taste, principles and standards.

She was an intelligent lady with a mischievous sense of humour. On one occasion, when in dispute with a neighbour, who'd moved a boundary fence, attempting to misappropriate a foot-wide strip from her garden, Nancy had received a letter from the neighbour's solicitor. Not impressed by the spelling and grammar of this missive, and totally ignoring its contents, the former school teacher marked the paper, 'three out of ten' in red pen. She wrote 'must try harder' at the bottom of the page before returning the correspondence to the lawyer. A subsequent note was received from the law firm giving an apology, and blaming a young secretary for the badly written correspondence.

On another occasion, while walking towards the town centre from her home, Nancy came upon workmen, discharging roofing material from a truck. The large adjacent property was council owned and required a quantity of porous roof tiles replacing. As she was passing, Nancy noticed the stack of new pantiles near the vehicle were purple.

"What are those for?" Nancy asked the foreman.

"They're to go on these buildings 'ere, Missus," he replied, pointing to the block of flats.

"But those tiles are purple," she said, indignantly. "The old ones were red."

"I know Missus, but we can't get any red ones for two or three weeks," the man replied, defensively.

"Well you'll have to wait," she said. "You can't put those on. They are not in keeping." Nancy promptly made a beeline for the Town Hall, seeking out and berating the Council Officer responsible for the project. "This is a conservation area, young man. Purple tiles are not allowed," she stated forcefully.

The job was stopped until the correct materials became available.

The lovely neighbour owned a little two-door, white, Ford Fiesta, which was housed in our garage, rather than on the street. The rent agreed for this parking arrangement was the provision for us of a weekly, Sunday newspaper. In addition, her little car was insured for both Dotty and I. If we needed the use of a second car, which wasn't often, a brief phone call usually secured its use.

94

A few weeks following her diagnosis, prior to her being admitted to the local, Saint Catherine's Hospice, Nancy rang to say, "Fred, you've both looked after my little car all this time. I've no further use for it and want Dotty to have the car. I've signed and posted the documents."

I had tears in my eyes and was left speechless.

On her admittance to the hospice, a very peaceful, almost new, purpose-built construction on the edge of town, surrounded by gardens, Nancy was not to survive long. She was given medication to ease the pain, but simply closed her eyes and waited for the end.

I would attend each day for a short while and hold her hand and talk, giving her the local news and talking about Dotty, the kids or the weather: anything so she wouldn't feel alone. I wasn't sure she could hear me but presumed so, as I sometimes thought I felt very gentle squeezes in response.

Following Nancy's death, I received a phone call from Sue, her friend saying, "Nancy asked if you would say a few words at her funeral."

"Ah'm pleased about that, Sue," I replied, "because ah was goin' to ask if ah could."

"She's left you a letter," Sue went on, "telling you what you can and can't say."

How typical was that? Even from the 'other side' Nancy was being stroppy.

The contents of the missive paraphrased to, 'I don't want to be 'bothering God', so won't be having a religious service. Please don't read out a CV, but I'd like you to say a few words about me at my funeral'.

Well that was fairly straight forward, or so I thought.

I penned the stories of the fence and the roof tiles, said she had enjoyed skiing and walking in her younger days and had been a sailor and filled a couple of pages with, what I hoped would be a fitting and amusing tribute to this remarkable lady. I read and re read the eulogy, hoping the tales would be well received by the congregation of her friends.

The day of the funeral arrived and as expected, the crematorium was full, plus there were people standing at the back, underlining the esteem Nancy was held in.

I had my two pages safely stowed in the inside pocket of my jacket, though nervously kept checking they were still there. Five minutes before the service was due to commence, I took the place reserved for me in the front row, beside Sue and waited. There was no sign of a humanist preacher. The clock was ticking. It was now almost two o'clock.

Leaving my position, I walked to the rear of the hall, looking for the Superintendent of the premises. Outside, I noticed the cortège was in sight and drawing close.

I knocked on the opened glass door of the office and the lady at the desk turned in my direction.

"Hello, can I help?" she said, smiling.

"Excuse me, I'm Fred Normandale and ah'm readin' a eulogy for the late Nancy Hines. Can yer tell me who's takin' her service?"

The lady consulted the list on her desk then turning back to me, smiled again and said, "it seems that you are."

I felt I'd been hit by a thunderbolt. "Oh 'ell! Just a minute," I said and dashed outside, indicating to the undertaker to give me a couple of minutes before entering, then went back to the office.

"It's quite alright," the lady said, kindly. "You'll be fine. Miss Hines has selected the classical music she wants playing. Do you want the whole CD or just the first eight-minute track?"

"I'm sure eight minutes will be fine," I replied, thinking, eight minutes is a long time for a piece of music.

As I departed, the official indicated where I'd find the button to close the curtains at the end of service.

I gave a thumbs-up to the pallbearers and returned to my place at the front. This was going to be interesting.

The music began and the congregation stood as the procession came through the doors and down the centre aisle. After raising the coffin onto the dais, the four bearers, each bowing, departed through the exit door at the side.

I didn't move. The music continued. I turned to Sue, whispering, "Nancy will be laughin' 'er socks off up there."

She smiled and nodded.

People were looking round wondering what was going to happen, and still the music played.

Eventually, eight long minutes later, the piece concluded and I walked to the pulpit. "Please be seated," I said, smiling at the relieved faces before me.

Taking out the two sheets, I began my eulogy to Nancy Hines.

I really enjoyed giving her the special send-off and hoped I'd pitched the tribute just right as, while not daring to look up, I could hear people either laughing or concurring with my sentiments.

Finally, I did look up and said, "thank you all for comin'. Ah'm sure Nancy is up there watchin' an' havin' a good chuckle. She's left some funds for drinks and nibbles, so if any of you would like to come back to our home in Castlegate, we'd be pleased to 'ave you along to share your memories." I pressed the button under the pulpit where indicated, and was pleased to see the blue velvet curtains surrounding the dais, close, encompassing the coffin.

Expecting a dozen or so guests and catering for twice that number, we were extremely, and pleasantly surprised to be inundated, when half the congregation turned up. There was some very hasty rounding up of additional glasses, extra food and more wine, but our dear neighbour had a lovely send off and left memories that are still shared to the present day. Her little car lasted till 2019.

Nancy Mary Hines died in December 2004

* * *

Standing on the balcony of the café, above the fish market, for once I ignored the magnificent view of the harbour and of my historic hometown, below the ancient castle. I was looking at the much-diminished Scarborough fishing fleet. Not many years ago this had been a bustling port where hundreds of men and scores of boats of all sizes plied their trade. These men, plus the ancillary support workers made for a thriving industry and a special community. Now it had all but gone.

There were still some smaller vessels, fishing for crab and lobster and three or four under ten metre trawlers worked daily from the port, but there was only one large trawler remaining. She was *Emulator,* fifty-nine feet in length, which I'd commissioned to be built in 1982 and launched in February 1983. She was the sole remaining vessel from about thirty-five similar sized craft, fishing from the port in the 1970s and 80s when I'd been her Skipper. How times had changed.

Sean Crowe was now Skipper and part owner of *Emulator.* He'd been a sixteen-year old deckhand when she was new, and this was the only vessel he'd work on from leaving school.

* * *

I was brought from my reverie by the local fisheries inspector, stopping on the pier above the *Provider*, the red painted, under ten-metre, multi-purpose vessel belonging to Mally Ward and Bluey Sheader, my former Skipper partners in *Independence* and *Allegiance*. They'd sold their shares in the two boats to me, and together bought *Provider*. I watched the unfolding scenario with interest. Mally, like most fishermen, was not keen on authority.

The young, naïve Officer boarded their vessel, asking the men if they'd measured the lobsters in the basket, which they'd just brought into the port.

"Of course we 'ave. We wouldn't bring undersized lobsters into t' 'arbour. We're not daft," replied Mally. He reached for, and held up a plastic measuring gauge, recently issued to their vessel by the inspectorate.

"You won't mind if I check them with my gauge then," the inspector stated pompously. "It's more accurate than that one."

Mally, looking at the man, then at the measure in his hand said, "so this one's no use then," and promptly threw the gauge into the harbour.

The man stood open-mouthed, then spluttered, "but they're alright."

"Not accordin' t' you. You've got a superior model."

The disconsolate, inspector, totally lost for words to defend his actions, and finding nothing wrong with the shellfish he'd measured, left the vessel in quick time. He wasn't to know there was a precision, aluminium gauge hanging on a piece of twine inside the wheelhouse door.

CHAPTER 12

AMERICA

Dotty and I were bound for America, a continent we could only have dreamed of visiting earlier in our life together. Then, a few years ago while on holiday, we met a retired United States Naval Officer, Capt. Ray Atcheson who, while his rank was Captain, had never been master of anything bigger than a launch. Strangely, Ray's seniority came from his being aircrew on carrier-based aircraft for many years. Ray had joined the US Navy as an enlisted man, and during his long career this amazing character had flown as a navigator in both the Korean and Vietnam wars.

Ray lived in New England and each year organised a large circle of friends to travel to Europe for sightseeing and skiing. These were a diverse group of interesting and pleasant people and we began to coincide our trips to France with the American group.

On one occasion when we'd met up, Ray said, "hey Freddy, I've been to Europe about fifty times and I've been to Ireland, where my family were originally from, but I've never been to England."

"Yer don't want t' go there, Ray." I replied. "It's a dreadful place. Yer should come t' the People's Republic o' Yorkshire. Come over an' see the real world in God's own county." For Ray, that was the start of a series of visits each Summer to Yorkshire, England and Scotland.

Now we were paying a return visit, flying into Boston. Before we left home, our daughter, Paula said, "if you're going to New

England, you should visit my friend, Douglas, in Washington. He'd be really pleased to see you. I've told him you're going to the East Coast."

Paula had been studying herbal medicine at a college in Sussex when she'd met Doug, and having a similar sense of humour and attitude, they'd hit it off and were good friends.

We said we'd be pleased to visit Doug, and Paula gave us his contact details and confirmed our visit with him. He, in turn sent directions to his house in Washington.

Following our landing into Boston we had an inauspicious start. Having laboriously cleared customs, then successfully found our medium-sized vehicle at the hire car firm, we left the airport and almost immediately were stopped at a toll road. We needed US dollars to pass, and realised we had none. I'd intended to get some before departure, then from the airport on arrival, but due to the security delays, had completely forgotten. An embarrassing U-turn and swift return to the airport to an ATM machine rectified this. "Brits abroad," I said to a less than impressed though, non-committal Dotty.

It didn't help any that Boston city centre was in the middle of a multi-million dollar, several years duration, 'big dig', where underpasses and new roads were being constructed, while attempting to keep traffic flowing.

A frustrating hour or so later, after travelling bumper to bumper, we were able to reach sixty miles an hour, the maximum allowed on a quiet, five-lane highway. We eventually turned off for West Hartford and soon after, found a small hill leading to a group of four or five large wooden houses, each on an individual plot of land. Ray's place was quite distinctive as, instead of the Stars and Stripes flying from his flagpole, I spied the Union Flag.

We'd hardly stepped from the car when our friend was out of the door welcoming us to the USA with an enthusiastic hug. He'd arranged for a dozen or so pals, who were part of his group, to meet up in a nearby restaurant that evening. He said these people all lived close, within a hundred-miles radius!

101

Distance seemed no object to these Americans. Again, the lovely people welcomed us as old friends.

The next few days were a whirlwind as Ray showed us his version of New England, in the fall. Our feet had hardly touched the ground each morning before we were out of the door and on tour. We'd catch a light bite of breakfast, en route to our destination. The exception to the light bite was when Dotty ordered pancakes, expecting two, and was served a stack of twelve.

The first stop on our tour was to *USS Nautilus SSN-571*, America's original nuclear submarine. This was the famous US ship that in August 1958, had travelled under the Arctic icecap; the first vessel ever to achieve this feat. It was almost impossible to believe this ship had once been the most sophisticated underwater vessel in the world. Now she seemed so small and old fashioned. Her computers were huge but had so little memory and power. A modern-day mobile phone had much more memory. How fast the world of electronic science had changed in so few years.

Not far from this historic ship was the massive US naval base of New London, where modern nuclear submarines were based. This was our next destination.

Ray drove slowly towards the security gate. The sentry, observing a naval sticker on the car's windscreen, stepped aside and saluted as we drove past.

"Wow," was all I could say.

Further into the base we came to another security gate where, this time we were stopped by a guard with raised hand.

Ray lowered his window to hear the guard say firmly, "I'm sorry Sir, you don't have clearance beyond this point. I do apologise, Sir."

"Don't apologise son." Ray said with a smile. "I understand." He turned the car around and pulled up a few hundred yards away, outside a regulating office. Leaving the vehicle, he entered the office, returning a few minutes with a chit of paper in hand.

"I do now son," he said, smiling again at the guard who had stopped us earlier. The sentry quickly scanned the paper then allowed us through the gates into the sub base; another salute welcoming us as we passed through.

Another, "Wow!" from me.

At this point I was really excited. I was in a nuclear submarine base and heading for the quayside. My enthusiasm quickly turned to disappointment when we discovered the wharf was devoid of subs! The saving grace however, tied up at her berth, was the 295 foot, white hulled, three-masted Barque, *USS Eagle*, the renowned Coastguard sailing vessel.

This tall ship was built in 1936 as *Horst Wessel* at the famous, Blohm and Voss Shipyard in Hamburg for the Kreigsmarine. She had been a training ship for cadets of the German Navy. Adolf Hitler and Rudolf Hess had attended her naming ceremony and launching. The next ship to come from the stocks of this renowned shipyard, following the barque's launch was *Bismarck*.

Horst Wessel served the German Navy throughout the war until captured and retained by the Americans in 1945.

Though Ray asked, he was informed it wasn't possible to go aboard *Eagle* at present, as a reception was due to be held on the ship shortly. As if on cue, two coaches pulled up close to the ship and a series of elderly gentlemen began to disembark.

Now it was Ray's turn to be surprised. He stood open-mouthed, looking at the growing crowd of old men. Each was wearing a single medal, the 'US Congressional Medal of Honour'. This was a band of heroes standing before us. Our host quickly came from his reverie and, moving over to the men and began shaking their hands. To each, he simply said, "thank you."

Immediately after, by way of explanation, Ray, clearly a patriot said, "my father was wounded on D-Day on Omaha beach. He'd only been in the United States for two years after emigrating from Ireland, when he enlisted. Dad nearly died on the bloodiest of the Normandy beaches. Whenever I see a decorated serviceman, I always thank them for what they did for our country."

He went on to say, "This has been a great day for me, Freddy. I could never have hoped to see so many holders of the Congressional Medal in one place, ever."

Soon after, we relocated to the recreational area of this huge base for a late lunch, but Ray didn't eat, he wanted to be on the road again, but he did take a beer. Raising his glass, he said, "to John Paul Jones, Father of the US Navy."

Taken aback by the toast, and knowing John Paul Jones had been the victor at the Battle of Flamborough Head, I blurted, "e was a bloody pirate!" invoking a glower then silent wrath from my host. I did attempt to mitigate my statement, saying he'd attacked a merchant convoy off Flamborough, but it was too late.

"I guess it depends on whose side you were on," I muttered defensively.

My gaff was soon forgotten, though for years after, whenever we met, in good humour, he'd always give the same toast, and I'd give the same response. The Yanks would always rise to the bait when I, non-too subtly, suggested that we Brits had given the United States their Independence!

The replies were loud and varied, but the sentiments were always the same. "You gave us nothing! We took our Independence!" They knew me well enough to know I was teasing.

Next, Ray took us to New Bedford. This port, along with Nantucket, were the wealthiest ports in New England, built solely on the capture of whales and the production of whale oil.

We visited the New Bedford Whaling Museum, which was superb and a really worthwhile visit. I was totally captivated. The voyages these little vessels made were incredible. Some of the ships sailing from this port were as small as ninety feet. From initially hunting whales close to home off the coast of New England and southwards, eventually, when the 'right whales' were almost hunted out, these small vessels began rounding Cape Horn. These little whalers roamed the vast Pacific Ocean, some visiting the Galapagos Islands, where they captured live, giant tortoises, feeding on fresh meat for months, when back at sea.

These tiny ships sailed as far west as Japan, with voyage durations lasting between two and six years. The longest voyage recorded, was by a ship called *Nile* and she was away from her home port for eleven years. Young boys signed up for a voyage, returning home as grown men. Our visit to this museum left me with a thirst for more whaling knowledge.[5]

The following day found us at Mystic Seaport; a recreated nineteenth century village, where we discovered a real whaleship, *Charles W. Morgan*. From reading about the work, looking at photographs and artefacts of whaling, to then go onboard a ship that had previously caught whales, was a huge bonus.

This visit underlined just how small the ships were, and how few men manned them. Depending on the number of whale boats the little ships carried, the crew would number between sixteen and thirty-six men and boys. I'd fished on boats that were almost the same size, but never spent more than seven or eight days at sea on any voyage.

Listening to the guide on board, I was captivated, and could imagine a 'Nantucket sleigh ride'; this when a whale was first harpooned from the small boat then, tethered, took off and sounded, dragging the boat behind. The line, attached to the harpoon, was allowed to run out as required, with slack turns passed around a timberhead in the bows. Water was constantly poured on to the smoking rope and post to prevent both rope and wood from burning from the friction. Additional coils of rope were bent on as required.

If the whale didn't sink or break free, the crew of the boat would gradually haul the rope back until the 'fish' was in sight, when more lances would be stuck into the helpless creature. When mortally wounded and with blood spouting from the blowhole on the mammal's forehead, the call, "chimney's afire" would be shouted enthusiastically by the harpooner.

Sometimes the boat and dead whale would be many miles from the ship when finally killed, leaving the crew with no option but to tow the huge beast, tail first, at no more than a mile an hour, back to the mothership.

Rudimentary outrigger staging was fixed to the ship's hull so men could stand outboard to 'flense' the dead whales (strip the blubber from the carcass) while the floating creatures were

---

5   See page 290

lashed tightly alongside. Sometimes the men would be waist deep in water as the ship rolled. The long strips of blubber would be hauled onto the deck by block and tackle from the mast head, to be cut into chunks small enough to fit into the boiling pot, to be reduced to oil, before being stowed in barrels below. The stink of a whaleship could sometimes be smelt miles away, even before the ship was in sight.

Another ship tied close by at the quayside was the fully rigged ship, (having square yards on all three masts) *Joseph Conrad*.

This vessel had been bought from Denmark by author, Allan Villiers in the 1930s. Originally built as *Georg Stage*, in 1882, she had more recently been a Danish cadet training ship. Renamed and refurbished, with a small permanent crew and many cadets, Villiers had circumnavigated the globe in this old vessel.[6]

In the ships' chandlers store, which was stockpiled with all manner of nautical gear, the smell of hemp, sisal ropes, Stockholm tar and oil was strong, and so evocative of the days of my youth, before synthetic fibres became available. I briefly felt quite melancholy for the lost way of life.

Close by the *Conrad* was the cooper's workshop, where various sizes of casks were constructed; this place too was extremely interesting and informative. The staves and hoops were skilfully assembled into watertight units. When rendered down, the whale oil was stored in barrels. I was interested to learn that a barrel was a volume of measurement. Eight barrels are the equivalent of one tun. One tun is two hundred and ten gallons.

There was only one building constructed of brick in the entire Mystic Seaport settlement: the bank, and for obvious reasons. It was much more difficult for a brick building to catch fire, so banknotes couldn't burn.

* * *

The Pilgrim Fathers arrived in America in 1620 on board the three-masted ship *Mayflower* at what is now Province Town on Cape

---

6   See 'Cruise of the *Conrad*' by Allan Villiers. A great read.

Cod, but they later settled at Plymouth Rock. It was in this place, courtesy of our host, that we discovered a replica settlement, with people dressed in period costumes acting the parts and speaking in old English dialect. The actors were very convincing and appeared to be living the life of the first settlers, though I doubt they'd be working in Winter. Half of the one hundred settlers who landed in December 1620 had died before Spring arrived.

"Is there anywhere you haven't been, that I can take you?" Ray asked, not expecting a positive reply. He was aware we were exhausted with our relentless sightseeing. We'd hardly stopped travelling since arriving in the US, thanks to Ray's kindness. We couldn't believe the energy our old friend had, though he was surprised when I said I had one more request.

"Is there any chance we could go t' Gloucester Ray?" I'd recently seen the film, 'Perfect Storm' and read the book. "It'd be great t' visit." I had visions of having a beer in the famous, 'Crow's Nest' pub where all the crews of the boats congregated. This reminded me of how pubs used to be back home, when we had a fishing fleet.

I should have known better. We visited Gloucester the following day and I saw the fishing boats, but from the car window. We had a fleeting glimpse of the Crow's Nest pub as we shot past. We did stop briefly at a very emotive bronze memorial statue, depicting a fisherman's wife with two bairns at her skirts, looking out to sea for her husband's return.

On my return home I suggested something along these lines to the Town Council, to be mounted on the seafront in Scarborough, though the idea came to nothing.

* * *

Gloucester's maritime history is phenomenal. The early settlers constructed ships and smaller fishing boats, reputedly from as early as 1713 from the timber growing close by, quickly exploiting the massive cod stocks. Cod was to be found in huge shoals along the entire eastern seaboard from Cape Cod to Newfoundland. These early fishers were the pioneers of America's 'Banks' fishery. The Portuguese had been fishing the 'banks' pre-Columbus.

Soon after this, the recent settlers in Lunenburg, Nova Scotia, now a province of Canada, were also building schooners to fish the abundant seas. Initially the ships didn't leave sight of land, while catching huge quantities of fish. These cod were headed, gutted then split, ready for drying on wooden frames on shore. Bait was plentiful; the waters teemed with herring and squid.

It wasn't long before ships got bigger and began carrying salt to preserve the split fish onboard, allowing vessels to travel further afield. Initially fishing with hand lines from the boat's deck in the shallow, nutrient-filled waters, vessels later carried dories powered with oars and a single sail, allowing the fishers to spread out. Later, long-lines with scores of hooks were used, permitting the little craft to work further away from the 'mothership' as the Portuguese did. This had its benefits, but also drawbacks.

With the cold Labrador currents and warmer waters from the Gulf of Mexico colliding in this region, dense fogs were frequent and extensive, and many dories and men were lost, unable to find their mother-ship. Literally thousands of men were swallowed by the sea; a few lucky ones making land, distressed, frost bitten and starving. Miraculously, some men were picked up by eastbound merchant ships; returning years later to wives who, having given their man up for dead, had remarried.

As the schooners worked further out into the Atlantic to fish the various shallow banks, they encountered the notorious Sable Island, about 150 miles East by South from Lunenburg. Crescent shaped, like a new moon, approximately 22 miles long, Sable Island is a huge shifting sandbank, hardly rising above sea level.

Frequent hurricane force winds, combined with shallow waters, created huge breaking waves. The weather in the region could be appalling and changed quickly from calm to storm. It's estimated by historians and researchers that more than a thousand vessels have been wrecked, and tens of thousands of fishermen, mariners and settlers have perished on the inhospitable shores of Sable Island. Some ships were just listed as missing. Heavy-laden craft with huge catches of fish onboard were simply swamped.

The loss of life in the North Sea in the great gales of the 1880s-90s was also immense, but the casualties reduced dramatically in later years with the introduction of steam.

108

Schooners without engines, but with a massive area of sail were still being lost from the eastern fishing ports of New England and Nova Scotia into the 1920s.

Six vessels and over a hundred and twenty men perished from Lunenburg alone in the two violent August storms of 1926-27.[7]*

These schooners made three trips each year between late February and October, making staggering individual vessel catches of 250,000-350,000 fish, that when split and salted, weighed in at over 100 tons. Amazingly all these fish were caught on hooks.

It was only following this tragic loss of vessels and men that the schooners began installing engines. Owners had been reluctant to lose carrying capacity in their vessels.

The Fisheries Museum of the Atlantic in Lunenburg is an amazing and extremely emotive place. The little chapel lists the hundreds of vessels and thousands of men, with dates of tragedies; this a highly recommended visit.

* * *

We left Ray's home early next morning, heading south, with fond memories and with an insight of New England we couldn't possibly have had without the knowledge, enthusiasm and generosity of our host. He must have gone to bed for a week following our departure. As we headed for Washington to meet Douglas, by-passing New York, rest was uppermost in our minds. Little did we know what was in store for us in America's capital city.

Reaching the outskirts of Washington, we began following Douglas's written directions. For the first few miles we were doing quite well, but hadn't appreciated some of the distances involved, and instead of skirting the main part of the busy city, found ourselves somewhere in the centre of Washington, lost and confused.

Fortunately, Doug was responsive to my phone call for help and in his 'hot-rod' mini, found us illegally parked, a few hundred

---

7   The book, The August Gales by Gerald Hallowell highlights much about the historic vessels and lost lives in this region.

yards from the White House. This inauspicious meeting was improved on about twenty minutes later when we arrived at Doug's unassuming, old three-bedroomed house where proper introductions were made.

It was immediately obvious that Doug, six feet in height, unkempt brown hair, glasses and permanent mischievous grin, was not like our friends further north in the US. His humour was zany, off the wall and certainly not P.C. I liked him at once and could see why Paula had made friends with him.

After his friendly welcome with coffee and cake, we unpacked, but there was no relaxing. "You really must see the Washington memorials," Doug enthused, "but the best time to see them is after dark. We'll visit them tonight. First, we'll go visit my mother. She'll be pleased to meet you. Have you watched any of the television programmes like Dallas, Knot's Landing and the other ones about the mega wealthy in America? You really should have. My folks live in a different world."

I thought this was a huge exaggeration, but it most certainly wasn't.

Doug, drove us about thirty minutes to where the buildings thinned, and soon we were driving up a private road. "Mom and Dad are divorced," Doug explained. "Mom lives with a nephew."

We pulled up at a huge, single story ranch-style wooden house with well-maintained gardens and grass. "This is Mom's place," our host said, with an expansive sweep of his arm.

"Wow! It's certainly impressive." I said, and meant it. To own a property like this, on the edge of Washington was phenomenal. This must be an astronomically valuable piece of real estate.

Doug's Mom, Jan answered the door. The lady was petite, attractive and had impish eyes, which explained Doug's mischievous countenance. Her nephew, Valentin, six-feet plus, blond, broad shouldered and wearing bib and brace overalls with a tee shirt underneath, looked like someone from a strongman competition. His handshake underlined this image. I thought my knuckles would crack when he buried my hand inside his huge paw.

Jan said, "you're just in time folks, we're about to go to the Country Club for a late lunch. Douglas, I hope you and your English friends are going to join us."

We protested we weren't dressed for dining out, but the decision was made on our behalf and shortly after, Doug, driving his mother's big motor with the five of us seated comfortably, headed for the private club, pulling up outside the sprawling building, fifteen minutes later.

And what an opulent establishment this was. Plush, deep pile carpets and heavy, dark wood furniture, gilt fittings and expensive ornaments filled the place.

"We're out of our depth 'ere," I whispered to Dotty as we were shepherded towards some ornately carved wooden seats with thick, red velvet cushions.

A waiter immediately appeared and hovered with menus and a wine list. Doug's Mum took the wine list, immediately handing it to me.

"Will you select the wine, Freddy please?" the lady asked, smiling warmly.

I reluctantly took the leather-bound folder and looked at the list. I didn't look at the variety of selection, just at the prices and gave a large gulp. First, I looked for the cheapest, expecting to pay for the meal. "White or red?" I asked with false confidence, looking for an indication of what to select.

There were four takers for white and one abstainer, Doug, a non-drinker. I'd rather have had a glass of red, but wasn't going to run to two bottles. It would be churlish to go for the cheapest I thought, and I didn't know much about wine, so opted for something mid-range, described as crisp and fruity. I could have spent a week boozing in the Leeds Arms for the cost of this bottle.

As it was lunchtime, albeit late, the food was quite light, except potentially on the wallet. The presentation and service were immaculate and typically, as we'd already discovered in the USA, very swift. All the meals were excellent and I was complimented on my choice of wine, though I don't think anything on the list would have been unpalatable.

Jan made us all laugh when she said her neighbours, an extremely good-living, religious, but disagreeable family, had 'adopted' a local road and had their own plaque erected. She said these people would spend each Saturday cleaning this section of the district giving them the 'feel good' factor.

Jan said she wanted these people to feel even better, so regularly scattered household rubbish and grandchildren's soiled nappies along the road at night.

Doug certainly got his wacky sense of humour from his Mom.

Following coffees and a plate piled with chocolates, the bill arrived, held out on a silver platter by one of the attendant waiters. I fumbled for my wallet but Mom beckoned the man over with a hand gesture. There was no credit card or rummaging in a purse, just a well-practised, scribbled signature on the sheet. Job done!

"Wow!" I thought once more.

After dark, Doug took us to see the totally breath-taking memorials. These commemorating the hundreds of thousands of American servicemen and women who'd lost their lives in the many theatres of war the USA had committed to during the past century.

Each memorial we visited seemed to surpass the previous one. The monuments marking the Second World War, Korea and Vietnam were all floodlit, some with water flowing, but what they all had in common was the feeling they evoked, of the futility of war. Thousands upon thousands of names, and each had been a person, a serviceman or woman. Each one of these names was someone's son or daughter, husband or wife, brother or sister, and all had given their lives for the USA. The visit left me with a feeling of great sadness.

Late morning on the following day, Doug said, "I'm going to take you to see how some Americans eat. You'll be amazed, though not impressed."

Slightly perplexed, we got into the little car, to be taken to Chesapeake Bay, to a crab house restaurant. The white-painted, wooden building was on the waterfront, giving panoramic views of the Delaware River. I was quite surprised that though there were only five steps to the door of the eating house, there was also a small escalator at the side of the steps.

On entry we were shown to a window table, from where views of Autumn colours on the riverside were spectacular in the midday sunshine.

On the menu I noted an 'all you can eat' item for a set price, but Doug suggested we order a crab cake and maybe a small blue crab each. We took his advice, also requesting a small beer each. Doug took a coke.

Sitting at a table close by, were four extremely large, rotund men, all wearing lumberjack type shirts with broad braces, supporting denim jeans. Tall glasses of light beer were being heartily quaffed by the assembled group.

As we chatted amiably, Doug constantly making us laugh with his observations of American life, I noticed a waiter's back appear from the swinging kitchen doors. As he cleared the entrance, he turned, hoisting a huge silver tray of steaming snow crab to shoulder height, heading towards the adjacent table.

"Bloody 'ell," I exclaimed, and couldn't help pointing. "Look at that 'eap o' crab. They'll never get through that lot."

Our host smiled knowingly, and said, "just watch them, but don't make it obvious."

Armed with nutcracker type tools and long silver skewers, the men appeared to descend upon the tray of food, and within minutes the platter was reduced to a small pile of broken white and orange shell. The waiter reappeared, wordlessly removing the carnage.

I'd been attempting to watch the adjacent party surreptitiously, but I'm sure my open mouth was a giveaway. At that moment the first part of our modest meal arrived. The crab cakes, about three inches in diameter and half an inch thick, were coated in breadcrumbs and came with a selection of relishes. Mine was tasty, though mostly filled with brown crab meat.

"Bloody 'ell!" I said again, as another tray of snow crab appeared. The piece of bread bun I was chewing almost left my mouth as I spluttered the words.

This second tray of snow crab didn't last long and had vanished by the time our blue crabs arrived. These were small: not much bigger than the little green shore crabs back home, and smaller than the minimum landing size of the brown, edible crab. Fortunately, the species we were eating had the same biology and were easy to dissect, though yielded little meat.

A third tray of snow crab arrived across the way, and this was attacked with the same vigorous tenacity as the previous heaps, and I was almost lost for words.

"Where the 'ell are they puttin' it?" I asked. It was a rhetorical question.

The waiter was soon removing the remains.

With no other takers, I opted for a scoop of ice cream. The vanilla blob arrived at the same time as a fourth tray of crab. The only words I could find were, "fo' fucks sake!"

We had coffees and enjoyed more of Doug's stories then asked for the tab.

Minutes later, having settled the account, we rose to leave. The fourth tray of snow crab was now empty and being returned to the kitchen. The four men were now leaning back, thumbs under their braces, bellies extended, their challenge met. Mission accomplished.

"Do you see what I mean," Doug said knowingly, when we were out of earshot. "We were in the place early, and there's a ball game on today. Normally the place is full of people like that on weekends. All you can eat for a set price isn't a good thing for the American waistline.

* * *

We'd seen many of the tourist sites and it was our last day in Washington, but even with all the excitement we'd had, there was more to come. We were going to meet Doug's Dad, Dwight.

We left the house in the early evening, heading for his Dad and Stepmom's place. Twenty minutes into the journey, we stopped in a darkish area with the headlights illuminating a pair of large, black, spiked double iron gates. An equally big wall led off into the darkness on either side of the gates.

Our driver left the vehicle, heading towards the gatepost, where an intercom was located. Pressing the button, he received an immediate response and before he was back in the car, the big gates slowly began to open. We crept through the gap, taking in the view of a huge, illuminated house to our right. "Colin Powell lives there," Doug said, taking a hand off the wheel to wave in the direction of the building.

"Colin Powell?" I exclaimed. "Wasn't he Chief of Staff in Iraq during 'Desert Storm?'"

"Yup that's right," Doug affirmed, then, pointing in the opposite direction said,

"That's Caspar Weinberger's house. He was Secretary of State for Ronald Reagan."

"Bloody 'ell," I said once more, and not for the first time was unbelievably impressed. "I've 'eard that name dozens o' times on international news bulletins."

Doug, now in full flow, pointed back to the right and said, "Senator Robert Kennedy used to live there, before he was assassinated. Dick Cheney[8] bought the house later, demolishing the property to re-build on the site."

Dotty, who'd been sitting quietly in the back, listening to the conversation, chipped up with the classic line, "was it a slum clearance?"

When he'd recovered his breath from laughing, Doug pointed ahead to a massive building in the headlights. "This is Dad's place," he said, pulling under a portico that would have covered four or five large cars. "Dad's a property developer," Doug said. "He developed this entire gated complex. That's how he got the best house."

I'd ran out of new exclamations.

---

8   Dick Cheney was later to become Vice President under George W Bush.

"This is as big as our street," Dotty whispered in my direction.

The statement was a slight exaggeration, but not by much.

Entering through one side of the large, mahogany double doors, we were met by Doug's father, Dwight. He was a big man, but proportionate, not fat. He was a slightly larger and older version of Doug, but had a certain presence. Dad was definitely a man who was used to giving orders and commanding respect.

Incredible, meteoric business success had seen Dwight rise from farm boy to billionaire, owning one of the country's largest home building companies and was a shareholder in the Washington Redskins, American football team.

Doug must have introduced other friends to his parents, as his Dad said, "and where are these people from, that you've brought to meet us, Douglas?"

We were introduced and I shook Dwight's hand, looking into his eyes, as he looked into mine. It was as if he could read my mind.

If he could, he'd have read me thinking, "what the hell are we doing here?"

Stepmom Martha, was tall, slender and elegant, dressed in a smart jacket and skirt. Her hair was beautifully coiffured and her manicure perfect, as I noticed when we gently shook hands. When the lady smiled her teeth were perfect. Her eyes were piercing.

Doug went over the top with his flattery to his Stepmom, kissing her hand and making outrageous complimentary comments about her appearance, which were enjoyed immensely.

We were offered drinks and accepted wine from the bottle already opened and which Martha said was wonderful. Poured into crystal glasses, the chilled sharp, dry wine was wonderful, though I'd no idea what it was.

Dwight asked me what my profession was, but I don't think he could comprehend a fishing family from a little town on the North Sea Coast, any more than I could imagine the sort of wealth that could develop a huge, gated complex in the centre of Washington for internationally renowned politicians.

"We're going out for dinner at the club this evening." Stepmom said. "We'd be delighted if you could join us."

I looked to Doug for direction.

"Sure, that'd be great," he said. "I've not been there for a while. These folks will love it."

I thought we might be a bit under dressed, but didn't realise where we were going. It wasn't the same place we'd been with Doug's Mom, Jan.

"We'll go in my new car," the lady said. "I'll drive."

We continued chatting with Doug and his Dad while finishing our drinks, then stepped outside to find Martha sitting in a new, sleek, top of the range, white Jaguar.

We were driven into the city then up a small driveway, where we stopped outside the entrance to a flight of stone stairs. As we vacated the car, a uniformed chauffeur stood waiting to take the Jag' away, to be parked until our departure.

I felt another, "Bloody 'ell," coming on, but swallowed, and stifled the words.

We began making our way up a broad, now carpeted spiral staircase, where I was immediately aware of life-sized, coloured, head and shoulders caricatures painted on the walls. Each had the name of the subject adjacent, and I recognised important politicians from the national and world stage from years past.

Where were we going? We were most certainly under dressed.

"It's a long way from Hessle Road," Dotty whispered, as we approached the opened doors, looking into the lavish furnishings of the dining room.

Dotty was referring to the part of Hull where she grew up. Hessle Road was a long thoroughfare leading west from the city centre, with many streets and terraces leading off. Most of the families who manned and serviced Hull's huge trawler fleet lived on or off Hessle Road. This was a densely populated area of old, two up, two down terraced houses. Severe wartime bombing of the nearby docks and many houses in the district, plus tragic losses of many trawlers and crews at sea, made this a close community.

We couldn't have been further from Hessle Road, entering into this establishment where the rich and famous, the movers and shakers of Washington D.C. frequented and dined.

The maître-d hovered by the doors to welcome what were obviously special VIPs. He turned, and with a sweeping arm to direct, escorted our party to a prominent table with crisp linen tablecloth. Rolled napkins were held in chunky, silver rings. Smart waiters hovered, assisting with chairs, then when we were comfortably seated, handed out impressive menus, not just for their physical size, but also for the range of food listed.

Once more I was handed the wine list, this time by Dwight and I muttered thanks. Once more I scanned the prices, realising at once that on reflection, the wine at the Country Club a couple of days ago had been reasonably priced. I mentally gave another curse.

"You must try the soup," Martha said, putting her hand on the back of Dotty's hand, when the waiter had announced the day's specials. "It's divine."

"Be careful what you order," Doug said. "The lobsters are huge, and so are some of the steaks."

I ordered shrimp and the smallest steak, rare. Dotty, on Stepmom's advice, requested the soup plus a starter portion of Chicken Caesar salad.

The maroon jacketed waiter raised his eyebrows at this choice until Doug, seizing the moment said, "don't worry, she's anorexic."

Dotty rolled her eyes and said nothing. The waiter smiled knowingly.

Studying the wine list, I intended to request one white and one red, then, biting the bullet, inspirationally asked the waiter for his advice, relying on my credit card.

The waiter suggested we have a sharp, dry, Californian white with the starter, saving a rich red for those having steaks, and I gave myself a mental pat on the back. I think I got brownie points from the company, and certainly won a smile from Dotty.

The conversation was very light hearted. Doug and his Dad made us laugh when they were recollecting Doug's childhood. The pair, against Dwight's better judgement, had been persuaded by Mom to attend an Indian Guide Summer Camp for fathers and sons. None of the participants were native Americans but everyone in the company had to have American Indian names. All wore costumes from the period.

Dad, laughed, saying, "I was 'Big Buck' and Douglas was 'Fast Buck'."

Doug said, "instead of feathers in our headdress, we had heaps of dollar bills stitched together to form the plumage. This sacrilege didn't find favour with the parents."

"I took a heap of firewater too," Dwight added, laughing again. "I invited the fathers to cocktails round the campfire, resulting in many drunken Dads."

Pleasingly and not surprisingly, this was the pair's first and last Indian Guides experience.

The first courses arrived and Martha took a taste of her soup. "Mmm!" she exclaimed. "Delicious." A minute or so later, the lady took another small spoonful. Much to our surprise, after one more taste, she pushed her bowl away, having had sufficient.

Dotty and I managed to hide our shock, but no one else seemed bothered or surprised at the waste.

My mountain of shrimps, that at home were prawns, was a meal on its own, and I wasn't going to waste any, though wished I had when the main courses arrived.

I thought my steak was big, till I looked at Doug's and Dwight's; these were huge. I cut into my ribeye, and the piece of meat was juicy and cooked to perfection, though didn't seem to have the taste I was expecting and strangely, seemed a little bland.

The wine was excellent, and did compliment the red meat perfectly. Dwight certainly enjoyed the selection.

Dotty was hidden behind a mountain of lettuce with half a chopped chicken atop, into which, she was struggling to make inroads.

Martha had finished her meal, though there was little evidence she had started.

There were desserts to follow, then coffees, followed by liqueurs, after which, I felt totally bloated. Maybe Stepmom had a point?

It was time for the dreaded bill and, fishing for my wallet, I really did offer to pay. Fortunately for me, Dwight would have none of it and didn't even look at the bottom line, just annotated a gratuity then initialled the tab.

Judging by the smile on the waiter's face, the tip must have been a good one.

The white Jaguar was waiting outside and Doug had the pleasure of driving, though Martha, in the back with Dotty and I, and concerned for the welfare of her vehicle, made helpful driving suggestions.

Through the iron gates again, we didn't go back inside Dad's house. After saying a huge, thank you for their wonderful hospitality and unique experience, we were quickly back in the little hot-rod, heading for Doug's home and our bed. I was so full of food, I'd have to prop myself up with pillows to assist the digestion of the feast.

The following morning, we gave huge hugs and grateful thanks before saying goodbye to Doug and to Washington, though not yet to America. We'd had an unrepeatable experience, but still had one more engagement. We were going to Newport, Rhode Island, home of the New York Yacht Club. It was the conclusion of the Single-handed, Round the World Yacht Race, and we had an invitation to the celebrations.

Back in Scarborough before our departure, I'd been talking to Tom Pindar, patriarch of the family run, Pindar' Print and Communications Group, telling him we were going Stateside soon, and giving the dates.

"Hey" he said, "our company is sponsoring Emma Richards in the single-handed race. At present she's in third position overall. The race finishes while you're in the U.S. If your dates coincide and you get chance, come to see us in Newport. We'll book you a room."

"That'd be wonderful," I said. "How hospitable is that? Thank you," and was determined to work the given date into our programme.

The drive to Newport, skirting New York again, was better than expected, though on arrival we needed directions to find the Hotel Viking, despite its size.

Checking in was easy; we were expected, and were pleasantly surprised to find a welcome basket of fruit and bottle of wine on the table to greet us; this from some of our New England friends; really thoughtful.

Down in the crowded bar we met up with Tom Pindar and his son Andrew, who along with other company staff, were with the young yachtswoman, Emma Richards, who must have been feeling extremely hemmed in and claustrophobic after her extended passage of solitude. Disappointingly, the talented young lady had been pipped into fourth place on the final day of her amazing voyage.

Tom passed me a two-tone drink in ice, saying "here Fred, try a 'dark and stormy'. The drink, in a half-pint glass with ice, had ginger beer on the bottom, with dark rum floating on top. Very tasty it was, and versatile, as the drink could be mixed by degrees or not at all, according to taste. Tom, grinning said, "the ginger beer is only there to hold the rum up. When you taste ginger beer, it's time for more rum."

The reception was really good and food excellent but, not for the first time, we felt quite out of place. Our hosts were extremely busy dealing with their many commitments and we didn't know anyone, or have anything in common with those around us. Nevertheless, it was a wonderful privilege to be here. Several dark and stormies and glasses of wine later, we felt more mellow and relaxed.

The remainder of the evening went swiftly and we managed to spend some pleasant time with our hosts. Tom asked if we'd seen the big houses along the coast and suggested we should have a short excursion to view these properties before departing in the morning.

I tried to explain to Tom that we'd seen big houses in Washington, but again I was to be proved totally wrong.

All too soon the night was ended and we said goodnight, thanks and farewells to the Scarborough people we knew, and the friendly folk we'd met during the evening.

Next morning early, feeling slightly weary, we packed what little we'd used, and not wanting anything other than coffee, soon left the Viking. Taking Tom's advice, before heading for Boston, we took the coastal road to inspect the big houses.

"Wow! Look at that place," I exclaimed, pointing to a huge mansion on the left. "It's like something from a film set. Doug's Dad's 'ouse is little, compared t' that."[9]

This phenomenal mansion was The Breakers, commissioned by the 'Vanderbilt' Family at the end of the nineteenth century.

Commodore Cornelius Vanderbilt (1794-1877) had amassed great wealth building steamships and founding railroads. His grandson Cornelius II, who became Chairman and President of the New York Railway Company, bought a wooden, Summer House on this site, which burned down. He replaced the destroyed building with, The Breakers. There are no words to describe this 'pile', and also, The Elms and The Marble House. These properties were the stuff of fairy-tales, and there were other mansions. Needless to say, these were breath taking, and we were so pleased we'd taken the diversion. These were further examples of America's extreme affluence.

Following our tour of the area we lost our way a little, making us late for the airport, but we eventually found the five-lane highway heading towards Boston. Luckily the road was quiet and we were making good time. I was feeling less concerned about missing our flight.

I should have known better. Traffic began to build up as we approached the city. All five lanes seemed to slow down together and I braked to maintain a safe distance from the car ahead. Unfortunately, the vehicle behind me didn't, and we felt a dull thud when hit in the rear by a driver unable to stop in time.

---

9   See www.newportmansions.org

"Shit," I shouted, then quickly checked that Dotty was ok. It wasn't a big bump and she was fine, though was already anxious about the time this bump was going to lose us.

The traffic around us was all stopped and I got out of the car to assess the damage, looking at my watch as I did so. We were certainly going to lose more time here, and had none to spare. The driver of the other vehicle, a small sports car, had also left his car and was already apologising profusely and offering to give me his insurance details. He was looking at the two cars and had stopped speaking.

I gave our car a cursory glance and strangely, but fortunately, there didn't seem to be any visible damage. The other guy said nothing. He just watched me examine the rear end of our vehicle. "There doesn't appear t' be any damage," I said. "An' we're in a hurry. Ah'll 'ave t' let it go."

He must have thought I was from a different planet, judging by the lack of comprehension on his face. The traffic had begun moving again and cars were swerving round us, sounding their horns. I left the confused man standing in the road and went back to our vehicle, started the engine then drove off.

We seemed to crawl through the 'big dig' but eventually made it to the airport and the hire car section. Following a sign saying, 'returns' I parked behind a big car that was being examined. Opening our doors, we both exited and I was raising the boot to extract our cases, when the attendant arrived to inspect our vehicle.

Gazing into the void where our luggage had been, the observant young man looked in my direction and said, "this car has been in a rear end shunt, buddy."

I was taken aback and was speechless at first, but then muttered, "ah know. Ah've jus' been bumped on t' 'ighway as we were comin' in t' Boston." At the same time, I was wishing I'd taken out full insurance with voluntary excess.

"It's nothing to do with me buddy," the attendant said, neutrally. "I come across these bumps all the time. I just report what I see to the office. Take it up with the people over there." He pointed to the building where I'd originally hired the car.

I looked at my watch, knowing we couldn't afford much more delay. Leaving Dotty to keep an eye on the bags, I rushed to the car rental office.

All the operatives were busy behind the long desk when I walked in. I looked at my watch again without seeing the face, but then within seconds a member of staff became available. "Phew," I sighed, moving towards the smart young woman.

She was a pretty, young, blond girl with a warming smile and I was greeted with, "can I help you, sir?"

"'Ello," I said, feeling guilty, for no sane reason. Handing over my agreement papers I said, "Ah've jus' brought a car back. It's outside, but some bloody idiot ran in t' back of me this mornin' as we were comin' in t' Boston. I 'aven't even got 'is details."

The young lady smiled again, which was reassuring. She said, "that's alright sir. I'll just get out your details." She turned to a filing cabinet and in no time at all was putting the papers down on the counter. "There's a four hundred dollars excess on this agreement sir," the lady said. "But don't worry. We have your credit card details and you've already paid the $400 excess. We'll just refund anything due after the repair. Have a safe flight."

It was that simple. Job done! As I rushed out through the door, I thought, Ah won't see that four hundred dollars again, but at least there's no delay. Great! New flights would 'ave cost a lot more.

Dotty had loaded our cases onto a luggage trolley and was waiting outside for the verdict.

"It's all sorted an' ok," I said, smiling for the first time since Newport. "We can still make that flight if we 'urry."

"Thank goodness for that," Dotty said with relief. "It wasn't even our fault."

I took the trolley, and we set off at a run for the check in desk, arriving only three minutes later. There was no queue and I was worried we'd missed the plane, but the attendant was still there.

"If you're for Heathrow, you've just made it sir. I'm about to close the flight," said the cheery lady behind the desk.

"We're fo' 'Eathrow," I said breathlessly, handing over our passports, "and we've made it. Fantastic!"

The two bags were given labels and disappeared down the conveyor and we were handed our papers with a friendly, "have a good flight" from the helpful attendant.

Boarding passes and passports in hand and with pulses still racing, Dotty and I looked at each other and we both laughed out loud. We'd made it, and now, checked in, we could head for security and the departure lounge at a more leisurely pace. The flight wouldn't go without us now.

The overnight Atlantic crossing was quite uneventful, and we both slept most of the way. Even the transfer across London was easy, and we had time for coffee and cake in Kings Cross Station before catching the train north. The onward journey to York and Scarborough was smooth and the remainder of the day went in a blur, as we attempted to catch up with the backlog of family affairs, mail and business.

In the evening, despite jetlag, we made time for an hour in the Leeds Arms and to regale our friends with our tales, and oh-boy, had we some stories to tell. What a holiday it had been.

"We'll never top that one," I said to Dotty, at the end of our tales in the pub.

"How could we?" she replied with a big smile.

* * *

Conversely, a couple of months later we were looking to have a warm break in Portugal, and at short notice could only get a flight from East Midlands airport. We opted to stay in an airport hotel overnight, for the early morning flight.

Arriving at the check in at 0700 hours, we then proceeded to the security section for hand luggage inspection. Dotty went to the left side conveyor and I to the right. Listening to the officious man behind the rollers, shouting instructions to the people ahead of me, I just knew there was going to be trouble. The man was obnoxious.

"Take off your belt" he barked at me when I drew face to face with him.

I wasn't wearing a conventional belt. My trousers were supported by a permanently attached belt made of webbing, with small interlocking plastic ends. Two thin, pronged, plastic wedges entered a receptacle on the opposite side, clicking closed. I opened the sections, holding them apart, saying, 'the belt doesn't come off mate. It's attached."

"Take off your belt," was the uncompromising instruction.

I clipped the belt shut then unfastened it again, holding both ends for his perusal. "Look! It's plastic. There's no buckle. It's hollow."

For the third time the odious official spewed out his mantra, "take off your belt."

A red haze came over me in frustration like nothing I'd ever experienced before. In an instant I kicked off my shoes then dropped my trousers, placing footwear and slacks in the grey plastic box, then shoved the container in the direction of the scanner. "Are yer bloody satisfied now," I asked of the now less vocal tyrant, as he stepped back in shock and surprise.

I could no longer see his face, only red. I stepped through the portal in my underwear towards a surprised, waiting Officer, who didn't need to search me.

Meanwhile Dotty, with her back to me was totally oblivious of the happenings behind her. It was only when a much more pleasant inspector, looking over her shoulder in my direction said, "well I've worked here for ten years and I've never seen that before."

Dotty turned, looking at me as I stepped into the x-ray canopy and, raising her hands to her head said, "oh noooo!"

On the other side of the scanner, I waited in pants for my stuff to reappear from the conveyor, oblivious to the staring and comments I was attracting. As my tray appeared, I grabbed and donned the light grey trousers then quickly slipped on my shoes. I turned, to be faced with a large, portly, uniformed man.

"Do you have a problem sir?" he enquired.

"Oh! I have a problem alright" I replied loudly. Pointing at the cause of my anger, I added, "I 'ave a problem with 'im." The odious, self-important dick heard me and looked in my direction, but quickly averted his gaze.

Unclipping my belt again, I held both ends in my hand. "Could you remove this belt if you were wearing these trousers?" I asked the Officer.

Looking at his belly, overhanging his belt, this was the perfect question. The man couldn't see his belt.

"I don't think I could sir," he answered, reasonably.

"Well tell that twat through there then," I said loudly, pointing to the cause of my outburst. I was starting to calm down a little now I'd found someone who'd listen to my complaint. "'Ee needs sackin'."

"I don't think we can do that sir," the man said softly, "but I will have a word. And next time, please, just ask for the supervisor. We don't like people taking their trousers off."

Dotty was now at my side and said, "what was that all about?"

I explained the circumstances, and as if it was an everyday occurrence, she simply said, "oh!"

The man following me through the booth, and who'd had an easy passage, tapped me on the shoulder and said, "nice one mate. He was asking for that."

Now calmer, I said, "thank you," but it was hours before I was finally back to my usual humour, and it was days before I could finally laugh at the situation.

CHAPTER 13

LOSS OF *CRIMOND II*

"Have you heard anything from *Crimond II* recently?" the Coastguard from Falmouth asked over the phone. "You're the named contact that we're obliged to call in the event of her EPIRB[10] going off."

I was unable to help, saying that I'd had no communication from the vessel, but that she was at sea with two men on board. I gave the Officer *Crimond II's* phone number.

I'd had a few calls of this nature in recent years, usually when the 'float free' beacon had become dislodged from its bracket in port, causing the device to transmit and the signal to be picked up by satellite. This time the vessel was at sea and her emergency beacon was apparently operating, so I tried ringing the boat's phone. The line was dead. Falmouth Coastguard would have got the same response, and would now be taking urgent action. It wasn't bad weather, but there was a fresh offshore breeze, maybe force three or four.

The boat's young Skipper, Thomas 'Tammy' McEwan, a Scot with a broad Glaswegian accent, who now lived in Bridlington, was a slight, energetic fisherman with short, dark hair and sharp features. He and I had travelled to Newlyn in Cornwall, a few years earlier to view *Crimond II, KY 246*, for Tammy to fish on the Yorkshire Coast grounds he was familiar with.

---

10 Electronic Position Indicating Radio Beacon.

I'd set off to drive the four hundred and eighty-five miles to Newlyn in the early hours, collecting Tammy in 'Brid' on the way. A couple of hours down the motorway, I pulled in for fuel, plus coffee and sandwich to go, then handed the keys to Tammy.

"You can drive for a bit," I suggested.

He passed them back, saying, "Ah lost ma licence, las' week, so ah canna drive."

"Oh great," I groaned. "It's gonna be a long day."

We arrived in Newlyn after noon and, finding *Crimond II*, met up with the surveyor we'd engaged. For a fee, the man was to provide a professional report and valuation on the black-hulled vessel, as required by the bank.

The three of us spent a couple of hours, checking out the engine room, fish hold, cabin and wheelhouse of the vessel. I remembered this sturdy little boat from 1973, when she was newly built and coated with light varnish.

Crimond II was a 55-foot, wooden boat from the Fraserburgh yard of James Noble, where my *Independence* was built four years later.

Crimond newly painted – Unknown

Her first owner, Billy[11] Boyter from Pittenweem, had successfully fished out on the 'North West Rough', seventy miles north east of Scarborough, fly-shooting with a seine net, landing good catches of haddock back into Scarborough. Since then her 230 hp Gardner engine had been replaced with a 310 hp Caterpillar.

Billy had eventually sold *Crimond II*, retiring to spent his time as a volunteer on the old herring drifter, *Reaper FR 958*, sailing around Scotland and occasionally as far south as Yorkshire in this historic, floating museum. In her day, *Reaper* had visited many of these ports as a working vessel.

Survey completed and minor defects noted, we stopped for a meal in a nearby fishermen's café. The surveyor said he'd compile his report and valuation in the region of the asking price and would mail the documentation in the next few days. We could then formalise the paperwork with our bank; a good job done!

It was now late afternoon and with the departure of the surveyor and nothing further to do, we decided we'd head back north. The plan was we'd stop somewhere en route to find a B&B. In the event, we stopped only for food and fuel. After dropping Tammy back in Brid, I arrived home at 0100 the following morning, having driven nine hundred and seventy miles. Annoyingly, I gained a speeding ticket on the M18, an hour from the end of my drive.

* * *

Talking to an operator at Humber Coastguard, which monitored the regions shipping and waters, I discovered that *Crimond II* was no longer in radio contact and they, and several fishing vessels had been attempting to make contact with her.

The last communication heard was by Skipper, Pete Ibbotson, on board *Wayfinder*, also from Bridlington. He'd picked up a garbled message from Tammy, saying they were making water and were trying to pump out.

A helicopter had been scrambled from RAF Leconfield and was fast homing in on the satellite signal.

---

11 Billy Boyter died on the same day *Crimond II* foundered.

It was an hour later when I heard from the Coastguard that Tammy and his crewman, Major Clark (the third generation of his family bearing the name) had been picked up from the water by the chopper. The pair were being flown to Scarborough hospital.

"Are they OK? How long had they been in the water? Why weren't they in the raft?" The Officer had no further information, and I feared the worst. It was late April and the North Sea was at its coldest.

It was hours later when I was able to get a response from the hospital. I learned that both men were suffering from severe hypothermia, but were alive. I was refused permission to visit as the pair were very weak.

They were alive! The pair had survived an extended immersion in the North Sea in April, but they were alive! That was incredible!

The following day I visited Tammy in hospital to learn his story. Major had been released a few hours earlier. As a big, strapping lad with a bit more fat on him that Tammy, Major had fared best of the two.

The Skipper said they'd discovered the boat was making water and the engine pump wasn't coping. The pair began using the deck pump, and Tammy had shouted a message on the radio, though hadn't, at that point sent a Mayday.

The pair realised they were fighting a losing battle when the engine stopped and power was lost. At that point they had no communications. Tammy and Major donned lifejackets then threw the life raft over the side. Pulling on the painter line, the raft quickly exploded into shape, but it was at this point they made what was almost a fatal mistake.

Rather than abandoning ship and taking to the raft, they made the painter rope fast to the railings on top of the shelter deck, until they felt it was time to leave.

The foolishness of this plan was quickly realised when *Crimond II* suddenly lurched and began to capsize. Now there was no time for the men to get into the raft, or even unfasten the securing line as the stricken vessel turned turtle. The two men were thrown into the water. The sinking craft dragged the raft under.

All life rafts are fitted with automatic, hydrostatic devices, fixed to the cradle which, in the event of a rapid immersion, release the capsule, allowing the raft to float free. *Crimond IIs* raft was already floating, so this was no longer relevant, but on the other end of the line, where attached to the raft, is a sacrificial strip. This patch, holding the rope, will tear off without damaging the fabric, releasing a submerged raft, allowing the lifesaver to surface.

The pair in the water never saw the raft surface. Their heads, on the surface, mostly between swells, gave them hardly any visible distance.

Fortune finally smiled on the pair when, along with a buoyant propane gas bottle, the floating EPIRB was close by. The men grabbed both these buoyant objects. Tammy said the water was bitterly cold, and it wasn't long before he'd lost consciousness. The young Skipper said had no recollection of being rescued. When he was hoisted into the helicopter. his core body temperature was almost at the point where life was extinguished.

I caught up with Major at the harbour later in the day and got his version of events. Young Major looked weary, and would have been better at home resting, but wanted to be on the pier with his pals. His constant smile was back in place.

"What 'appened Maj? Ah've jus' been t' see Tammy an' 'e's goin' to be ok, but 'e doesn't remember anythin'."

Major concurred with Tammy's story until they were in the water, then said he'd had to keep his arms around Tammy, who'd lost consciousness. He'd waved as the helicopter approached. Major had undoubtedly saved his Skipper's life.

"They never saw us Fred," he said, the smile disappearing. "They went right over t' top of us. It was ages before they came back. I was 'olding on t' Tammy and t' EPIRB. We wouldn't 'ave lasted much longer."

Apparently, the chopper had run down on the bearing of the beacon, then lost the signal and had to wait for the next satellite to pass. The technology of this baffled me, but the time loss was almost fatal.

This was the third vessel we'd lost in a few short years, but at least we'd not lost any crew. Boats can be replaced, though this had been another close-run thing, and we were not too popular with the insurance company.

* * *

As fish quotas continued to be reduced and policing grew more stringent, with massive punitive fines or worse for transgressions, fishermen began to look for alternative methods of surviving. The Skippers who couldn't adapt, sadly, left the industry. The UK fleets continued to contract and good men became jobless.

This coincided with the huge expansion of the oil and gas industry, and both the SFF (Scottish Fishermen's Federation) and NFFO (National Federation of Fishermen's Organisations) formed 'Service Companies'. These bodies would charter fishing boats to the oil and gas industry to guard unmarked, sensitive sub-sea installations. These were usually exposed or new pipelines and pipeline crossings.

Boats were paid a daily rate, which though not lucrative, accumulated over extended periods up to twenty-one days. Fuel consumption was low and more importantly, no precious quota was being used. This was a boring job for crews, who were used to working round the clock.

During the day, while the Skippers gave out radio warnings to approaching shipping, the crews cleaned, painted bulwarks, decks, cabins and engine rooms. They mended or made new nets and even made crab pots. The days were filled, and there was time for reading and watching videos. Later, satellite television would become universal.

The arrangement between the boats and service companies was mutually advantageous. The federations, with declining membership, still had huge commitments to represent members at national and international level. The small percentage levied from guard work subsidised membership costs and helped to keep the federations effective.

All this was a far cry from the earliest oil exploration in the North Sea during the 1960s, and at a time before fishermen needed to negotiate with politicians. Herby Nicholson, in the old keelboat, *Protect Us, GY 640* was given the job as chase boat to one of the earliest seismic survey vessels. Modern day exploration vessels use air cannons to penetrate the strata, then to record the returning echoes. The survey vessel Herby was following was using explosives and these charges killed many fish, propelling them to the surface. Herby, and son Brian gaffed the dead fish, earning additional pocket money.

Subsequent to this, an exploration jack-up rig arrived and was located a few miles off the Scarborough coast. Local boats, in turn were paid £80 a day to stand by the rig while the activity was taking place.

The Skipper of *Vigilantes GY 179* decided to save fuel by dropping his anchor and stopping the engine. Unfortunately, when the next vessel arrived to take her turn, *Vigilantes* crew couldn't start their engine and embarrassingly, had to be towed back to port.

On board *Success II, SH 112*, where I was a deck hand with Skipper Bob Walker, our turn came to be the guard vessel. We spent two days overhauling nets, meticulously cleaning the cabin and engine room, then endless reading.

We were bored, but to make matters worse, a loud, irritating, Texan drawl, was frequently transmitting over the radio from the rig, "*Sussex, Sussex,* move in closer there, boy."

We'd had enough and our Skipper requested to be relieved. We had the trawl down and were fishing within an hour of the relief boat's arrival.

* * *

Some years later, much to my surprise, I received another letter, in pink pen from the 'presumed' old boy who'd written when the Spanish fleets were pillaging the Grand Banks.

My dear Frederick

You will doubtless recall our brief correspondence some years ago following your appearance in my morning Telegraph.

I was a younger man in those days and eagerly volunteered my services to deal with those Dago boats robbing our fishing grounds, damn em!

You thought you could do the job without me and see where it's got you.

Anyway, it is all water under the bridge now and I spend my days in front of the gas fire reading any trash that comes along.

It has been a great delight to discover your excellent books and have just been brought your latest effort by my daughter, the same one that knits the sweaters. I believe she is half way through one for you. It features a fish body with a finned human skull or such.

Your book is brightening the Winter days and making an old man happy. Jolly good photos too.

I intend to make a journey north, someday soon and will look forward to a night out in the old town with you and your shipmates.

I know you will be able to help me with the wheelchair and empty the bags etc.

Very kindest regards, Reggie Walmer

PS sorry about this bloody awful pen.

To this day I don't know if these were spoof letters. I never met this character, but if he was real, I'd loved to have done so. If it was scam, well done!

* * *

Dotty and I had just arrived into a busy Leeds Arms and were standing at the bar next to a large, thickset chap with a round face and receding hair. He was accompanied by a good-looking, elegant, blond lady, possibly in her late thirties.

I was attempting to attract the attention of Moira the barmaid, as the small, dark-haired server was pulling a pint from the beer pump in front of me. I whispered, "when you've a minute, lovely lady."

I wasn't sure Moira had heard me, as she continued serving customers. "When you've a minute, please," I said again, the next time she was close.

"Yes! I'll be with you shortly," said the barmaid, acknowledging me, but beginning to get flustered. "I do have other customers."

True to her word, a minute later, Moira stood before me. "Yes Mr Normandale," she said pointedly, attracting the attention of the adjacent couple. "What can I do for you?"

I requested a glass of wine for Dotty and my usual drink, now a 'dark and stormy'.

The drinks arrived and were placed on the counter. Thanking her, I tendered a note and received my change.

"Now Mr Normandale," she said in the same tone, "is there anything further I can possibly do for you?"

"Ah suppose a shag's out o' the question?" I replied audibly.

The tall chap next to me had just put glass to lips, quaffing a mouthful of beer. Hearing my comment, he coughed, and unable to swallow the liquid, sprayed the beer forth, spraying the mirror behind the bar. The big man continued to cough for several seconds with beer up his nose.

"I'll ask my husband," replied Moira, now entering into the banter. "He's over there. What do you think he'll say, Dotty?" She addressed my wife.

As ever, Dotty, looking in my direction, just rolled her eyes.

The adjacent couple introduced themselves as John and Melanie. They'd recently moved back to Scarborough, where the man's family were owners of a seafront arcade. His family were originally fairground people. John and Mel had just discovered their local pub.

Crimond II sank on 24th April 2001 30 miles North East of Scarborough.

CHAPTER 14

OBAN WITH DAD

Six months later with sea gear loaded in the car, Dad and I set off for Oban.

On the way north, during our conversations I said, "Remember Dad, yer seventy-seven, an yer back's been givin' yer a bit o' gyp. If they ask yer if yer want t' climb up t' mast, tell 'em no."

"Aye, alright," he replied.

We had a good drive north and west, including a couple of brief pit stops, arriving about 1900 hours on the North Pier, where *Nelly* was berthed. She was very distinctive among the smaller, motorised vessels.

We took our gear on board then, leaving the bags near the main mast, walked into the upper mess. Dinner was finished and the permanent crew were unwinding, enjoying some down time. They'd waved the previous voyage crew off earlier in the day, and the next group were not due on the ship until the following afternoon. Bosun's mates were required to report a day early, and I didn't think they'd mind me bringing Dad along too.

It was pleasing to be greeted like as an old friend by the crew, making me feel quite special.

A small, cheery, rotund lady with short, straight, dark hair and sparkling eyes, dressed in checked chefs top and trousers, introduced herself as Mary Ann; the Cook for the next few voyages.

While chatting, Mary Ann informed us her main occupation was teaching in a catering college in London. One of her pupils had been Jamie Oliver, the TV chef.

"There's some 'spag bol' in the galley. I can put some in the microwave, if you'd like a portion?" the little Cook offered.

I accepted for us both, with thanks.

"What's spag bol?" Dad whispered, when Mary Ann had returned to the galley.

"Spaghetti Bolognaise," I replied, while at the same time nodding to Marco, the Engineer. It was Marco who'd been on some of my previous voyages, and had stashed the old bottle-screw in my bag.

"It'll be good," I assured Dad. "You'll enjoy it."

"Bloody foreign muck," he muttered. "Ah was expecting some proper grub."

Despite his lack of enthusiasm, Dad tucked into the bolognaise sauce with enthusiasm, mopping the plate with a couple of slices of bread. He seemed less keen on the spaghetti.

Following dinner, I took the car to a long-stay car park at the top of the town, a ten-minute walk away then, returning, unpacked my kit and made my bed, suggesting to Dad that he did the same. I'd learned my lesson in Lisbon.

"Never go ashore t' pub till yer've made yer bed," I said, speaking from experience.

Dad and I went ashore with a few of the crew for a couple of drinks, though it was a comparatively quiet night for us in the little, Oban Inn, an old pub full of character and characters. I'd visited this friendly place many times previously with divers from the Sub Aqua Club.

Leaving the crew in the pub to continue enjoying their free time, we said our good nights and Dad and I were back on board by ten-thirty, weary from our travels.

It was early afternoon when the new voyage crew joined, and along with the other Bosun's mate, Ross, a stocky, cheerful

Irishman, I was again busy doling out sea gear to the new arrivals. The last member of the voyage crew to arrive was to be Dad's buddy.

"Hullo, ah'm Bill," said a big, powerfully built, ginger-haired, bespectacled Scotsman.

"Bill what?" Dad replied.

"Yes, that's right," said the big guy grinning, in what must have been a well-used routine, "Ah'm Bill Watt. Ah'm a fisherman frae Macduff."

A common bond between the two was struck immediately when Dad replied, "I used t' be a fisherman. Ah fished from Scarborough most o' me life." He then explained that I was on board with him, and was also involved in the industry.

Dad introduced me to his new buddy and as ever, when two or more fishermen meet, there's no shortage of conversation. During several discussions we discovered we had many mutual friends in Scotland. We talked at length about the many problems facing the fishing industry.

Bill was Skipper/part owner of *Fertile*, a new, purpose-built, twin rigged trawler, (towing two nets) fishing Rockall, in the Atlantic. I later discovered Bill's nickname was 'Fraggle', because he fished at, The Rock. His mates had named him this, after the children's TV programme, 'Fraggle Rock'. In his previous, much smaller vessel, also *Fertile*, this crazy guy had fished at the Rock. He'd seen and been caught in some horrendous weather, and survived storms that could have caused larger boats to founder. Everyone was pleased when his new vessel arrived.

It transpired that his voyage on *Nelly* was a fortieth birthday present from his wife, June. Following this trip Bill would come back several times as a Bosun's mate, and I enjoyed sailing with him immensely. June said, "it was the gift that just kept on giving."

Following the usual introductions and prior to the safety briefing, Captain George Mills, a tall, round-faced man with short, brown hair, announced he would attempt to get *Lord Nelson* out to St Kilda during this voyage.

Wow! This was a place I thought I'd never get to. A visit to this little archipelago was on my wish list. St Kilda was Britain's most north-westerly inhabited island.

Hands aloft was announced. This was the first opportunity for the voyage crew to climb the masts and the four watches were instructed to assemble at the fore and main masts. I'd be assisting the for'ard watches to climb to the fighting top.

I hadn't seen Dad for a while, as he was in an aft watch, so was gobsmacked when I looked aft to the main mast, to see him waving from the platform. He must have shot up the mast like a rat up a drainpipe. So much for his bad back!

We let the ropes go, two head-lines and two springs for'ard, which were coiled and secured atop the upper mess and simultaneously, a pair of stern lines and springs aft, these to be coiled and lashed on the stern platform.

Our ship headed out into Oban Bay then into the Firth of Lorne. Crossing this waterway, which goes north to Fort William and the Caledonian Canal, and south to the Clyde, instead we entered the south-eastern end of the Sound of Mull, heading north-west, passing Duart Castle to port. This imposing building, historically protecting this entrance, was the ancient home of the Clan McLean.

I knew these waters well. The Scarborough Diving Club made an annual Spring trip to the Sound of Mull, bringing their RIBs (rigid inflatable boats) on trailers, and using Lochaline or Tobermory as a base. It was important to read the tides correctly in the Sound as some of the wrecks could only be dived at slack water.

I made a mental note of the wreck locations as we passed each in turn, while working at various tasks on deck. To port we passed the site of *Breda*. She was a large cargo vessel of 400 feet in length and nearly 7000 tons. The wreck lay close inshore at the south end of the Sound, on the island side. In late December 1940, *Breda* was straddled by a stick of bombs, dropped by a German Heinkel III. These explosions ruptured a major inlet pipe on the ship, causing her to flood and sink.

Her mixed general cargo, including hundreds of tons of cement and war materials were still to be seen in her five holds. I recalled it was essential to avoid getting close to the deck of the ship. There was no tide here and the silt on her decks was thick. The smallest touch created a cloud in the water for subsequent divers, which took ages to settle.

Soon after, on our starboard, mainland side, was the wreck of *Thesis*. She was 167 feet and 378 tons. The brass letters, *Thesis* from her port bow were on the Sub Aqua Club wall back home. She was an old wreck, sinking in October 1889 when she hit a reef, drifting ashore and sinking. *Thesis* had only been launched two years previously.

She's now badly deteriorated and from inside the wreck a diver can see daylight through her rotting plates.

With a fair, southerly wind, *Lord Nelson's* tops'ls, t'gallants, royals and fore course were set and the passage down the Sound was fantastic. The narrow entrance to Lochaline to starboard was soon in sight. The car ferry to Fishnish, in the middle of Mull operated from Lochaline, here on the mainland.

This big, conspicuous inlet was a safe anchorage from all weathers and must have been a rendezvous for vessels from time immemorial. We'd found pieces of amphora and old bottles when diving in the loch, when the weather had been too stormy to dive out in the Sound.

To the present day Lochaline is a recognised safe anchorage with a slipway and mooring buoys. Jean's caravan teashop was a favourite with divers and travellers waiting for the Mull ferry. Her venison burgers were a special treat.

Crossing the entrance to the loch, then sailing a little further north and west, on our port side was a rocky island in the middle of the Sound, with a white lighthouse atop. The wreck of *Rondo*, 264 feet and 2363 tons lay here. Her stern is not far below the surface and brightly coloured wrasse swim, unafraid, around here. Her bow goes down beyond fifty metres. *Rondo* had parted her anchor cable in Aros Bay, south of Tobermory in a blizzard. She had drifted ten miles down the Sound on a strong tide, going ashore on to this island. *Rondo* had been partially salvaged when she slipped off the rock. Her lateral bulkheads are the main features as a diver swims steeply down the wreck.

Beyond this little islet is the village of Salen. The drive from Salen to Tobermory is one of the most beautiful, scenic journeys in the UK. High up, overlooking the Sound of Mull, sedate yachts with colourful spinnakers and busy, Calmac ferries can be seen. These black-hulled ships, with red and black funnels are constantly rushing up and down the Sound, on passage to and from the outer isles.

Next, close inshore to starboard was the wreck of *Shuna*, 240 feet, 1426 tons. She was a small collier with a cargo of coal onboard and had sunk in this location. Shuna sat upright on the seabed and could be dived at any time, though clear of tide, there was some silt on her decks.

The last of the known wrecks in the Sound is *Hispania*, 236 feet, 1323 tons. She was a general cargo vessel, which sank in December 1954 after hitting a rock in a severe Winter storm. All hands were saved when they rowed ashore, but the Captain chose to go down with his ship. She lays listing to starboard, close to a port-hand navigation buoy, where the water shoals, south of Tobermory. *Hispania* can only be dived at slack water. The Captain's bath is still in situ, though now damaged. Scallops can be found off her starboard, shoreward side, protected from scallop dredgers fishing in the deep water. Her foghorn is on the Sub Aqua Club wall.

Soon after passing the port-hand buoy, we were off Calf Island, which sheltered the lovely little town of Tobermory, set in an attractive bay. Folklore has it that a Spanish galleon from the Armada had foundered here, and the prisoners taken to Duart Castle. I'd been into Tobermory many times with diver friends and enjoyed the location immensely.

Looking into the gap at the top of Calf Island, the many coloured shops, pubs and houses were clearly visible on the waterfront. The bright yellow building was the Mishnish pub. This hostelry was known to yachtsmen and divers throughout the land. I'd had so much fun in the 'Mish' over the years. Hopefully we'd call in here on our passage back. Tobermory was a great run ashore.

We passed a large, white lighthouse, Rubha nan Gall, on the shoreline a couple of miles to the north of the little town. A narrow path made for a pleasant walk along the coast to this unmanned signal station, and this was a great, isolated picnic site.

The next hour would be extraordinary. Between the ship and the lighthouse, we saw a couple of grey seals, then minutes later a school of dolphins were playing across the ship's bows. These friendly creatures stayed with us for five or six minutes. Soon after, as we headed north-west between the Isle of Coll and Ardnamurchan Point, Britain's most westerly mainland position, a pilot whale surfaced, spouting then sounding several times. The added bonus, after these sightings was a basking shark, swimming on the surface, just a couple of hundred yards from the ship, as we headed for the top of the Isle of Coll. Amazing!

Passing the north end of Coll, we headed due west across the wind towards the Atlantic, the southerly wind still in our favour. *Lord Nelson* was heeling wonderfully to starboard in the fresh breeze, aiming to pass Barra Head, the southernmost point of the Outer Hebrides.

The water out here was really clear and the wreck of *Tapti*, 416 feet and 5504 tons, ashore on Coll was a great dive. She was badly smashed up, being wrecked in January 1951 in a gale, so there was plenty of nooks and crannies to explore. The visibility was a pleasant contrast to some of the silted wrecks in the Sound of Mull, though the weather and forecast had to be fine to get out to the island and back safely from Tobermory in a RIB.

The rocky outpost that was St Kilda was north north-west from Barra Head, out into the Atlantic Ocean. The next land to the west was America.

Lord Nelson sailed overnight with a star-filled sky and a favourable, but falling wind. Next morning the little isles and stacks that was St Kilda, were in sight.

Thousands of noisy seabirds, gulls, kittiwakes and fulmars filled the sky and the surrounding water was dotted black with guillemots, puffins and several other diving birds. I identified, and pointed to skuas. I remembered seeing these big birds while a teenager, trawling in *Whitby Rose* off shore from Filey Bay. These big, brown speckled bandits awaited nesting birds returning with food for their young, dive-bombing, to make the poor parents regurgitate the sand eels they were bringing ashore.

The wind had eased and drawn to the west with the daylight, as Captain George had predicted, and we dropped anchor, a quarter of a mile offshore in the lee of the main island, Hirta. A smaller, uninhabited island, Soay, lay unseen to the west, hidden by cliffs. Dun was to the south of our position, and looked part of Hirta, though a small sound separated the two. The other main landmass, also uninhabited, was Boreray, to the north north-east. All the little islands were treeless; not surprising with the winds that swept in from the Atlantic. In addition, several stacks protruded vertically from the sea, white-caked with bird droppings.

From the ship's deck, a row of little stone-built houses was visible up the rough, unmade path from the shore. At the top of the highest point on the island, at 430 metres, was a big military radar station.

There was no landing place or beach out here in this remote outpost, but there were people. A few soldiers, in battledress were waving from the shore.

This was great. We'd be able to get ashore. There were very few days in the year when it was possible to land in this remote location, out in the North Atlantic.

The DOTI boat was launched and the Captain and Second Mate, Jerry went ashore as the official party. Jerry was driving the rubber craft. I was taken along to mind the boat while the Officers were ashore. We were all wearing buoyancy aids, now mandatory when using the small boat.

A bunch of military personnel walked down to the water's edge to greet us. The boat hit the sloping shore and I jumped onto the stony, weed-strewn rocks, bow painter in hand, holding the rubber boat steady so the Officers could step ashore without getting wet feet.

There was some handshaking and the group went up the hill, entering a bigger building, which it transpired, was the Puff Inn. The hostelry served as a bar and community centre for the island's current inhabitants. These consisted of service personnel, and during the Summer months, representatives of the National Trust for Scotland and volunteers from the RSPB.

Half an hour later the ship's Officers returned, boarding the DOTI boat. I waited till the engine was started, then pushed the rubber boat off from the shore. A few minutes later we were again tied up alongside *Nelly*.

All hands were summoned to the lower mess and Captain George addressed the ship's company.

He gave a brief, but thorough outline of the history of the little settlement, of a unique, exceptional group of people, close to, but completely separated from the UK. These people had lived in isolation for thousands of years. The main source of sustenance for these islanders were seabirds, numbered in hundreds of thousands, nesting in St Kilda's islands and stacks, though the isolated inhabitants also grew vegetables. Their livestock were cattle and a couple of ancient breeds of hardy sheep that survived in this hostile environment.

In Spring and early Summer, the men climbed the cliffs, barefooted. Their toes, prehensile, having evolved over many centuries, were immensely strong, enabling the folk to harvest thousands of seabirds' eggs, which were kept airless, buried in peat ash.

Gulls were caught in nets by hand, as they flew close to the cliffs. All the food, and other supplies were stored in 'cleits', hollow stone cairns, throughout the year. The almost constant wind blew through the gaps of these rudimentary structures, drying the food. Hundreds of these cleits were scattered around the islands.

Strangely the men didn't do much fishing, though some were caught and dried. Perhaps the uncertainty of the weather influenced this activity. The people had homemade boats, enabling them to row to other islands and stacks.

The nineteenth and twentieth century saw a rapid demise of this unique settlement. Visitors brought disease that the community had no immunity from. A church minister and school teacher were dispatched to the island in the nineteenth century, for the good of the heathens, bringing religion and education. This enforced learning took away valuable food-gathering time and the work the younger folk could provide to the community became limited. These children would not learn all the skills their parents had been taught.

The ability of the islanders to survive diminished, and the last of the starving populace requested to be taken to the mainland in 1930. St Kilda is now a World Heritage Site.

The voyage crew, excitedly lined the decks ready to be taken ashore, supervised by the Mate. All held personal bags or rucksacks, containing cameras and wet weather gear. It would take four trips in our small boat to ferry them all ashore.

The aluminium ladder was deployed and the first ten passengers, including Dad, clambered down, their bags would follow. Jerry was at the helm and I was in the bows, as before. We quickly shunted these, then two more boatloads ashore. In the boat for the last run we had Geoff, a watch-leader. Though in a wheelchair, the man had massive, upper body strength. He'd been a farmer until an accident with a large hay bale had ended his career. Geoff was one of the few who could manoeuvre his wheelchair up and down the gangway unaided.

We also carried little Jenny, a pretty, young dark-haired girl with a permanent smile, who'd been struck by a debilitating, life-changing illness.

Both chairs were pointing forward in the boat, with the other eight personnel divided equally on either side. At the shoreline, the able-bodied personnel disembarked, but the two wheelies had a pleasant surprise. A large, yellow JCB digger was waiting at the water's edge. The driver loaded the two people, still in their chairs, in to the vehicle's bucket, then drove steadily and carefully over the small, slippery rocks. The digger continued up the slope to the settlement, where the pair were lowered, beaming, onto the gravel path.

Our work done, we took the boat back to *Lord Nelson,* then Ross ferried me ashore, so I too could enjoy this unique site. There were fixed times posted on a whiteboard by the gangway, giving the hour of returning boat runs.

The little village and its history were amazing and it was hard to believe this settlement had existed for so long, and had lasted well into the twentieth century. The first stone building I approached was a museum with fascinating photographs and narrative on all the walls, plus informative literature about the settlement. There were rudimentary farming implements and other very basic tools; these required to survive in this inhospitable place.

An enthusiastic gentleman from the National Trust for Scotland gave additional information to the visitors. This onsite representative, who was on the island for several weeks during the Summer months, was so keen to impart information, it would have been difficult not to be interested.

The representative said the island's men-folk would meet each morning to decide what the day's programme would be, and what work was required. It must have been a spartan way of life, but it was all they'd ever known.

Next door, the hovel had been restored to its original condition. The room must have been extremely smoky from the peat fire, and little comfort was to be found. The wild Winters, when incessant gales screamed out of the Atlantic, must have seemed interminable.

Most of the other buildings that had provided accommodation were in a state of disrepair and one was locked. The earlier inhabitants would never have seen a lock. The church and school room had been restored, though were bleak.

Opposite the museum was a restored cleit, an example of the hundreds erected over the centuries. I couldn't image what fulmar or gannet meat must have tasted like after a couple of months stored in this improvised stone fridge.

The Puff Inn was the only building that could be recognised as modern. The splendid hostelry, decked out with ensigns, bunting, nautical memorabilia, ships photos and prints, all donated by visiting vessels, was most welcoming. So was the barman. As each group finished their tour of the settlement, all had gravitated here to the pub. I was one of the last to arrive.

Everyone having seen this exceptional site, it was obvious what the conversation would be, and all hands were avidly discussing this great visit. Getting a drink from the bar, I found Dad, glass in hand, at a table with his buddy, Bill and some watch-mates.

"What d' yer reckon t' that Dad," I asked, nodding my head up the hill. "That was amazing."

He'd clearly enjoyed the visit and the boat ride. "Ah can't believe all that 'appened in mah lifetime," he said seriously. "What a way o' life."

Gradually the gathering reduced as the ferryboat shuttled the voyage crew back on board. As much as I'd have loved to remain in the convivial company, I had a couple of drinks then joined Geoff and his buddy heading back. No digger was required. The tide had flowed, the weed-strewn stones were covered and the boat was now more accessible.

Nelly looked fabulous with the sun, still high in the sky, shining on her white masts, yards and sails. This was our home for the time being, and there was nowhere I'd have rather been. It was an easy hoist on the davit to get Geoff back on board, despite his size. Willing hands hauled on the tackle, and once on deck the powerful guy headed directly for the accommodation door unaccompanied, his strong arms thrusting at the wheels of his chair. "Gangway! Toilet required," he yelled.

Before weighing anchor to depart this strange, wonderful, historic place, the Captain handed me a coloured print of *Lord Nelson* and her sail plan. Rolling the picture up, he put an elastic band around the roll then placed this carefully in a plastic bag. "Fred, take this ashore to the Puff Inn with our thanks, please."

Getting into the boat, I started the engine, then, asking someone to cast off the lines, headed for the shore. I fastened the painter around a big stone then walked up to the hostelry where, entering the brightly lit establishment, I handed over the print to the barman, who accepted the gift with thanks.

"To add t' yer collection," I said, smiling. "Thanks very much fo' yer 'ospitality."

Refusing a drink, thinking the ship was waiting to sail, I headed back, ensuring the engine was running before casting off. It was quite special to be given this roving commission, and looking back, I'm aware this couldn't happen now. Only permanent crew are allowed to drive the DOTI boat, and understandably, from a safety perspective, a minimum of two crew are required at all times.

Dinner was served before the anchor was recovered. Ross, who'd also managed to get ashore during the afternoon, was now down in the starboard focs'l with a team of four, flaking the heavy chain under the deck in the cable locker. The linkage came from the windlass on the foredeck, down the hawsepipe and into the locker.

Heading out from St Kilda, then passing close to Boreray, we made a north-easterly course to round the Butt of Lewis, approximately a hundred miles distant. The sun was still high in the sky. In this position, 57 49' North and 08 35' West, it would remain daylight until after eleven in the evening.

Motoring overnight, then setting sail after breakfast in a light breeze, we arrived in Stornoway on Lewis, late in the afternoon. It was my turn to lead the shore party, one from each watch, to be put ashore by the small boat. We'd take the ship's lines as she came alongside, then haul the gangway ashore when the ship was safely moored to the quay.

I caught the well-thrown heaving line, hauling the thick, eight-stranded, platted rope ashore with the assistance of an enthusiastic young girl, Maggie. Though still in her teens, this girl was competent in every aspect of her work on board, whether cleaning ship, rope handling or climbing masts.

Together we put our stern line on a bollard that a smart, thirty-foot motor cruiser was also using for her head rope. The shiny, white nylon rope, with a shaggy, frayed end, was fastened on the bollard with a small eye, made with a bowline.

The eye in this rope was too small for us to dip our thick line through, which would have allowed either rope to be cast off. I pulled some slack, unfastening the thinner line, making it fast again below ours with a rolling hitch.

"That's a locking knot," said a tall, scruffy individual, speaking in a local accent, as I stood up from the task. "Ah'm wanting a bowline in ma rope."

I attempted to explain that if our rope was on top of his and under tension, he wouldn't be able to release the line. If his was on top, we wouldn't be able to release our rope without letting his line go first.

The man was having none of it and insisted on his bowline.

I gave up and left him to it. I was muttering unpleasantries while smiling and rolled my eyes at my young friend. Maggie must have sensed my frustration, or heard me muttering. She gave a sweet, girly giggle.

A couple of hours later I was talking to the Harbour Master, a cheery, elderly Scot with a weathered face that had seen some sea-time. The short, stocky chap was standing admiring our beautiful ship when I approached. After sharing his sentiments and observations, we discussed the ethos of the Jubilee Sailing Trust.

I told the old boy I'd been a fisherman in the North Sea, and we discussed fishing operations in this out-of-the-way port, which he said was thriving on catches of prawns.

I mentioned to him the bizarre episode I'd encountered with the owner of the adjacent cabin cruiser.

"He's no' the owner," said the Officer. "He's just a 'chancer' that's managed tae land the job o' looking after the wee boat fo' her owners. They're awa hame fo' a wee while. He's a strange wan."

"Yer can say that again," I replied, as I waved goodbye, making my way back on board.

Early that evening, Dad and I, along with Marco, Jerry, Ross and a couple of other crewmen, went ashore looking for somewhere for an evening meal. Strangely, in this out of the way little port, the only place we could find was an Indian restaurant.

On realising this was the only option, Dad began to tut. "Do we 'ave t' go in there?" he questioned, knowing the answer.

"We do if we want to eat tonight," I replied. "We've said we were eatin' ashore. It'll be alright," I reassured him.

We were led to a large table and when seated ordered beers all round. Six of us scanned the menu, then ordered a selection of meals to share, while Dad, without looking, said, "ah'll 'ave chicken an' chips."

The small bottles of 'Tiger' beer arrived, and were tasted.

"It's lager," Dad said with distaste, "an' can I 'ave a glass?"

The communal poppadum's, with various dips, arrived for starters.

"D' ya wanna try one o' these Dad?" I asked, thinking I already knew the answer.

Surprising me, he replied, "ah'll 'ave one o' them big crisps, but ah don't want any o' that coloured muck on it," he stated emphatically, pointing to the sweet and spicy tubs of dips.

Six varied meals turned up with shared rice, and looked quite appetising. Next the chicken and chips arrived, placed in front of Dad by an apologetic waiter.

In what can only be described as Scottish Punjabi, the frowning Indian said, "I'm very sorry Sar. The only chicken we 'ave is already cut up."

Poor Dad looked crestfallen as he gazed on his plate of diced chicken that had been destined for the curry pot.

"Ah told yer it'd be foreign muck in 'ere," he muttered, before demolishing the entire plateful in short order, followed by another beer. He then tried a few spoons of the communal food, not saying anything about 'foreign muck'.

Some mixed tinned fruit, including lychees was disappointing, but devoured, then we left the Indian restaurant to visit the adjacent pub, The Star.

We laughed at an amusing chalked sign on a blackboard outside the door, which read, 'Husband creche'. Leave your man here for free. Just pay for his beer when you collect him! We didn't need collecting.

Ready for departure again on the next leg of our voyage, I was back with the shore party, ready to throw off our mooring lines. The shiny nylon rope with shaggy end had a bowline in place again. This was atop of our stern line and was tight.

Hauling on the white line, I gained some slack as the small vessel drew closer, before her stern line became tight. Putting my foot on the rope to keep the slack, I unfastened the bowline. Passing the rope under our line and back round the bollard, I made a round turn and two half- hitches, then added a further eight half hitches for additional security. If only I could have seen the face of the boat's minder when he came to check his moorings.

Leaving Stornoway, we motored out in to the middle of the Minch to find a fair wind then, setting 'everything', we sailed 'hard on the wind' south down the Minch, heeling wonderfully to port, passing to the west of the huge Isle of Skye, the grey, Cuillin Mountains, stark on the eastern skyline.

The following year I was to go into Loch Carport on Skye, on what was advertised as a *Lord Nelson* 'whisky cruise'. This would be another great voyage, though I didn't drink whisky.

A further treat was in store on the voyage. We were to spend the night anchored off the Isle of Rum, the largest of the Small Isles. The others in this group were Canna, Muck and Eigg. Furthermore, we were hoping to 'sail' on to the anchorage in the bay.

Nelly came slowly into the bay under tops'ls only, her bow gently cutting the smooth water, then she was brought quickly round, up into the wind, the sails going aback. When the way was off her, and *Nelly* was going slowly astern, the hook was dropped into the shallow water. Three shackles (each 90 feet apart) were paid out as required by the Mate, then the brake on the windlass was screwed tight and the safety slip secured around the rigid cable.

Ashore, a red bricked building was easily visible close by, inland. This was Kinloch Castle.

There was a barbecue dinner on board that evening, which was something special. The Engineers, Marco and Alan, his volunteer assistant, a former RAF aircraft fitter, (awarded an MBE for a long career in the service, and charitable fundraising), had put a large asbestos blanket on the stern platform. In the centre of the fireproof material, a tall, iron tripod was erected, with a circular metal tray and mesh grill attached, low down at working level. Bags of charcoal had been disgorged into the tray earlier and were now glowing hot. An extinguisher, buckets of water and a fresh water hose were on hand for emergencies.

Mary Ann had supplied the temporary chefs with various cuts of meat and chicken, plus salmon and peppers for the non-carnivores. The men were enthusiastically flipping burgers, chicken legs, lamb cutlets and steaks. This was warm work, but the two were keeping cool with a supply of bottled beers from the fridge below. A pair of loudspeakers blasted deafening pop music throughout the area.

When the diners had collected their main items from the barbecue, trestle tables by the mainmast bulged with salads, various cold dishes and sauces, plus a mountain of the Cook's freshly baked bread to compliment the meal. Most of the permanent and voyage crew sat on the deck or on small benches, brought up from below, chatting amicably. Fresh fruit salad and cheese followed. Wines, beers, teas and coffees were available. All hands were content.

There was no time to relax yet for Bosuns mates. Our job, with assistance from the designated galley team, was to round up the crockery and cutlery, rinse and channel these, in trays through the steriliser. This machine was exceedingly fast and the contents came out hot and pristine, to be stored in their lockers and racks.

The galley team were dismissed and Ross and I set to, scrubbing and vacuuming the upper mess and galley. Twenty brisk, sweaty minutes saw our work completed and we too could relax.

"It's time for a shower an' a change of clothes, then we can party," my Irish cohort, said, heartily.

"Bring it on," I replied, equally enthusiastic, "the young is yet night."

Ross looked at me, perplexed.

Half an hour later we were sitting on the foredeck among shipmates with music, drinks and good banter. We were relaxed and here we stayed. It was the perfect, relaxing evening. A light, warm breeze came from the land and though still daylight, the down-lights on the masts were already lit. The rig glowed wonderfully.

This changed rapidly when a swarm of midges descended on the ship. Initially no one noticed, but the invasion continued until, eventually inundated, slapping the insects, we retreated to the bar below for a nightcap, before bedtime.

Next morning almost everyone on the ship was complaining of midge bites. The blighters had permeated the ship. The offshore breeze and ship's lights had attracted the wee beasties, and they'd invaded in force, leaving their mark. I knew the reputation of the Scottish midge, and had always tried to avoid them using sprays, but hadn't brought any, thinking myself safe on the ship.

There was an opportunity for the voyage crew to go ashore to visit the castle, and I helped to man the DOTI boat. I wasn't too bothered about the visit personally, but many were. All hands were required to be back on board for lunch, ready for departure.

This visit turned out to be a huge success and the organised tour very informative. Kinloch Castle was built over a period of four years between 1897 and 1900. The building had been commissioned by Sir George Balloch, whose family had made their fortune manufacturing textile machinery in Lancashire. He'd bought the island of Rum, building the castle as a Summer residence and shooting lodge. In its day this place was the talk of society for its lavish, risqué, allegedly scandalous, private parties, with wealthy guests and minor royals in attendance. The staff were never allowed to see what took place at these soirees. All food and drink were either pre-laid, or passed through panel doors from the kitchen.

When Sir George passed away leaving no issue to inherit his estate, the building fell into disrepair and is now owned by the National Trust. The house is in need of much restoration.

Nelly was prepared for sailing, and we were to 'sail' off the anchorage. The wind had shifted enough to give a slant out of the bay. The cable would be hauled till straight up and down, then tops'ls set and anchor weighed.

I'd see none of this activity, as it was my turn in the cable locker. I was below, in the foc'sle, starboard side, with the team of muscle and a 'hooker'. We'd lifted and removed the two bottom panels in

the deck, exposing the rusty chain lying below. There were three
shackles out, so there were four lengths of cable still down in the
locker. A piece of thick, heavy-duty nylon rope was spliced into an
eyebolt at the after end of the locker. The other end of this line,
buried under chain, would be spliced into the, 'bitter end' of the
cable.

Holding the long, thin, metal hook with a length of knotted
line hitched into the ring at the other end, I addressed the anchor
party. "Ok folks, listen up. 'Ere's the plan."

I explained that we'd allow an amount of chain to pile up at
the bottom of the hawse-pipe at the fore end of the locker. Next,
the hooker, Alison, lying on her tum on the deck, facing forward,
looking into the for'ard void space, would take the hook when I
passed it under the deck from the after space.

"Ah'll shout, 'ook on' to Alison when some chain's settled, then
we do nothin' 'til more cable 'as built up. On the shout, "aul away',
we pull like 'ell and drag a bight o' chain t' back o' t' locker. It's
'eavy work, but yer get a breather between pulls. OK?"

The four big people nodded their understanding.

"When ah shout, 'come up', drop the rope. Then ah can unhook
it. If yer keep tension on, an' ah can't do it, ah'll be very cross."

There was the odd mistake, when enthusiasm caused the troops
to pull too soon, or not let go of the line, interrupting the smooth
running, but a terse yell, followed by a qualified apology restored
the routine.

Three shackles of cable, each length ninety feet, each shackle
painted white, were the minimum amount used, so this wasn't an
onerous task.

Lots of "well done everyone, thanks and first-class job", left
the anchor party with a good feeling of achievement, and willing
hands manoeuvred the deck sections back in place.

"Form a circle an' pat yerselves on the back," I called out, as I
left the locker.

Years later I had some unofficial certificates printed, which I
issued to the ladies who'd done the hooking. I'd write the name

of the recipient on a line at the top, then below was printed, 'was a hooker onboard Lord Nelson'. In small brackets below read (in the cable locker) then gave the ship's location, date and Captain's name. These were signed, 'Fred the Fish BM'. The documents were always received with pleasure and coveted.

I grabbed a mug of tea from the upper mess then went on deck. There was plenty of activity, as more sails were being set. Rum was to starboard, Eigg on the port bow and Muck beyond. Another few miles and we'd have Ardnamurchan abeam and would have circumnavigated the Outer Hebrides. We were heading for Tobermory, where we were to berth at the ferry terminal for the night. We'd have to leave early the following morning, before the first ferry arrived.

Back in the Sound, all the sails had been handed and *Nelly* passed through the gap between Calf Island and the shoreline, motoring with the lifeboat station to starboard. The calm water in the bay reflected the colourful buildings along the shore ahead. This was the perfect chocolate box picture. The pier we were to berth on, lay just beyond the afloat RNLI boat.

Ross was ashore to receive the lines with his team. I was for'ard with the Mate and selected voyage crew, ready for coming alongside. With no wind, the berthing went smoothly and the gangway was quickly deployed. The voyage crew were free to go ashore.

Minutes later, when all was quiet, Marco said, "hey Freddy, you're a diver. How d' ya fancy diving over the side, here on the berth? We have two sets of diving gear aboard. The scallop dredgers that fish here in the Sound, tie up alongside this pier at night to sort their catches. They throw all the small ones over the side, and the small ones keep growing."

I never mentioned my recent 'bend' and was up for the fun. The water's shallow so I should be okay.

We kitted up with the gear and I prepared to drop over the side. There were some concrete steps on shore, close to the ship, which would be our exit from the water. The Engineer handed me a wrist computer, similar to the one I'd owned, then passed me a netted bag for the catch.

Sitting on the ships side with fins dangling, I dropped into the water, hand on facemask. Marco dropped beside me and we surfaced, both gave the ok sign then submerged. The water was only ten-metres deep and I felt sure I'd come to no harm.

Scallops were immediately in view and I was delighted. This was one of my favourite diving pastimes, and I thought I'd never do this again. I began filling the bag. Marco wasn't far away and I was sure he'd be doing well too.

In about ten-minutes my bag was half full, and the shells were getting scarcer. I inflated my buoyancy aid to compensate for the extra weight I was carrying. Marco swam to me and, waving, beckoned me to follow him. I followed in his wake, breathing heavily with the exertion. After a minute or so he stopped and turning, gave a large, theatrical shrug. His finger circled, indicating something in the vicinity.

I looked around, scanning in all directions but saw nothing of interest, apart from one or two more scallops, which I hoovered up.

The Engineer had accumulated a pile of scallops on the seabed, then come for me to bag his catch. Now he couldn't find his heap again. We never did find them.

Working together, we managed to harvest more shells, filling the bag, then dragged our catch between us to the steps. We humped bottles, fins, masks and the sack to the ship's gangway. Back on board, we hung the bag of scallops overboard to keep them alive, then disaster! I lost the computer from my wrist. The instrument dropped into the water with the smallest of splashes.

"Bugger," I yelled, knowing I'd have to kit up again. The computer wasn't mine, or I might have left it.

With the diving gear back on and without a word, angry at my stupidity, I dropped over the side again. I didn't surface, just rolled forward dropping to the bottom. The computer was immediately visible and grabbing it, I surfaced again.

Having already had 'a bend' at Scapa Flow, I was aware this shallow 'bounce' dive wouldn't be good for my body. Repeat dives are taboo, but I hoped for the best. I'd been very quick and it was shallow.

Back on board we carried the bottles below, stowing them away in the pump room. Following this exertion, I thought I could feel a little niggle in my back, where I'd felt the previous hit, but I couldn't be sure. There was nothing to be done right now. I wasn't sure I had decompression sickness, and there was no chamber here in Tobermory, so no point in worrying. It was time to shower and to go ashore for the last night of the voyage. I'd monitor the situation.

There'd be few people eating on board tonight. Most voyage crew and permanent crew would want to go ashore, though there was nowhere in the town able to accommodate all hands. We'd be heading back for Oban and home tomorrow.

Everyone gathered in the bar, partaking of a couple of quick drinks while the slower hands arrived, then half a dozen of us went ashore to dine. Mary Ann, the Cook was on good form, knowing there were no dinners to make and only sandwiches to prepare in the morning.

Dad was in his element with a place that served, 'proper grub'. The little restaurant was in a small passage, off from the waterfront and seemed busy, though this was due to a table of ten from our voyage crew. This group, across the room as we entered, were already dining. Looking in our direction, the group were immediately vocal, and loud interaction commenced across the room, the gist of which was, "what are you lot doing here?"

"If we'd known you were 'ere, we wouldn't 'ave come," I replied. "Is there any wine left?" Fortunately, there were no other diners.

We ordered drinks while scanning the menu, but then our shipmates, saying they appreciated the permanent crew's camaraderie and assistance, sent some wine to our table. Dad, sensibly stuck to his beer. The choice of local fish, Scottish beef and mussels from the bay, was wonderful. Scallops were on the menu too, but we had some on board.

As expected, the food was superb and the wine, in excess, was of quality and went down easily. Dad was tucking in to a large piece of haddock with gusto, not entering into the banter at all.

The crowd at the other table made ready to leave and were heading for the door. "See you in the Mishnish," Geoff called, as he manoeuvred his wheelchair up the stone step to the passage outside.

"We'll be there shortly," I called to the open door.

Bidding farewell with thanks, to the cheery staff, we headed for the yellow building. The music and noise from the 'Mish' were audible, long before we arrived. On the threshold of the door, Dad said, "Ah'm not goin' in there. It's too bloody noisy. Ah'll see yer in t' mornin'." He walked on, back to the ship, a hundred yards away.

Nelly looked fabulous with her downlights shining from the top of the masts and under the platforms on to the masts and yards.

Opening the inner door, we entered the Mishnish. The place was almost full of revellers and most of the ship's company were here too. This pub was unique in the Western Isles and its reputation second to none. Atmosphere is intangible but were it possible to bottle it, this place had the stuff in crates.

To the right, on the little stage, a rock band was belting out good music. To the left, half a dozen bar staff were working at full speed to satisfy the thirsty customers, three-deep at the bar. There were several large wooden kegs spaced around the room, doubling as tables. All were surrounded by groups of revellers. Seating was confined to the sides and window areas. The huge mantle shelf surrounded a large fire, which, when lit radiated heat, as I remembered from our cold, Easter diving days.

The evening was a fun one with much laughter, joking, interaction and singing along with the band. The time flew by and it was soon midnight. We, along with many others of the ship's compliment, made headway back to our ship.

Looking at the fabulous vessel as we walked, I asked loudly, to no one in particular, "who do yer know who'd live on a ship like that?" I felt a glow of contentment to be involved in her.

Reaching the gangway, Mary Ann, who had been chuckling for the past five minutes at some unknown joke suddenly, at a quip from Marco, sank to her knees and rolled on to her side, laughing loudly. She then rolled on to her back with her dumpy little arms and legs in the air, giggling uncontrollably. She reminded me of a tortoise on its back. It was with difficulty that we were able to get our Cook up the gangway.

The night went by in an instant, and the tannoy calling all hands, sounded through the ship at 0700. An early breakfast of sausage and bacon sandwiches was served on trays by the mainmast, with tea and coffee on tap. There was no sign of Bosun's mate, Ross. I'd not seen him since he was talking to some local girls in the Mishnish, prior to closing time.

Mary Ann showed little sign of the excesses of the previous evening, or was hiding the hangover well. There were plenty of stories of the previous night's frivolity.

Dad had been up since 0500 and had shucked the scallops. These would make a great lunch for all hands as we cruised down the Sound to Oban.

Nelly's ropes had been singled up for ages and the remaining lines were finally cast off as the ferry came into view. We slowly began to drift from the quayside when a cheer went up from the hands near the main mast. I was for'ard, looking down the deck in the direction of the yelling. I spied a young girl throwing her shoes ashore then, quickly hitching up her skirt, climbed on to the ship's side. Bravely, foolishly or with no alternative, she leapt across the widening gap, landing safely on the quayside, raising another cheer from the spectators. Ross, red-faced, half dressed and bare-footed appeared among the group, looking bewildered. The girl was already thirty-yards down the road.

The crew showed no mercy to the young BM.

"Did you get her name?"

"She didn't even say goodbye."

"What! No goodbye kiss?"

He was ribbed for the remainder of the passage down the Sound, but took the banter in good part and just grinned.

As we were leaving the picturesque, sheltered bay, passing the ferry, I looked back at the imposing Western Isles Hotel, overlooking Calf Island, down the bay and into the Sound. The terrace in front of the building had unsurpassed, panoramic views for miles.

During the war this building had been the residence and headquarters of Vice Admiral Gilbert Stephenson. At the outbreak of WWII, he was informed he was too old to take a sea-going command, though he'd been a pioneer of anti-submarine warfare in the Great War.

Instead he was ordered to take on the massive responsibility of bringing on stream, all the newly-built destroyers and corvettes from UK shipyards. He was to work these vessels up to service standards.

A submarine was seconded to his command, and each day the warships and sub would sail out into the Minch to exercise. Vice Admiral Stephenson would ensure these vessels were up to scratch before being signed off for active service.

Throughout the Royal Navy, Vice Admiral Stephenson was known as 'The Terror of Tobermory'.

The old boy was a stickler for security and would occasionally, surreptitiously sneak on board the ships at anchor during the night, attempting to catch the crew napping, without a sentry posted.

On one occasion, when the crew of a corvette were paraded on the ship's main-deck, Stephenson took off his cap and threw it to the deck. "That's an unexploded bomb. What are you going to do?" he bawled to the line of men.

An adjacent matelot, grinning, promptly kicked the headgear over the ship's side.

"Very good sailor," said the Vice Admiral. "Now it's a 'man overboard'. What are you going to do?"

The shocked sailor had to jump overboard to rescue the floating cap.

* * *

It was a glorious cruise down the Sound of Mull and there was no shortage of volunteers to stow the tops'ls and fore course on top of the yards. This was a harbour stow and a strip of sacrificial sail cloth, permanently stitched to the top of the sail, was the only part of the canvas exposed to the elements when stowed correctly.

Crossing the Firth of Lorne again, we were soon tied up alongside in Oban and it was time for goodbyes. This was the only part of the voyage I didn't enjoy. There were hugs and tears. Friends and shipmates were departing and dispersing following their, in some cases, life changing voyage. People would keep in touch; others would arrange to sail together again, but there would never be another voyage like this one. Every trip was different. The destination, voyage crew, permanent crew and the weather would change.

I collected the car, parking on the quayside, by the ship. Dad was waiting with our bags. We loaded up, and having already said our farewells, with a 'toot-toot' of the horn and a wave in the general direction of the ship, we set off for home. Dad had a plastic box full of scallops, topped with ice.

It was a good steady run back and we managed a couple of short stops. I'd forgotten about the niggle in my back until we were at the summit of some high ground and I felt the tingle again. Maybe it was with sitting in the same position, but I couldn't be sure. What I did know for sure now, was I'd definitely made my final dive.

Half an hour from home and after intermittent conversations, I said, "what did yer reckon to it then Dad? What did yer think t' yer trip on *Nelly*?"

Taciturn as ever, he said, "Ah, it was alright."

Praise indeed! He'd later tell his pals, and others how good it had been, but he wasn't going to tell me.

* * *

It was February the following year when I next sailed with Bill Watt. We were Bosuns mates together in the Canaries and were to do two, one-week voyages. The first was a round trip, sailing from Santa Cruz de Tenerife, then, with a fresh voyage crew, we sailed for Las Palmas, Gran Canaria. As ever, Fraggle was in top form.

His laughter was loud, infectious and frequent and there was sure to be plenty of fishing talk and competition on the stern platform.

We had a good night ashore with the crew, drinking red wine and sharing a tapas meal, with everyone choosing three items. There was always lots of fun when the crew were free of responsibilities.

With the arrival of the voyage crew next day, an almost equal, male/female split, the ship was back into full swing. There were always one or two familiar faces, though it was sometimes difficult to remember names. We'd know almost everyone by the end of the trip.

The usual briefings took place then, apart from two-hourly night watches, which commenced at 2200hrs while the ship was in port, the new crew were allowed shore leave, where they'd start to get to know each other.

Following breakfast, we quickly did hands aloft then bracing and were ready for sea. Immediately following Smoko, with ropes let go, we motored clear of the harbour. There was a fresh, favourable breeze, so slowly, listening to the Officer's instructions, we set most of the sails, heading south to round the foot of Tenerife. We were then to head west for the little island of La Gomera.

The breeze stiffened and we heeled wonderfully on the starboard tack. As soon as the opportunity arose, Bill and I streamed our lines, game on! Fishing keen. We'd take a few small tuna and dorado before our first destination. There'd be fresh fish for dinner.

La Gomera is one of the smaller islands in the group, all of which are volcanic. On arrival, the voyage crew embarked on a coach tour to explore the island, including lunch. They'd be back at 1600hrs to rest up, ready for their evening in the town.

There'd be several groups ashore, watches and crew, visiting one of the delightful little courtyard restaurants. Our group would call in the local Yacht Club first. The club was housed in a spectacular cavern on the shoreward end of the quay. This building had been hacked out from the cliff face.

The barman welcomed our group when he heard we were from the 'Barco', *Lord Nelson*! Marco pointed to a photo of the ship on the wall, among other vessels. This print had been presented to the Yacht Club on an earlier visit by the ship.

It wasn't far from the quay to the town, where the main square splits into two charming narrow streets. We took the left lane, finding a courtyard with tables and benches. Above was private accommodation with balconies.

There were locals and a few of the voyage crew at the tables and local musicians in traditional garb were playing stringed instruments, singing ballads in Spanish. One of their number was collecting coins in a wooden box, hanging from around his neck.

The food was excellent, wholesome, tasty and filling. I opted for local fish with a tomato dressing which came with a large salad. Even with wine, the cost was very reasonable. It was a pleasant evening, though we didn't stay late, but did revisit the Yacht Club.

All hands, now familiar with the ship and getting to know each other, had enjoyed their exotic dinner ashore. There was plenty of banter and recollections of the run ashore while waiting for breakfast.

Following breakfast, the voyage photo was taken on the quayside, with the ship in the background. All hands, including Marco, now the official photographer, using time-lapse, were in the shot. Fancy dress shirts were popular.

Almost everyone would buy a copy of the photograph as a memento of their voyage, boosting funds for the Trust. Venue and date would be recorded in golden lettering on the mounting. Captain Mills took this opportunity to give the morning briefing to everyone, giving the plan for the day. This programme was always prefaced by, 'this may be subject to change'.

It was a leisurely casting off mid-morning, and with only a gentle breeze, all sails were quickly set. We were now heading for the north-westernmost of the Canary Islands, La Palma and the port of Santa Cruz, on the eastern side. There seemed to be several towns named Santa Cruz in the Islands.

At the western side of this inverted triangle shaped island, is a massive fault line, that at some point, maybe hundreds of years in to the future, will fail. This rift, in the side of the mountain, will slip into the sea creating a tsunami of astronomic proportions. The resulting gigantic wave will take out the entire eastern seaboard of North America and much of the Caribbean.

I recalled the last time we were in La Palma, most of the crew were given a half day off. Alan, the occasional Second Engineer was my opposite Bosuns mate on the voyage. He'd suggested we hire a car to explore the island. Strangely, I appeared to be the only one of our quartet on board with a driving licence. Along with Ali' the Cook's ass', a tall, blond, long-legged girl and our Engineer, we set off out of town on the only road.

In discussion we'd decided the trip wouldn't take too long, as the island was only 20 x 30 kilometres. We'd been informed there was an astronomical observatory at the top of the island and the view was fantastic.

What we didn't realise, until we'd set off, was that there was no road around the coast, but a narrow zigzag road leading up the mountain. We had to drive twenty miles to travel five, and the turns were so steep and frequent, we could never go more than thirty miles an hour. We'd been driving for what seemed an age, yet when we looked down, could still see the ship in the harbour, way below.

Spotting a bar as we motored through a little village, we pulled in. It was mid-afternoon and was cooler at altitude. The hostelry was unattractive and only inhabited by a couple of locals, apart from hundreds of flies. We didn't stay long.

Back on the road, knowing we were no longer circumnavigating the island, we pursued our quest for the summit, and getting higher, hadn't far to go to our new destination. A sign on the roadside said, Observatory, 1 kilometre. We were nearly there.

I drove around the next bend to find the road blocked. A big red and white sign stated, 'Road Closed, Snow'.

We exited the car, immediately realising it was freezing cold. Looking up the hill, there was a pile of snow ahead. We were wearing, shorts and tee shirts. So much for our day out. We return the car and found a bar.

* * *

Back home, when I told my adventurous, yachtie pal, Arthur about our visit to La Palma, and the height of the island. He said, "I know the place. I sailed to the island in *Alison* a couple of years ago. I walked to the top, up to the observatory, though didn't follow the road. I met some Germans coming down. They said I was a crazy Englishman." This came as no surprise.

* * *

Santa Cruz de La Palma was another good run ashore for everyone. There was a long waterfront with cafes, restaurants and bars, but the back streets, as in most places, were much more interesting and cheaper. Warm evenings and outside tables made for a great atmosphere. It was Winter at home.

The passage back to Tenerife was another good sail with a very strange occurrence. We sailed across the north end of the island with all sails set, altering course to starboard to draw closer to the land. Suddenly the wind freshened from a moderate breeze to gale force, with no indication of its imminent arrival. At once we were storming along at a huge rate of knots, heeling heavily.

I thought this was spectacular, until the bawling voice of Captain Mills came from the bridge. "Get the royals off her. Get the bloody royals off her."

The Mate and Bosun came running forward from the bridge, the on-watch voyage crew following. I ran for'ard to the royal halyard on the port side; Bill going midships to the main purchase. On instruction, we lowered the yards smartly. The watch and volunteers hauled on the furling line, rolling the sail into its groove. As the slack canvas was taken into the slot, both Officers slackened sheets at the fife rail at the bottom of the mast, spilling the wind and allowing the remaining slack sail to be wound inside the royal yards. The ship had slowed and was steadier. Panic over.

Extraordinarily, five minutes later, the wind died completely. It had gone from gale force to total calm in a minute. We'd experienced an 'acceleration'. Warning of this phenomena is marked on the Canaries navigation charts. The wind funnels between the islands, causing these sudden surges then, in the lee of the land, the gale dies just as suddenly.

Two hours later saw our arrival back into Santa Cruz de Tenerife and the end of the voyage. There'd be a crew meal ashore somewhere, where everyone could celebrate and relive the voyage highlights. There'd be a better one in Las Palmas at the end of the next voyage. We were more familiar with socialising on Gran Canaria.

Strangely, next morning before the voyage crew began to depart, I took a phone call from my sister, Christine who coincidently, was due to arrive in Tenerife on holiday with her friend, Joan, the following day. The pair needed no persuasion to come to the ship for a look round and a drink in the bar. I suggested they arrive about 1800hrs. The next voyage crew should have finished their briefings by then.

The time suited, as they were staying a distance away and would need to take a cab. There were hundreds of taxis on the island and a busy rank was close by the ship, so this wouldn't be a problem. I informed Chris it was the beginning of Fiesta Week today, and there was the huge, Mardi Gras procession.

It was a relaxed group of mostly permanent crew congregating in the bar in the evening when I brought the girls on board. The pair were immediately 'Marco'd' with ultra large gin and tonics.

Though both ladies are choristers in the Parish church, the pair enjoy a glass and a laugh. Bill was in his best, entertaining form, though when he got excited, his accent was so broad, he needed an interpreter.

Making our way ashore past the taxi rank, half a dozen of us, including the ladies, found a local bar on the procession route to while away an hour, before the parade.

A couple of drinks later the street outside was crowded with people and we joined the throng. The first of the spectacular floats was passing as we squeezed into the crowd. And there we stood for the next hour and a half, watching a magnificent parade with all manner of themed topics. There was lots of loud music, bright lights and streamers and many of the participants on the floats were holding bottles of beer. We weren't!

As the final float moved away, many of the crowd followed along in the same direction, leaving us with aching legs, hungry and thirsty. It was time to find food and refreshments.

All the restaurants close by were busy, but we managed to find a little tapas place in a narrow back street and enjoyed some excellent local food and quality Rioja. There was some great fun and the girls were enjoying being the centre of attention.

Before we realised, it was past midnight. Chris and Joan were weary and wanting to get back at their hotel.

We supped off and headed back on the short walk to the ship and the taxi rank. There were no cabs, but even stranger, no queue. Bill and I said we'd wait with the girls. The others in our party would get turned in.

We waited and waited but no taxis. Eventually Bill wandered over to the taxi sign and shouted, "Hey mon, there's nay bloody taxis gaan frae here atter midnacht."

That explained the absence of a queue. It was now 0130.

"What are we going to do?" Chris asked. "We'll have to walk, but it's miles."

"Yer'll 'ave t' sleep aboard," I said. "Yer can 'ave our bunks." I'd volunteered Bill's bed without consulting him, knowing he wouldn't mind.

The big Scotsman nodded his agreement.

Had it been the previous evening, there would have been plenty of empty beds, but now the ship was full.

The girls followed us up the gangway and were embarrassed at the top, when confronted by the two night watchkeepers, serving their stint. Both men looked sceptical when I introduced my sister and her friend! There were raised eyebrows again when I jokingly turned, saying, "what's yer names again?"

One of the guys requested the girls remove their heels to protect the teak decks, then, shoes in hand, the pair followed us down the dimly lit companionway.

Below, small safety lights penetrated the darkness, fingering down from the deckhead. We pointed out our two bunks, high above the tables in the lower mess, on opposite sides, mine to starboard. Bill directed the girls to the 'ladies heads', and while the pair went off together, we salvaged our toilet bags.

On their return, Chris came to my side of the ship and Joan went to port.

"How do I get up there?" asked my five-feet nothing sister, timidly.

"Stand on t' seat-locker, put a foot on t' edge o' t' table an' roll in," I said quietly, not wanting to wake whoever was in the next bed, for'ard. I held cupped hands, inviting a foot, then raised Chris steadily up into my bunk.

I looked over at the other bunk, then laughed loudly, waking a grumpy watch-leader in the next bed when I caught sight of Bill, unsubtly projecting Joan up into his bunk with a hand on each of her buttocks.

Both Bill and I slept on the cushioned seat-lockers below our respective bunks. These weren't uncomfortable berths, though were a little narrow.

I was disturbed about 0700 when I heard movement above my head. Sitting up, I made space for Chris to step from the table edge to the seating. Her pal was vacating the berth opposite.

The pair didn't hang about. Pausing only for another visit to the heads and a drink of water, shoes in hand, the girls followed us up to the deck, then bridge and gangway.

We met two elderly, lady watchkeepers, who had no idea of the circumstances when our two, now red-faced guests arrived at the gangway behind us, keen to disembark.

Bill and I gave the girls a little kiss and a wave goodbye.

Giving each other knowing looks, and quietly tutting, the old ladies watched the departing friends.

Chuckling, I shouted, "ah promise not t' tell anyone about this," to the pair, now fitting shoes on the quayside, then added, "till ah get 'ome."

There was a solitary taxi on the rank and before getting in, the pair turned and waved.

"Maybe we'll see you tonight?" I yelled, waving back for the benefit of the sentries, and knowing we'd be at sea.

"What was yours called, Bill?" I asked, grinning, in earshot of the now gawping watchkeepers.

"Ah canna remember," came the reply.

When I saw Chris back at home, following the next voyage, she said it felt like the, 'walk of shame' leaving the ship and again when they entered their hotel foyer before breakfast.

* * *

In the event, we didn't sail, as there was a problem in the engine room requiring urgent attention. The ship remained alongside. Some of the new crew went ashore, but most stayed on board for a meal of roast beef with all the trimmings.

When everyone had vacated the galley after stowing cutlery and crockery, Bill and I set to, scrubbing the upper mess and hot galley floors.

I liked working with Bill because we were on the same wavelength and got stuck into the work with a will. One would scrub, the other would follow up with a wet vacuum cleaner.

In the corner, on the galley floor, Bill found a large saucepan, containing the remains of the earlier meal, that had been left to soak. "What'll ah do wi' this, Freddy?" he asked.

"'Ave a look through t' galley door, down t' deck, outside," I said in a stage whisper. "If there's nobody about, just fire it over t' side, an we'll wash t' pan up."

Coast clear, Bill grabbed the handles of the huge pan and, inverting the large utensil, tipped the contents over the port bulwark.

"Hey Freddy" he called, on his return. "We ha' wee problem. I hoyed the stuff o'er the wall, but ah didna hit watta."

Not looking overboard, and expecting nothing untoward, Bill had tipped the dregs in the pan over the side, but into the DOTI boat, tied up alongside.

"Oops!" I said, laughing. "It wasn't us!"

Next morning, Jerry, the Second Mate, attending the small craft, discovered our blooper and came to find us. "What's that stuff in the DOTI boat?" he challenged.

"Och! Sorry Jerry, it's ma fault." Bill said. "Ah wer sick o'er the side las' nacht. Ah never noticed the wee boat. Ah'll clean it up."

Still laughing at our earlier faux pas, we set to and mopped out the little rubber vessel.

We were at sea again by mid-morning and were bound for Las Palmas, Gran Canaria, but first, after an overnight sail we anchored off Los Cristianos, on the south coast of Tenerife. The little harbour was too small for *Lord Nelson* to enter, but once anchored, we ran the voyage crew ashore in the boat. They'd spend the day ashore, walking, wining and dining. There were frequent, timed collections for those wanting to return to the ship. If we got ashore early with the small boat, there was time for a quick beer in the sun, outside a quayside bar while waiting.

All hands were back by 1800hrs in readiness for the sundowner punch on the bridge, and one of the ship's famous barbecues.

Next morning, following breakfast, Bill was in the cable locker with his team and a happy, 'hooker'. I was on the foredeck helping to set the tops'l once we'd sailed off the anchor. We were now to spend a couple of nights at sea.

I was quite surprised that after the first night, looking astern, I could still see snow-topped, Mount Teide quite clearly. Curious, I went to the bridge, asking the Officer of the watch, "'ow far are we from Tenerife, Mr Mate?"

Checking the radar, and aware we were a considerable distance from the island, he said, "thirty-four miles. It's surprising, isn't it."

"It certainly is," I replied, quite shocked. I'd been used to looking at land when at sea, but the air must be so clear here that distances were deceptive.

The second morning passed pleasantly, and following happy hour and Smoko, Bill and I held a 'bends and hitches' class by the main mast, where interested parties could learn useful knots and an eye splice. It was peculiar that we could teach seven or eight handy hitches and most pupils would grasp them all, then later practise with the short ends of rope. At the end of a voyage, they might remember two of them.

There was sad incident after lunch when someone washed the Captain's mug. The 'Old Man's personal mug was stained dark brown inside from the tannin of many brews of tea. It was a golden rule that no one was allowed to wash this receptacle.

Unfortunately, word hadn't got around the voyage crew and one unsuspecting member of the galley team thought he'd do the Captain a favour. Ten minutes of hard work with a pan scrubber revived the mug to its original, pristine condition.

Expecting praise, the poor chap was devastated when the Captain blew a fuse on seeing his mug. He acted like a spoilt brat and the poor unsuspecting man, his voyage ruined by the outburst, vowed never to sail again.

In the evening there was a quiz in the bar, which was always well supported. The four watches competed against each other and the permanent crew also had a team. There was much prestige in winning, though the box of chocolates prize didn't last long.

The honesty bar was well supported and seldom knowingly abused. One Bosun's mate would abstain from drinking if the sails were set, in case he or she was required to go aloft.

The following morning, we sailed across the top of the island and, turning to starboard, approached Las Palmas from the north. Excited crew were now out on the yards, enjoying putting the sails to bed.

With the sails handed, we approached the massive port. To starboard, over the long pier wall, I could see huge oil rigs. Ahead of us, anchored in the bay, were several large ships of varying types, tankers, bulk carriers and large fishing vessels.

Turning ninety degrees to starboard, we began to motor across the vast harbour entrance. The oil rigs were visible now and all had floating oil-spill booms encompassing them.

To starboard was Astican Dockyard and Slipping Company. On the ways were several ships, some of immense size, drawn out from the water. A vast tanker, with ant-sized people working from scaffolding around the wall-sided hull, gave some perspective to the ship's size.

Half a dozen small, white Korean fishing craft were tied up waiting for maintenance work. These vessels worked all over the world, hardly ever returning to their country of origin.

Considering Las Palmas was a port on a small island in the South Atlantic Ocean, this was one of the biggest docks for slipping and maintaining ships in the world.

It took a further thirty minutes motoring towards Santa Catalina, where we were to berth. The DOTI boat was launched and, as usual, a member from each watch climbed down the pilot ladder, ready to go ashore as linesmen. Bill was in the boat to show his team 'the ropes'.

I was surprised how many fishing vessels of different nationalities were in the huge port. There were Dutch built and registered ships, Russians and even a Fraserburgh registered vessel. I presumed these ships were catching sardines off the African Coast.

To port, ahead, three old frigate-type warships, flying the Spanish flag, were tied up to the quay in a secure, military base.

Next we passed a huge, white-hulled cruise liner with hundreds of individual balconies. The top of our main mast didn't reach the first promenade deck of the leviathan. This ship, and its type reminded me of large pigeon cotes with individual boxes. A few passengers were waving to us from their balconies, but most would be ashore. These people could all see us on board our ship, but strangely, they couldn't see each other.

There were plenty of bars, restaurants and beaches ashore to interest the passengers and most wouldn't go too far from the ship. They would all be back on board by 1700hrs and were not allowed to bring alcohol back. The ship would sail at 1800hrs and the passengers would spend their money in the ship's bars at sea.

Beyond the liner, we could see Bill and his shore gang on the quay, waiting for our lines. Behind them, partly constructed, was a huge, five story, luxury shopping complex, which, once completed, would be frequented mostly by cruise ship passengers.

Across the harbour lay a group of old, rusting, derelict reefers, tiered alongside each other, awaiting a passage to the scrapyard.

I was for'ard in the Mate's mooring party when *Nelly* drew close to her berth and was poised with a heaving line. This was a job I enjoyed, and it was very pleasing to get an important line ashore, especially when the wind was off the quay. The ship carried a huge amount of windage with all the stowed sails, yards and rigging aloft and would swiftly blow off the pier. She had no thrusters to counter this, though the Second Mate in the DOTI boat, with a voyage crew bowman, would use the boat to push for'ard or aft wherever required. The Captain, with hand-held radio gave instructions.

With little wind, we were soon alongside and the shore gang securing our hawsers on the bollards.

Once we were 'one and one', with single lines and springs, the ship was secure, and we could double these ropes up at leisure, then hitch chafing gear in the form of old, split hosepipe around the ropes where these passed through the panamas in the ship's side.

With *Nelly* tied up, most of the mooring team went midships to help hoist the gangway ashore, while a few finished lashing the chafing gear, then coiled the inboard, slack ropes away.

The two sections of gangway, in turn were hoisted aloft by the crew for Bill and his team to haul to the quay, where they were assembled. One end of the completed gangway was then hauled back onboard where safety nets were attached.

The local Customs Officers came on board immediately, but it didn't usually take long to give clearance, then the voyage crew were free to go ashore to explore. It was the end of another voyage.

This evening would be the last night party. All hands were due to meet at 1900 hrs at the Casa Pablo restaurant, known to the regular sailors as 'El Cids'.

The Bosun gave Bill and I a short list of essential jobs on a 'job and knock' basis. The work was finished by mid-afternoon so we quickly showered, and with several other regulars headed up to the main, Santa Catalina Square, where several open-air cafes were available and inviting. Our favourite was 'Jackie's Bar', operated by a Chinese family. This was a great place to while away a few idle hours in the sun. There were outside televisions mounted on the wall for special sporting occasions.

Our group would begin with a table of three or four but could grow to twelve or more seated at three tables. I don't know how Jackie managed to keep the tab up to date, but the bill never seemed excessive and was easily divided up.

It was only a short walk around the corner from Jackie's to El Cids, and we were there dead on time, finding the bar area at the front of house, full of *'Nellies'*, all in good humour and very loud. It was impossible to believe most of these people didn't know each other a week ago.

I waved to Miguel, the head chef, as he passed through the bar. When first introduced to him by Marco, we'd shaken hands. The Engineer stepped back to watch me cringe, as my fingers were crushed mercilessly. This only happened once.

Dinner was announced and the crowd drifted into the back room for food, each jockeying for a seat with their pals. The choice was meat or fish. The six or seven permanent crew interspersed among the troops. Everyone felt part of the team and loved the interaction. Wine flowed free and freely and though we paid for our food, we were not allowed to buy drinks. It was the voyage crew's way of saying, thank you.

There was the odd bit of naughtiness with flying bread rolls, and someone always spilled red wine, but it wasn't excessive: there were no other customers and the restaurant would never be full on a Sunday or sell so much wine. The staff were extremely friendly and always acknowledged us when we called in for drinks and tapas.

There were some headaches at the early call for breakfast at 0700 hours when all hands were called from their bunks. Folks would dress, then beds were stripped and the linen deposited by

175

the washing machine, where Jane would soon make a start with the laundry.

Everyone would pack, deposit their bags in the bar then have a quick, reluctant happy hour, cleaning below decks. Only then were there egg or bacon rolls available, served by the main mast. The voyage was over. The memories would linger and remain. Folks were free to leave their bags on board and wander into town, retuning for their kit in time for shared taxis or bus rides for the half hour trip to the airport.

It always seemed strange to have an empty ship when the voyage crew had left. We were so used to the hustle and bustle of a full crew. The next voyage crew wouldn't arrive until the next day, and Bill and I were leaving. We'd work until mid-afternoon then we were free again, but would have a gentle day. A few drinks and light bites at Jackie's would make for a pleasant evening.

The following morning, we were on the bus in the massive, state of the art, underground bus station, which was totally invisible from the road. The express bus, every thirty minutes to the airport was a fantastic service and extremely good value.

My body would be home in six hours, my head would take a week. After any length of time on the ship my brain became scrambled, and I couldn't focus on other matters for days.

It really made me think about the poor American soldiers who were airlifted back to the States from Vietnam, to be dropped back into home society. No wonder so many had mental health issues.

CHAPTER 15

TWO DEREKS

The 'Cook's assistant' on my next trip was Derek Gibb, a short, stocky, bespectacled, cheery old boy from Great Yarmouth with a wonderful, broad Norfolk accent. Derek was universally known as, 'Dad'.

The old boy had recently retired from the sea, having served as a seaman on the twin steam engine, Trinity House vessel, *Warden*. This famous ship serviced navigation buoys, marks and lights around the coast of England and Wales. Derek had also been a lighthouse keeper when younger, and was aboard the *Sunk Lightship*, anchored off the Thames in November 1954 when the *South Goodwin Lightship* parted her cable in hurricane force winds. The stricken vessel had drifted, helpless in the storm, before washing onto the Goodwin Sands and capsizing with the loss of seven of her eight crew. The sole survivor, Ronald Murton, was rescued by a USAF helicopter after dawn.

Derek told wonderful tales from the days of his youth, when he'd been a crewman on steam-driven herring drifters, working out of Yarmouth, fishing the North Sea. He could remember the Scottish herring girls that followed the drifters, which, in turn pursued the vast shoals down the North Sea from Spring to Autumn. The herring that were off the Buchan coast in April and May, migrated south and were caught off the Tyne in June and July. By August and into September the drifters landed fish into Whitby and Scarborough, then during October and November the shoals and boats were to be found off the coast of East Anglia.

Five Old Hands
L to R: Derek Gibb, Alan Fisher, Author, John Gilbert, Colin Woodhead

The female workforce, travelling to the ports by train, would live in lodging houses close to the quayside, processing the fish wherever they were landed.

These dexterous, efficient ladies, sharp knife in hand, could take the throat and guts from herring at the rate of one a second, before salting and barrelling the little fish ready for export. The back-breaking work was undertaken from early morning when the boats came into harbour until the last of the fish were barrelled, sometimes late in the afternoon. Their hands, with multiple cuts, despite bandaging, never got chance to heal and must have been extremely tender with the constant immersion in salt.

Derek, laughing, said one of his pals had pointed to a large, red-faced herring lady and said, "I bet yer can't 'it that ol' woman wi' a herrin'."

"Course ah can ol' boy, easy," he'd replied, swiftly hurling the fish about ten yards at the lady, hitting her firmly on the side of the head. Realising the full extent of his accuracy and crime, Derek quickly turned to run away, but not before he'd been identified.

The shocked lady turned towards Derek with venom in her eyes. "Right ya wee bugger, yer card's marked! Ah've got yer number, an ah'll ha' ye!"

The young lad had forgotten all about his bull's eye as the days passed, but the formidable lady hadn't. Walking nonchalantly along the quayside the following week, heading for his boat, Derek was quickly 'scragged' by the large lady, who, with the assistance of a couple of other strong women, swiftly inverted him into a half-filled barrel of herring.

His hair, eyes, ears and nostrils were filled with scales, blood and slime, and his entire upper torso was coated with the same vile substance.

"What 'appened t' you, bhoy?" the Skipper of *Ocean Rambler* had asked, looking at the state of his crewman, on his return.

The young lad, his head and shoulders still contaminated with slimy gunge was unable to speak. Revenge had been sweet and this was a lesson Derek has never forgotten.

Now, many years later as he told the tale, the old boy had tears of joy in his eyes, but I think the tears must have been very real at the time.

These industrious ladies and young girls worked six days a week and when fish was in short supply or the weather bad, these same women would fill their days knitting ganseys, stitching and looking after their laundry and personal effects. Sunday was their day of rest and many of the ladies could be seen, arm in arm, singing traditional folk songs as they promenaded along Yarmouth Quay.

Derek said some of the younger girls were quite flirtatious and would be happy to go out with the local fisher-lads. Laughing loudly again he said, "one Sunday arternoon, ah were alone wi a bonnie young herrin' girl behind one o' the fish huts near the quay. We were gettin' on famous an' were in a real clinch," he chuckled. "Ah were almost at the point o' no return when she whispered, Jimmy, yer can put it in, but ya canna squirt it!"

* * *

I met another Derek on the ship, early in my sailing days. Derek Norton was a tall, elderly Londoner who'd sailed on the ship for several years as a watch-leader. Seeing my interest, he made a point of walking round the main deck with me, attempting to explain the miles of rope hanging from the three masts. This old boy knew the ship intimately and had recently spent several days serving some new wire footropes, wrapping them tightly with thin, tarry twine; a laborious, time-consuming task.

Sitting in a little group in the ship's bar one evening, Derek made all laugh with a story of working for a railway company, and being responsible for a railway crossing signal box on a branch line, on the outskirts of London. Derek said the line was busy during each morning, but on afternoons he only had two trains passing through.

One day, after the first afternoon train, and nearly three hours before the next one, Derek thought he had time to visit the nearby cinema, to take in a current, 'must see'. He'd sat through the film, occasionally keeping an eye on the clock at the side of the screen.

Eventually, realising the timepiece had stopped, and having no idea of the time, he'd dashed back to the signal box. He was dismayed to see the train stopped at the gate, whistle sounding and steam emitting from the smokestack. Hurriedly, Derek released the gates, allowing the locomotive to pass, but a few days later, he'd received a visit from a railway Inspector, wanting to know the reason for the delayed afternoon train.

Thinking quickly, he replied that some boys had come to his signal box with news there was a blockage down the line. Derek said he'd left the box and hurried down the track to check out this report. He'd found an object straddling the rail and had been able to clear the obstruction.

Satisfied with this information, the Inspector left to make his own report.

A couple of weeks later, the signal-box was again visited by the Inspector, this time presenting Derek with a safety award, but advised him that in future, he must alert his superiors by telephone, before taking any unilateral action.

Derek was a widower and quite frail, but still spent quite some time on *Lord Nelson* now he lived alone, using his numerous skills for the benefit of the vessel and the JST. The ship's crew were his friends. The old boy found difficulty in swallowing dry food, so would always ask for plenty of gravy or accompanying sauce with his meals. The Cook accepted this situation, just as he looked after the entire ship's company with their dietary requirements.

One of Derek's past pleasures was ballroom dancing, and he'd often speak of going to various venues in and around London when in his prime.

The old lad came onboard in a state of great excitement one day in Southampton, saying he'd heard that the cruise liners sailing from the port would take elderly male passengers for free, if they were able to dance. It seems the ships always had an excess of ageing widows and unaccompanied ladies. Derek was going to apply.

There was much joking at his ambitions, including the lack of gravy on the ships, too much excitement, or that maybe one of these game old birds might see him off.

Nevertheless, our erstwhile shipmate joined one of the big ships, sailing off down the Solent on his new adventure.

We never saw the old boy again, but did hear that on his second voyage, Derek was taken seriously ill and was brought ashore. He passed away shortly afterwards, in hospital. There was much speculation on our ship as to the cause of Derek's demise, but we all agreed he must have left this life doing what he loved most.

* * *

A few weeks later, a phone call from Jilly in the Jubilee Sailing Trust's office in Southampton informed me that Wilton Jones, my first 'watch-leader' had died at his home in Doncaster. Knowing I was only seventy-five miles from his home, Jilly asked if I'd like to be part of a group representing the JST at the old boy's memorial service. This was to be held at the college where he'd been a House Master.

"I'd be delighted to attend." I replied. It'd be a privilege to pay my respects, and it was thoughtful of the people at the Trust to inform me of his passing. I'd sailed with Wilton on several voyages since we'd first met, and I'd always had great respect for him and his wealth of knowledge. Despite being elderly and in poor health, Wilton had continued to sail almost to the end. His demise came as no real shock.

The small contingent was due to meet in a pub close to the college and I was pleased to see the group of old *Nelly* shipmates when I walked through the door, and that Jilly was in attendance. Jilly had been Cooks ass' on my first voyage and at the time, worked as a bank clerk. Such was the pull of the JST that the young lady had taken employment with the Trust. Jilly had been on board *Lord Nelson* on the ship's maiden voyage in October 1986. We became good friends, and this lovely lady would be our guest in Scarborough on many occasions.

All the people working in the JST's office were extremely caring, and the work for these long-serving, underpaid staff was more vocation than employment. All the staff sailed on the ship, not only to gain experience, but for pleasure.

I recognised and waved to Piles, then spotted Ian Wester, a tall, heavy set man with a round, red face and thinning hair. Ian was a frequent Bosun's mate and in real life, an electronics specialist, who'd saved the JST many thousands over the years with his skills. Ian was fun to sail with, and had also visited Scarborough to experience a fishing trip on *Independence*. On his return, he said he'd enjoyed the experience, but didn't want a second voyage.

Ian was talking with Andy Spark, the Ships' Operations Manager. Andy was another who'd sailed on *Lord Nelson* as a volunteer, then joined the staff. Universally, but totally non-PC, Andy was known to all on the ships as 'Leggo', due to his prosthetic leg, fitted following a motor cycle accident. Pale of face, with very long fair hair, tied in a ponytail, Andy had a slight stutter but a great sense of humour. His surprise party trick for the uninitiated, was to stab himself in the leg. Usually the false one! Andy had been heavily involved in the building of the Trust's new vessel, *Tenacious*.

Also in attendance was Steve Higgs, who sailed as Bosun. Steve, a former Royal Marine, bearded with tousled hair was short, stocky and powerful. He was a great teacher and had an amazing ability to make his talks and briefings to voyage crews interesting and amusing. It was almost impossible not to absorb his information. Steve had the most prodigious capacity for red wine, though seldom drank at sea. The ex-marine would go on to become Mate on *Lord Nelson* and later on the newer, wooden vessel, *Tenacious*.

Wilton's service, in the college chapel, was a celebration of his life. He had no surviving family. His college and the Jubilee Trust were his family.

The memorial was well attended, mostly by staff and former pupils. We did feel many eyes in our direction in an, 'I spy strangers' situation.

It wasn't until later, at a wake of tea (or sherry) and sandwiches in the college library, that several of the staff came to talk to us, realising we were from Wilton's other life.

One of his ex-pupils made us laugh with a recollection of his former tutor's accuracy with the blackboard rubber. He said, "if it whistled past your ear it wasn't meant for you. If it got you between the eyes, it was!"

A small, table-top display of some of the old boy's possessions was on display but a receipt for 7/6d for six Malaccan canes stood out and spoke of a no-nonsense House Master.

There was no opportunity for me to toast the old boy with anything but a small sherry, as I'd be driving home shortly.

Wilton Jones had sailed on ninety-nine voyages on his only love. His shipmates gave the old boy a good nautical send off for his hundredth passage, when, after a short ceremony, they scattered his ashes from the stern of *Lord Nelson*.

This loyal supporter left his lifesavings to the Jubilee Sailing Trust.

* * *

Dotty had been driving back from visiting her Mum in Hull, as she did weekly, sometimes twice-weekly when, on the radio she heard an article relating to DNA and how it was possible to find the origins of ones' ancestors by sending a saliva sample and fee to a specialist company. Knowing my Dad had always said we were from Viking stock, my wife made a note of the address then sent for a kit as an unusual Christmas present for me.

The little pack arrived and I followed the instructions, returning the sample in the stamped, addressed envelope provided.

One of the principles of the DNA test is that a male can get the lines of both parents, but a female gets only the maternal side of hers.

The results, which arrived a couple of weeks later, were printed on five sheets of A4 paper. The first four sheets were generic, relating to the origins of man, stating that everyone in the world came out of Africa. The human race then spread to all points of the compass as the planet warmed, ice melted and land mass moved.

It was the final page, specific to me, giving personal data that was extremely interesting. The Normandale line was indeed 90%+ from Scandinavian and North German extraction, but Mother's side originated predominantly from the Levant and Palestine region. That was a surprise, and there were some in the family who did tan easily, and were not as fair of complexion.

I photocopied and printed five copies of the results, and with Dotty, took these to Mum and Dad's house on Sunday morning. Most of our family gathered for teas, coffees and a catch-up, each week.

The results were produced with a flourish from an envelope and I said, "Dad you were right, we're mostly from Vikings." He nodded approvingly from his armchair and gave a little smile.

Turning to Mum, I said, "your lot are different Mother, yer' all from t' Middle East and Palestine."

Mum turned on me most indignantly, and said, "It's a load of rubbish! How do they know? And anyway, our family came from Brid'.

The chatter was mostly the usual homely stuff of what grandchildren and great grandchildren were achieving and who was going, or had recently been travelling.

Dad would ask me of my exploits if I'd been sailing with the tall ships and what our boats had been catching.

The time passed, and we made ready to leave. As I was passing through the door into the hallway, I turned to Mum and said, "shalom, Mother."

She threw a shoe at me.

CHAPTER 16

TRIP TO HOLLAND

Dotty and I were visiting Great Yarmouth for the annual Maritime Festival, held in September. The occasion, on the quayside of the River Yare, was a popular fair and well attended. Good crowds and many visiting vessels from the region were present, including, this weekend, *Lord Nelson*.

We'd attended the event to meet up with friends I'd met and sailed with on the ship previously, and while here we'd visit shipmates onboard *Nelly*.

Bill, small, tanned with thinning hair, glasses and stubble beard was an artistic blacksmith and extremely talented, living with wife Jan in an historic cottage in the countryside, with adjacent forge. Some of Bill's art work was to be found in Norwich Cathedral. We'd sailed together as Bosuns mates on a couple of occasions and got on really well.

The other shipmate I'd catch up with was Keith, a marine artist who was exhibiting his work at the festival. Keith's specialty was his interpretations of the Battle of Trafalgar. His coloured, pencil drawings were detailed and gave the timing of the battle, hour by hour with ship names and narrative. Keith also took commissions to reproduce Royal Navy vessels past and present for retired and serving personnel.

He'd kindly sketched and framed a pencil drawing of the armed trawler, *Lord Inchcape* for Dad. This was the vessel he'd served

186

aboard in the Mediterranean, during the war. This picture took pride of place on Dad's staircase among his gallery of ships and family boats. There was also a photo of *Lord Nelson*, heading south with Scarborough Castle headland to starboard.

This was a pleasant break and there were some great stalls and exhibits, as well as other interesting museums on the Quayside Road. One of these was dedicated to the original Lord Nelson, who would possibly have been familiar with Great Yarmouth, being born in North Norfolk.

On board *Lord Nelson*, Cookie, Fiona was bemoaning not having a Cook's assistant for the next voyage. "I don't suppose you fancy being my Ass' for the next trip Mr Fish? It's not a long one. Yarmouth to Scheveningen, then back to London." She looked hopefully in my direction with raised eyebrows.

I looked at Dotty, also hopefully.

"What are you looking at me for?" My wife responded, "You know you're going to go. Just remember, you've a birthday party at home coming up. You'd better be back for that."

"T' ship's due in t' London on 21st. Ah'll 'ave 24 hours t' spare," I assured her. I looked back to Fiona. "It looks like yer've got a Cook's ass' for t' next trip, Fi."

The following day Dotty and I drove home; not the easiest drive. It's slightly over 200 miles via the Humber Bridge, but what a torturous route. The Fenlands are flat and there's an absence of motorway and with few dual carriageways for much of the journey. I'd never take this route again. The distance via the A1 and A64 is several miles longer, but at least the roads are better.

We arrived home after a great weekend, then I packed some sea gear and left by train the following morning, early. This was an equally torturous, four train journey, boarding trains at Scarborough, York, Peterborough and Norwich, ending on a forty-year old, clapped-out rattler. Including changes, this journey took most of the day. East Anglia must be one of the most inaccessible regions in the UK, as I know well, by experience. My arrival at the ship coincided with the voyage crew joining.

All the usual routines would be observed and we'd be sailing the following morning, bound east for the Netherlands under the command of Captain Mike.

The 'Old Man' for this voyage was tall, elderly, slightly stooped with greying hair and matching beard: an old mariner with many years sailing experience.

The tide had just turned high water, and the first drain of ebb was running in the river when we were ready to let the ropes go. *Nelly* was starboard side to the quay, pointing upstream.

Captain Mike ordered the ropes to be taken onboard in sequence, except the starboard spring, which was now tight, and a slack stern line from the port quarter. The ebbing tide gently pushed the ships head off the pier, then as the gap widened, more tide was brought to bear on her side.

When the ship was completely broadside across the river, her bowsprit was no more than twenty feet from the other bank. The nylon rope on her quarter stretched bar tight and the fender between the quay and the stern, protecting the paintwork, was squashed flat.

The tight spring was slackened, let go and quickly taken in as the ship drifted downriver. Now the stern line on the port side became tight and held, drawing the ship back parallel with the quay, and now pointing downstream. This stern line was let go, hauled in and we were underway. This was a slick operation, though I wasn't involved. I was watching the departure from midships with Fi, before going back to the galley to prepare lunch.

For hundreds of years past, each Autumn, the River Yare had been full of hundreds of herring drifters, local and Scottish. It had been possible to cross the river from boat to boat. Tens of thousands of barrels of herring had been filled and salted annually by hundreds of Scots lasses, ready for export to Europe.

Through the mess window, as we motored swiftly downstream, I could see several oil-related vessels and small, open, fishing craft. Towards the estuary, the Yare turns ninety degrees left before entering the North Sea. It must have been incredibly difficult for the sailing drifters of old to manoeuvre this entrance in strong winds and tide.

We were soon at sea, bound for Scheveningen and, in all directions could see production rigs. These would be pumping North Sea gas into the huge shore terminal at Bacton, 25 miles north. There were plans for massive wind farms to be installed, generating electricity from the Thames Estuary to north of the Humber, taking up many hundreds of square miles.

Scheveningen, historically was the premier Dutch herring port. It was now home to a fleet of beam trawlers and was a popular holiday resort. I'd been to the port several times previously.

The hundred-mile passage across the Southern North Sea was a good sail and the voyage crew enjoyed pulling on the halyards. We could see this undertaking through the mess windows, but from a Cook's ass' perspective, it was uneventful. That would change on the return passage.

Fi' was easy to work for. My main tasks were directing the mess team to ensure food was prepared, served promptly below, then dishes washed and stowed. I'd make several 'shopping trips' daily to the galley store, two decks below, in the bilge compartment. The most important task however, was keeping Cookie Fi happy and supplied tea during the day, gin after dinner.

Late morning the following day, we passed between the piers, red and green lighthouses on the ends, marking the entrance. To the north, were miles of tourist beach with a substantial boardwalk, housing dozens of wooden shacks. Some were restaurants, others, bars or ice cream parlours. A few were selling many of the Dutch food specialties.

At the extreme north end, beyond the boardwalk, in the sand dunes, was a Hippy Commune that I'd stumbled across on my previous visit when walking. I'd noticed plenty of drink flowing and drug fumes were in the air. The settlers were very friendly, offering beer but I'd declined and reversed my course.

Our voyage crew would have a great run ashore, though I doubt they'd require wacky baccy.

No sooner were we alongside the quay than three Dutch Customs Officers came aboard and were quite officious. Asking to see the bar, the Captain directed the Officers down the aft companionway, then

189

paged Marco to join them. The Senior Customs Officer seemed delighted when the Engineer showed his party the stock of wines and spirits, stowed beneath the seat lockers.

"This is not a secure store," the spokesman said. "This alcohol is now bonded and must be securely locked up and sealed. England is not part of the Schengen agreement," the grinning Officer announced.

"That's nothing to do with me mate," the Engineer replied. "You'll have to take that up with the Captain."

Leaving his two underlings to guard the booze, the Officer attended Captain Mike's cabin. This meeting can't have gone too well, because ten minutes later both men arrived in the bar.

"Marco, can you get a team together and take the wines and spirits and stack them in my toilet." Then through gritted teeth said, "this Officer will seal the door."

When the booze was stacked in the Captain's cabin and the toilet door secured with an official wax seal, the Dutch customs man added insult to injury.

"This seal must not be broken until you are twelve miles from the harbour entrance. There are serious penalties should you do so. You should have signed the Schengen agreement."

"I'll make a note to take that up with the Prime Minister when I get home," Mike said in total disgust.

This did seem an extreme measure. I'd sailed on the ship scores of times and visited almost every European country bordering the North Sea, Channel and North Atlantic, and some in the Mediterranean. I'd never known this rigidity to regulations.

We were to get twenty-four hours in port and the voyage crew would enjoy the visit. The permanent crew would. I knew of a fantastic, seafood restaurant, the best by far that I'd ever visited. I'd informed all the hands and pre-booked an evening table, for those available.

Simone's was a huge restaurant, immediately behind the port's fish market. I'd been here twice previously and was still amazed at the décor, artefacts and old photographs, but most of all, the spectacular array of seafood and the range of wines and beers.

We were a table of eight, with several bottles of quality wine, on ice. Three tureens of mussels were placed on the table in reach of everyone. I'd advised that three pots would be sufficient, as unlike in the UK, these tureens were filled to the extent that the pan lids lifted as the moules cooked. These tops became receptacles for empty shells.

There was bread to mop up the juice, but with four huge, mixed seafood platters to follow, few wanted to fill up with bread. There was no room for, or interest in desserts.

Everyone was thoroughly impressed with the venue and raved about the food, as I'd expected. There was lots of good-hearted banter and the odd quip at the Captain's expense about his lack of privy.

"We might have some seasick sailors tomorrow," Captain Mike announced, changing the subject. "There's a really nasty low, with a west to south-west gale coming in about sailing time. It'll be right on the nose."

This statement brought a few groans.

There was another groan from Marco, who, when he stood, was holding his stomach with both hands. His appetite was phenomenal. "I need a 'belly wheel'," he moaned.

Making our way to the entrance, we thanked the staff. There was no bill to pay, only gratuities, as everything had been prepaid when ordering.

It was back to the ship for most, including me. I'd be called at 0600 to start laying up tables for breakfast. Some would find a bar en route for a nightcap.

There was a smart breeze the following morning when I stepped out on to the main deck, mug of tea in hand, prior to turning to. The Dutch courtesy flag was flapping strongly on the halyard below the fighting top, as were the sails' clews on the yard ends. The Bosun's mates would have to put sea-stows in these before we departed, preventing them flogging in the gale.

There was a good attendance for breakfast, then hands were called to harbour stations to let the mooring ropes go. Soon we were outward bound, making for the Thames and London. The DOTI boat was quickly recovered and fastened down. *Nelly's* head was already lifting to the swell before we reached the harbour entrance.

No sooner were the ropes coiled and secured than Captain Mike's voice boomed over the speakers. "Bosun, get a party together and get that bloody booze out of my toilet."

Cheers were heard around the ship.

We were out through the piers and motoring slowly into the south-westerly gale, *Nelly* throwing spray high. Had we not been head to wind, the crew would have set the fore and aft sails to steady the ship, but on this course they would flog badly.

The Bosun's mates, Ted and Godfrey, a couple of old hands I'd sailed with many times, were saturated when they arrived back midships, shedding their oilskins after securing the anchors and closing the bow doors.

Fi had made a tasty meal of baked potatoes with chilli and cheese plus salad for lunch, and we fed most of the voyage crew. This wouldn't be the case at dinner, if this weather continued to freshen.

With the cutlery and crockery stowed away, Cookie and I were free until 1530. Fiona departed for her cabin and I took a turn on deck for some fresh air, before heading to my bunk for an hour's rest.

There was a full gale blowing now, the wind fine on the starboard bow. Spray was flying down the windward side. On the leeward side of the ship, aft from the main mast, three youngsters, part of the 'Youth Leadership at Sea' scheme, were sitting on a bench. All were pale and all had disposable sick bags in hand.

The girl was the first to succumb, retching into the bag, then as if in sympathy, the boys followed suit almost immediately.

I opened the accommodation door and, reaching inside, grabbed a few new bags from the wooden holder. Wordlessly, in turn, I relieved each of their messy handful, replacing new for old, then dropped the biodegradable bags over the side, receiving wry smiles for my assistance.

After washing hands in the 'on-deck' heads, I headed below for an afternoon nap. My bunk, the after-most of the pair of 'holes in the wall' on the starboard side was my favourite. I could still feel the ship's motion as she lifted her head, but it would be far worse in the foc'sle, where some of the voyage crew would feel the lifting and slamming at its worst. There'd be some seasick sailors tonight unless the wind eased, I thought.

For the next few hours, at intervals, the anchors would bang in the hawse-pipes. The BM's would trek for'ard four or five times into the spray, each time cranking the retaining bottle-screws as hard as possible, until the anchors were finally home solidly, no longer banging. At present the hooks were still in need of attention.

The wind didn't fall away, and by dinner, Fi was struggling with pans in the galley. There were spillages on to the hot oven, despite the fiddles on the range. Fiona didn't get angry; she was quite stoic and soldiered on, but the erratic movement made the work slow and very taxing. Two of the messmen had succumbed to seasickness, meaning we were short-handed to serve the food below.

Cookie had prepared dinner for all hands, but only about half of the people turned out to eat. The ongoing watch for the bridge was short-handed.

It was 1900 hours and almost dark when Fi and I left the upper mess, leaving Ted and Godfrey to sweep out. They'd only scrub the hot galley tonight, where spillage from the stove had made the deck treacherous.

I carried a mug of tea down to the bar, which was deserted. The tables and chairs were all lashed securely to the seat-lockers, against the weather. Supplying Fi with a G&T, we wedged ourselves in the corner, on the cushioned seating, where we'd spend half an hour unwinding.

It was going to be a long night in poor weather, and it wasn't a good idea to turn in too early. Yes, I was weary, but going to bed too soon would mean waking in the middle of the night. I'd done that several times in the past. I'd also climbed into my bunk for a doze, or to read after work, then fallen asleep, only to wake about ten, get out for a shower, then get back into bed but be unable sleep.

As I'd suspected, the night was a wild one. I could hear banging and crashing in the galley above whenever the ship gave a lurch. There were intermittent groans from the foc'sle, and articles sliding around on the lower mess floor.

The upper mess and galley were in a bad state when Fi and I met, within minutes of each other next morning. The weather was no better, but it was almost daylight again. First things first; a mug of tea and a quick look on deck. Once we started working, it would be non-stop until after breakfast.

There's a little dry place alongside the mainmast, close by the mess door, out of the wind and water and I tucked myself into this corner to take in the situation. There was still a gale blowing and spray flying. During the night, lifelines had been rigged on deck for additional safety. I began to wonder what progress *Nelly* had made overnight. We were supposed to be into the Thames this evening, but that was already looking unlikely. It was my birthday the following day, and I was expected to be home.

Back in doors there was a big mess on the galley floor. Fi was salvaging what she could and sweeping up various ingredients from containers that had jumped from shelves, despite their bungee retainers. Behind the serving counter, separating messroom from galley, the microwave oven was lying broken on the galley floor.

"Ah'll dispose o' that." I said, unplugging the tight cable. Picking up the oven, working my way to the main deck, I ducked under the lifeline, with the intention of taking the article to the stern platform, where the ship's general gash and galley waste were stowed. As I stood up, a bigger than normal wave shook the ship, throwing spray high and I was on the receiving end of the fall out. Swearing loudly and annoyed, I wasn't going to wait for the next sea. I promptly dropped the oven over the side, quickly retreating back indoors. The microwave would become home for various sea creatures for years to come.

Back in the mess and soaked, I said to Fi, "t microwave's gone over t' side. T' ship rolled an' it jumped out of me 'ands."

Cookie smiled knowingly and continued her cleaning.

We managed to get the galley and mess shipshape, getting rid of broken crockery and glass, and then mopped the deck, though Fi wasn't feeling too well. No messmen came to help, so we were on our own. I'd have to serve breakfasts below.

The Cook kept breakfast simple with scrambled eggs, baked beans and tinned tomatoes. There was unlimited tea and toast, self-service. Taking a chance, Fi had only prepared food for twenty people, not the full compliment. It was fortunate she'd unilaterally made the reduction, as there were only a dozen takers for breakfast; including permanent crew.

The morning meeting in the chartroom at 0845 hours was a sombre affair. Captain Mike announced that we'd only made thirty miles in almost twenty-four hours, since leaving port. There was no chance of making London today, even if the wind eased.

Someone suggested to the Captain that we'd only sailed so he could use his toilet. This brought a laugh.

I fervently hoped we'd make better time in the next twenty-four hours, or I was in deep trouble.

The wind moderated during the day and we did increase speed, but then a new announcement came from the bridge. We were no longer going to London, but were making for Dover! That was going to upset some people's travel arrangements, including mine.

We had a full house for dinner that evening, and four messmen. The weather was better and some of the folk onboard hadn't eaten anything substantial since we'd sailed. The ship was steadier as, with a shift of wind and course, the fore and aft sails had been set.

There was a good atmosphere in the bar that evening. Everyone was ready to socialise and seasickness would be a thing of the past for most. Hopefully this would be the memory they'd take away.

It was 1100 hours next morning when *Lord Nelson* slipped between the piers into the expanse of Dover harbour, slowly making for her berth. My bag was packed ready for a dock-head jump at the first opportunity. Unfortunately, the chance didn't arrive, as it was low water when we came alongside the pier. The quay was high up and there was no fixed ladder. I'd have to wait till the gangway went ashore from the bridge.

I was champing at the bit to get ashore, but the crew were having difficulty getting the gangway into place, so steep was the angle. After half an hour the aluminium gangplank was finally in position, though the stanchions and manropes were not yet secured.

"Gangway!" I shouted, and leaving my bag on the deck, scrambled up the sloping aluminium plank, grabbing the horizontal foot-bars with my hands.

"Hey, you can't do that," the Mate shouted, by which time I was almost at the top.

Dropping one of the heaving lines down, I shouted, "'itch me bag on please."

Ted was about to fasten my bag to the line when Fiona came running on to the bridge. "Wait a minute," Cookie called out. Opening my bag, Fi put a small package into the holdall and re-zipped.

"Just a little something, with thanks," Fi shouted, blowing me a kiss. I couldn't have managed without you."

"Thanks, Fi. You shouldn't 'ave," I called back, not knowing what was in the bag. No one is indispensable, and the ship would have sailed regardless, but it was nice to be appreciated.

"Thanks fo' the trip folks," I shouted down to the crew, as they continued fixing the gangway. "See yer again soon."

I received cheery waves and calls in return.

Turning, I was wondering how I'd get to the station, but immediately spied a taxi, parked close to the ship.

"Are yer booked, mate?" I asked, through the open window.

"Well I am, but I've been waiting half an hour already," came the grumpy reply.

"Ow far is it t' station?" I asked. "It'll be at least fifteen minutes before anybody comes ashore yet."

"I can get you there in five minutes and be back here in ten," the driver said, cheering up at the chance of the extra fare. "Hop in."

I'd paid the driver, including a good tip, before arriving, then ran into Dover Priory Station, looking at the announcement board as I entered. There was a train about to leave for Charing Cross, and I made it with minutes to spare.

It wasn't much over an hour to the Capital and, hurrying to the underground, checked the notice board. I ran down the steps to the Northern Line platform, stepping almost immediately onto a train. One stop got me to Leicester Square and I dashed to the Piccadilly Line. Again, within minutes, I was on a train heading for Kings Cross. Four short stops and I was at the main line station. Unbelievably there was a train heading north in ten minutes.

Hoping my out of date ticket would still get me home, I hopped on and we were pulling out, York bound. I'd lost no time so far. As soon as the train was underway, I felt confident enough to ring Dotty. "Ullo me darlin'. Ah know ah'm runnin' late, but ah'm goin' make it. Ah'm jus' leavin' Kings Cross."

If the train was on time into York, there'd a connection with the Liverpool to Scarborough train within fifteen minutes. Great!

Remembering Fi' had put a package in my bag, I now had time to take a look. An envelope contained a birthday card with a lovely, 'thank you' message and an aluminium foil parcel, which I teased open carefully, revealing a small cake in the shape of a fish. The cake had been iced, then decorated with coloured eyes, gills, fins and a smiley face. How lovely was that? When had Cookie found time to make and decorate this special gift?

I had a wide smile and big lump in my throat as I thought of the effort and secrecy Fiona had undertaken to spring this surprise. What a star she was![12]

My smile was wider still when the guard, seeing my birthday cake, and listening to my story, clipped the ticket and gave a cheery, "good luck."

Arriving on time into York, my connection was due to leave from the same platform, fifteen minutes later. Another fifty minutes

---

12 Very sadly, Fiona Spears, Ship's Cook and larger than life character died at her home in Weymouth 24/11/13. We gave her a great send off.

got me from York to Scarborough and with a short taxi ride, I was home. Phew! That was some journey. Unbelievably, I had an hour to spare.

Dotty was busy in the kitchen, but I'd time for a "missed you", kiss and to relate my epic journey. There was enough time to bathe, shave, then dress before welcoming the first of our guests. In my head I was still travelling.

* * *

The next time I was in the Netherlands on board, *Nelly,* she was in Amsterdam, attending one of the, five-yearly, Tall Ships Regattas. The Amstel was filled with hundreds of sailing craft of all sizes from small yachts to massive Russian square riggers that dwarfed *Lord Nelson*. The old harbour tugs in the port were completely transformed, decorated with flowers from stem to stern.

Imagination knew no bounds. Afloat in the harbour, powered by outboard motors, were a mini skip and a ten-foot wooden, yellow clog.

I was sitting in the ship's bar early one evening, prior to going ashore with a little group of our crew. One of the JST's lady Captains was in the company.

"I have to go to my cabin now, to make myself look presentable, ready for a television interview," the Captain said, self-importantly.

I caught glances from those in eye contact, then said, "'ave yer tried radio, Ma'am?"

It was only when I saw the eye contacts had turned to open-mouthed gawping that I realised the enormity of what I'd just said to the Captain.

"Bloody 'ell," I exclaimed. "Did ah really say that? I on'y meant t' think it."

The Master, stood, turned and stepped through the crew's accommodation door, heading for the stairs to her cabin, not saying a word.

The comments came thick and fast in her wake.

"You cheeky bastard!"

"You've done it now."

"How did you get away with that?"

What a 'foot in mouth' moment. I certainly hadn't made a new friend on that occasion.

* * *

The Western Isles is a beautiful part of the world, and sailing from Oban, 'round the top' to Aberdeen with a compliment of Girl Guides made this voyage exceptional. The occasion was the centenary of the 'Girl Guide Movement'. I'd travelled to Oban with Colin, who was sailing as 'Cook's assistant'.

Lord Nelson had been chartered for ten voyages of ten days duration, to sail around Great Britain and for the first time, the minimum age for sailing on the ship was reduced from sixteen to fourteen years. The permanent crew and volunteers on board throughout the period had been subjected to CRB checks. Mine disclosed three penalty points for speeding!

This voyage crew were a mixture of youngsters, senior guides and guide leaders. Quite a few of these ladies were Aberdonians, who'd joined the ship to sail back to their home port from the west coast. What almost all the guides had in common was their enthusiasm and love of adventure. No one needed prompting when there were tasks to be undertaken. The galley was inundated with volunteers, despite the set watches. With Captain Barbara Campbell in command, these sailors would derive the maximum benefit from this leg of the passage.

The wind was set fair for a swift sail down the Sound of Mull, including a brief sightseeing visit to Tobermory. (Known to some of the guides as Balamory, from the BBC childrens' TV programme)

Next day *Lord Nelson* was to the west of Skye, heading north to pass well clear of Cape Wrath. Captain Barbara was taking us to see Sule Skerry, an isolated, treeless outcrop of rock in the western approaches to the Pentland Firth, thirty-five miles north of the Scottish mainland, forty miles west of Orkney. The lighthouse marking this small island was first lit in 1895, after three Summer seasons of construction by the famous Stevenson family, who'd built many of our nation's lifesaving beacons.

From 1895 to 1982, when the edifice became automated, Sule Skerry was the most remote, manned lighthouse in the UK. Now the island was home to thousands of puffins, gannets and other nesting seabirds.

Today the weather was moderate and it was daylight when we approached the lonely, white-painted lighthouse. It took little imagination to envisage Winters with endless screaming, hurricane-force winds battering this remote outcrop, and the isolation faced by the keepers of the light. There must have been many occasions when these men would be unable to be relieved or re-supplied when their duty period was over.

Leaving the lonely outcrop behind, we were now bound for Scapa Flow. This would be a better experience than my previous visit.

Nelly spread her wings and with a following tide, flew towards the Island of Hoy and the western entrance to Scapa. The surface of the sea was flat, though boiling with the riptide, underlining the danger of the combination of wind and tide in this region, where the Atlantic Ocean shoals up to meet the North Sea.

There was a memorable moment for me after we'd handed sail on the approaches to the Flow. I'd been sent aloft with two very young guides onto the fore, port, tops'l yard to put in a sea stow. The ship was rolling, which didn't seem to bother the youngsters at all. Passing close on our port side was the large, white ferry, *Hamnavoe*, heading for Stromness from Scrabster. Passengers on her upper deck were waving. We all returned the salute, as did others from our decks.

On the landward, starboard side, we were passing the famous landmark, the Old Man of Hoy. This 450-foot, free standing natural stack has stood sentry on the western entrance to Scapa Flow for millennia. I hoped the Girl Guides would remember this special moment in time.

Girl Guides inspecting cooked crabs – Fred Normandale

Dressing crabs, Captain Barbara in blue – Fred Normandale

Once inside this massive natural harbour, we motored for about half an hour then dropped anchor close to the shore. Several of the young ladies needed little encouragement to deploy mackerel feathers, resulting in a couple of dozen fat fish. These were stored in the chilled, veggie locker.

The following morning, before picking up the hook, a small boat came alongside and an elderly, local fisherman held up half a basket of large, live male crabs with big claws. "Ah these ony use tae ye," the old boy asked. "Ah kin ony sell ma lobsters."

Taking the lead and nodding enthusiastically to remove any doubt, I replied, "they sure are, thank ya."

Our Captain, seeing the visitor and his gift, sanctioned a bottle of whisky from the bar in exchange, and sighting the bottle, the old Orcadian's eyes lit up as if he'd won the lottery. He steamed off towards Stromness, turned and waved. He was a happy man.

I distributed the big crabs between three plastic buckets, filling these with warm, fresh water, weighting down the brown backs to prevent escape. The crabs would soon drown and Cookie Dave in the galley would cook them up.

We tied up alongside in the old port, allowing our guides and leaders to explore the historic little town.

I'd been given the phone number of Jason Schofield, one of the top fishermen in Orkney, by my son, Danny. He'd suggested Jason may be able to donate some of his catch to the ship.

Extremely apologetic, Jason said his fish was already landed and had been sold on the market, but kindly arranged for fifty portions of vacuum-packed salmon to be delivered. Though invited, sadly, Jason was too busy to bring his family to visit the ship.

There was a frenzy of activity in the galley during the afternoon when, along with Captain Barbara and Colin, I attempted to teach a dozen or more girl guides to dress the cooked crabs. There were bits of shell flying everywhere as the strong claws were being smashed, revealing the tasty meat.

Cookie Dave pulled a couple of big bags of peeled prawns from the freezer below and he, Col and the galley team prepared fresh bread and some wonderful salads.

That evening, on deck in the sunshine, we all enjoyed the most amazing alfresco meal of mackerel, salmon, crab and prawn, various salads plus freshly baked bread. For those eligible, there was white wine. This was a spectacular meal in an amazing setting, that hopefully, everyone would remember.

The voyage ended in Aberdeen as planned, and the Girl Guides' departure was a tearful affair. The youngsters and their leaders had had an amazing voyage. The pair of plucky girls who'd been on the yard with me when we'd passed the Old Man of Hoy, unsurprisingly, would return in years to come as Bosun's mates.

CHAPTER 17

CAPE HORN

Anyone with any interest in tall ships and the days of sail must want to see Cape Horn. I most certainly did, so when the opportunity arose to join *Lord Nelson* in Ushuaia, on a leg of her round the world voyage, I jumped at the chance.

Along with Colin the baker and brother-in-law, Dave Mercer, I flew to Buenos Aires, then south to Ushuaia. It was Autumn in the southern hemisphere, raining, and the temperature was two degrees on our arrival. There was snow on the mountains beyond the town.

Nelly was alongside and newly back from her epic voyage to the Antarctic, under Captain Chris Phillips, having encountered an exceedingly stormy northerly crossing of Drake Passage on her return.

When she sailed down the Beagle Channel again, making for the Southern Ocean a couple of days later, Captain Barbara Campbell was in command. Adverse winds, though reasonable weather meant we motored to a position two miles from the bleak island that is Cape Horn, in approximate position, 56 degrees South. 67 degrees West. Everyone on board was captivated to see this world-renowned landmark. If this black landmass could speak, what tales this grim promontory would tell.

This was our westernmost position and *Lord Nelson* turned east with all sails set. We hadn't rounded Cape Horn, but had seen the awesome, grim, austere southernmost tip of South America. Countless ships and thousands of men had come to grief, lost without trace, while attempting to reach the west coast of the great continent. This sighting, for me, was a lifetime's ambition fulfilled.

Initially the voyage programme had said we were to sail along the Argentinean coast, calling in at various ports, ending in Buenos Aires. Sadly, the exorbitant charges in Ushuaia for harbour dues and pilotage, and the expectation of more of the same, made this plan cost prohibitive. It was time for Plan B. Captain Barbara charted a course for the Falkland Islands. What a bonus! This would be another tick in the book of life's experiences.

Many ships disabled by the ferocity of the 'Horn' beat a retreat to the Falklands for repairs and restoration. Some never left.

Under full canvas, we were making good speed, and were soon approaching the Straits of Le Maire, the passage between Tierra Del Fuego and the Isla de Los Estados, notorious for strong tides, fog and severe weather: another graveyard of ships and men.

At the first opportunity I put a speculative fishing line over the stern, not expecting to catch anything, but hoping. I was delighted when, within ten minutes a big fish took the lure. This specimen took some hauling in, and was just in photo range for cameras from the bridge deck, when the tuna dropped off the hook, causing strong language from me and several, 'awes' and, 'the one that got away' comments from the watch above.

With the line back out, twenty minutes later it was, 'fish on' again. This time a smaller (of course) big-eyed tuna took the lure and was landed on the stern platform. This fish was big enough to feed the entire crew, but sadly the fishing activity had attracted many large seabirds including boobies and albatross, so I was compelled to haul the line in.

The birds continued to follow the ship, and it was several days later before it occurred to me that a small, wooden paravane with lure extended behind, would dive below the surface, keeping the hook out of the reach of the birds. Dave and I made a device from a bit of wood and almost immediately began catching fish again. Albacore tuna made great sushi starters and superb dinners.

Big fish at Cape Horn – Dave Mercer

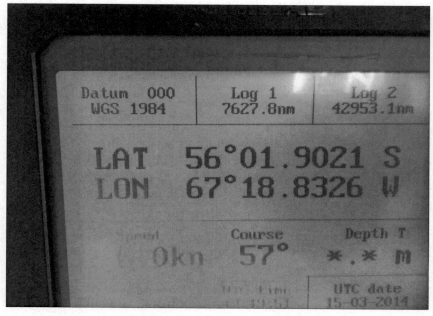

GPS Latitude and Longitude of Cape Horn – Fred Normandale

Colin the Baker – Fred Normandale

It was a sail-cracking passage to the Falklands, taking many days, and where we received a great reception from the locals. We were to spend the first night berthed at the Mount Pleasant Military Base then the following two nights alongside in Stanley.

Captain Barbara had been ashore on the first day and on her return, informed everyone that she'd walked about four miles along the coastline to a 'rookery'.

"We're in the Falklands," I thought. "Who wants to see rooks? And what's more, I haven't seen any trees." How was I to know penguins lived in a rookery?

Derek, the Cook on this voyage had a strange experience while shopping for provisions in Stanley. Among other necessary items, he bought potatoes, which, when he checked the bill, realized their cost was astronomical, as they were imported. He returned half of these to the supplier and bought rice. Potatoes were on ration.

Cookie also ordered lots of cuts of local lamb, which he knew was cheap and available, but these joints arrived in the form of three whole carcasses, to be dismembered. These were quickly strung up in the little galley, then a hacksaw and a fire axe, borrowed from the Engineers were utilised by Derek, with helpful assistance from Caroline, the Aussie doctor on board: professionally, a gynaecologist!!

All hands were given tours of the battlefields, which the locals took great pleasure in conducting, and at no charge. Donations were requested, and willingly given for the upkeep of the local Community Centre, where we were provided with tea and sandwiches. This tour was extremely moving for everyone, and for some, a tearful experience.

My impression of the Falklands in Autumn was of desolate, wind-swept, treeless islands, though with extremely friendly, patriotic inhabitants.

After three nights in port, we were due to depart and, 'sailed' off the berth. Vantage points around the bay were filled with islanders watching *Nelly* sail. This was an impressive, memorable departure. It was pleasing to be a part of the enthusiastic, waving and horn-sounding interaction that took place between the ship and spectators.

Once clear of the land, Capt. Barbara announced that, having been to the Falkland Islands, *Lord Nelson* would no longer be welcome in Argentina. Instead, a course was set for the north bank of the River Plate and for Uruguay. Another bonus! This, one of the smallest countries in South America, was also a country I never thought I'd visit.

The weather grew warmer as we progressed north and west and shorts were now worn by most. We continued to enjoy favourable winds, sailed well and still caught plenty of fish. This was now a welcome alternative to the constant lamb, prepared in its many guises. Cookie' had versatile ways of presenting both.

Fishing ceased again for a while, a couple days out from the River Plate, when a huge, black triangular fin was seen in the wake of the ship. Both lures and 110lb breaking strain line were snatched, parting like cotton. This shark must have been colossal in size.

Arriving in Uruguayan waters, we anchored off Piriapolis, a small resort town where the voyage crew were taken ashore in the boat to explore what was a very cultured and civilized country. The Spanish-speaking natives were extremely welcoming and friendly. A chairlift took many of the crew to the top of a large hill overlooking the bay, from where *Nelly* looked the size of a pinhead.

We stayed at anchor overnight, then sailed further up the mighty river to Punta Del Este and to the end of our fantastic voyage.

It wasn't a simple flight home to the UK from Uruguay. We were bussed to the capital city, Montevideo, then took a very short flight across the River Plate to Buenos Aires, from where we'd catch our return flight across the Atlantic. I looked hard from the window of the little plane, hoping to catch a view of the wreck of *Graf Spee*, but to no avail.

On our arrival in Argentina, we'd been instructed by the ship's office to say we'd been on a cruising holiday, ending in Uruguay, rather than sailing on *Lord Nelson*. This clearly worked, though the Immigration Officers were not happy to see 'Falklands Islands' stamped in our passports. (I was)

What a fabulous voyage this had been. It had indeed been the trip of a lifetime, and there was still fish in the freezer for the next leg of *Nelly's* epic circumnavigation.

* * *

Some months later, I met up with shipmates who'd sailed on the previous passage. *Lord Nelson* had crossed the Pacific Ocean and with the southernmost tip of South America getting closer and only a few days away, Captain Chris, at his morning briefing, announced that after dinner, there would be a showing of a 'Cape Horn' video in the upper mess.

One of the voyage crew with a hearing problem, loudly asked, "why does the Captain want us to watch a 'gay porn' video?"

CHAPTER 18

BOARD OF INQUIRY

An unusual phone call in July from a gentleman in the Aberdeen Courthouse was to open a chapter in my life that was to leave a lasting impression.

The clerk explained that some divers, a few years earlier, had discovered and identified the wreck of the *Trident PD 111*, an 85 foot herring trawler. This craft been lost with all hands (seven men) on 3rd October 1974 after rounding Duncansby Head, en route for Peterhead via the Pentland Firth. The vessel had been completed early the previous year, and was part of a syndicate of four herring trawlers, fishing on the west coast of Scotland.

I was a young Skipper at the time of the loss, but could remember the incident. The tragedy was extensively reported in Fishing News.

There had been a Board of Trade Inquiry following the sinking of the vessel, and this august body had reached the conclusion that *Trident* had been lost after being hit by a large wave or a series of waves. Despite an extensive search at the time, the wreck had not been found. Now, in light of the recent discovery of the sunken vessel, the Board of Inquiry was to be reopened.

I'd been invited to Aberdeen with a view to being an 'expert advisor' for the case, assisting the Sheriff Principal of the Highlands and Islands. The case was expected to last no more than three to four weeks. The main requirement was for a non-Scottish fisherman, with extensive knowledge of the fishing industry.

Intrigued, suited and booted with shirt and tie, on 21st September 2009, I flew to Aberdeen from Humberside Airport. This was an hour-long passage and, due to the demand for flights from oil workers, the fare was about £350 for a single journey, similar in price for a return flight to the USA.

I reported to the Court House at the eastern end of Union Street, the main thoroughfare of the Granite City and was surprised at the level of security to get into the building. This was like going through an airport, with scanners and inspectors. Once inside, I asked at the enquiries desk for the clerk who'd contacted me, then waited quite some time for the gentleman to appear.

I was pleased when an attractive young lady arrived. About five feet seven with a round face, sparkling eyes and a button nose, her hair was jet black with tight, shoulder-length ringlets. This was Janie. After introductions, Janie gave me an outline of the case and it was obvious to me that this bonnie and efficient young lady was well in control of her brief.

Janie concisely explained that the remit of the new inquiry was to find the cause of the loss of *Trident II* in the light of the new evidence discovered. The hearing was to provide information to assist other vessels of a similar size and design, that may not have benefitted from subsequent improved safety regulations and modifications. The lovely lady said this would be made clearer when the case began.

Presuming I'd already agreed to take the job, Janie handed me a volume of the preliminary findings of the JPE (Joint Panel of Experts). This group had been assembled as part of the new inquiry, and all had been involved in the proceedings since the wreck had been discovered. These people had met several times while compiling the volume, and had been present onboard the diving support vessel, *Fennica*, chartered from the Aberdeen company, Subsea, to survey the wreck.

I was shown into a waiting room and began to thumb my way through the tome, expecting to have all the answers by the time I was called to the court room. Fortunately for me, this was not the case.

It was almost an hour before I was summoned into the chamber, where a body of men were seated, facing a tall, lean, elderly gentleman who was sitting alone on the magistrate's bench. The man was the very picture of how I imagined a leading judge to be. He looked very serious, solemn and had the hooked beak-like nose of a wise owl. This was Sir Stephen Young, Sheriff Principal of the Highlands and Islands of Scotland. For some strange reason, as part of his remit, Sir Stephen was also head of the Northern Lighthouse Board. He would annually cruise the Western Isles to inspect his lights.

"Ah Mr Normandale," he greeted me. "Come and sit up here on the bench with me. You'll be doing a lot of this in the next few weeks."

Well this was a surprise, and it looked like I was taking the job. I was expecting to be a witness and be giving an opinion, not sitting up on the bench with the judge.

"This is only a preliminary hearing," the beak said. "Mr MacWhirter will be joining us when we commence the hearing proper, next month. He's an expert on ships' stability. We'll not be in this room. The full inquiry will be taking place in the Aberdeen Council Chambers, upstairs."

I was pleased to hear that someone with a knowledge of ship's stability was going to be present. I knew the principle of top weight being dangerous and about the timing of the ship's rolling period being critical. The faster a vessel rolls, the stiffer and safer she is, but the calculations on paper always confused me. I'd managed to scrape through my Skippers (limited) stability exam, though after much cramming, and I'd mostly forgotten the abstract calculations required.

Sir Stephen, ("call me Stephen when we're not in court") said I must keep all receipts and a record of my travel costs, hotel and food expenses for reimbursement. "This is not to include alcohol," he emphasised sternly. There was no mention of any payment for my services.

Four weeks later, on Monday, 19th October, 2009, soon after 0700hrs I flew out of Humberside Airport. This airstrip, though still small, had grown significantly since I'd flown from here while building *Independence* in 1976/7.*

The plane, a small, blue and white, twin turbo prop, Fokker Friendship in Eastern Airways livery, took an hour to reach Aberdeen. I carried a small bag of clothes for the week ahead and a briefcase for documents.

The flight, when visibility allowed, was superb, as it was almost completely along the coastline. The Humber Bridge, the River Humber, Spurn Point, Flamborough Head, Filey Bay, Scarborough and Whitby were easily identified early in the flight. It seemed strange to be flying over Scarborough, having left there only a couple of hours earlier.

Tees Bay, the Tyne, Berwick and the Scottish Coast were all viewed and put into perspective during the flight, which was pleasantly interrupted with tea and biscuits from an efficient, smiling hostess. Little did I know, but I was to do this flight many times over the next few months.

Landing into Aberdeen, to the north of the city, I discovered I wouldn't need a taxi as there was a frequent bus service to the city centre from the airport. I'd booked into the Carmelite Hotel, which had been home to an order of nuns in an earlier life. There was still stained glass in the windows of the staircase. The place was a reasonably priced, private hotel with a dining room and bar.

Located near the harbour, rail and bus stations and a five-minute walk to the Council Chambers, this was the perfect location. I'd stayed here several times previously while in Aberdeen on fishing industry business with the NFFO. This was a homely, cheerful place, unlike most modern hotels.

Checking in, I left my bag in the room and, briefcase in hand, made my way up Market Street to Union Street, then to the rear door of the large courtroom building, as instructed. Showing identification, I was escorted up a large staircase then along a landing to a small anti chamber, where I was left to knock on the locked door.

Seconds later, the door was opened by Sir Stephen. "Ah, Mr Normandale, come in. Meet Mr MacWhirter."

See Slack Water *

This tiny compartment was the robing room for the Provost of Aberdeen. It was to be sanctuary for the Judge and his advisors for the duration of the case.

"Hello, I'm Nick," said the short, stocky, bearded, balding, grey-suited man, holding out his hand. "I'm pleased to meet you. I do know of you. I've seen your name in the Fishing News occasionally."

Nick spoke with a southern accent and seemed quite a serious person.

Introductions over, the Beak said, "before we go into the courtroom, I have a few things to say that will give you some background to this case. There were seven men lost on board *Trident* on that fateful day. Their families are represented here today, as is the Solicitor General of Scotland and the Skipper, Mr David Tait, who was the major shareholder of *Trident*. We must bear this in mind at all times."

Mr Tait had survived the loss, as, fortunately for him, he'd driven home from the west coast to arrange for the slipping of his vessel in Peterhead. Sadly, the Skipper had lost his vessel and his crew and was to live with unwarranted guilt for the remainder of his life. He had spent most of his subsequent years in Canada.

Trident under construction – From the Trident inquiry evidence

The Judge went on to say that also in attendance as part of the 'joint panel of experts' were representatives from the Sea Fish Industry Authority, 'SFIA', previously known as the White Fish Authority. There was a WFA surveyor present through every stage of construction, launching and trials of *Trident III*.

I was aware of this body. The WFA was a Government quango, involved in administering grants and loans for the building and refurbishing of fishing vessels. I'd conducted business with this body and its successor organisation when building our three vessels, *Independence*, *Emulator* and *Allegiance*.

The Sheriff continued, "also present for this case, though now quite frail, is Mr Andrew Cumming, the designer of the vessel. He will assist the court wherever possible, represented by his barrister."

The preliminary brief went on, and other advice would follow on a daily basis.

There were two pieces of card face down on the table in front of the judge. He said, "Gentlemen, I'm going to share with you the most important advice I was given as a young lawyer. It is still as relevant today." He flipped the first card over and the word, SHUT, was written in large capitals. Turning the second card over, he revealed the word, UP. "I emphasise these words, gentlemen. You are to speak to no one about this case, except myself and each other. There are many people in the courtroom who would wish to speak with you, and to know our thoughts. Discretion is imperative, always."

Well! That was clear enough.

Our final instruction, as we approached the door of the court, was our order of appearance. As the Sheriff Principal was to sit in the middle, I would enter the chamber first. Nick MacWhirter would be third.

Melody, the Court Usher, robed in a black gown, was waiting for us at the door, greeting us with a pleasant, open smile. The bespectacled young lady was small, plump, cheerful, blond and bore a name that quite summed her up. Melody was delightful.

The young lady opened the door inwards, walked through, then, holding the door open, called out, "all rise."

There was a shuffling of chairs from within the room as those inside, stood.

I was first through the door, briefcase in hand and was surprised to see so many people present. Leading the small procession, I walked into the huge chamber, ascending the three stairs then crossed the bench. I waited until the Judge was seated, then I too sat in a soft, comfortable, black leather chair. The arms were at the perfect height for elbows. When we were seated, the other parties present also sat.

The bench was at the head of the room and on three sides were numerous groups, representing the varied interests in the case. I counted thirty-four individuals in the lower chamber. There were also several spectators upstairs in the public gallery, overlooking the proceedings.

In front of our position was Janie, also black-robed and fully attentive to the court. I was to rely on her knowledge frequently when looking for my copies of the numerous productions, submissions and other documents constantly put before the court.

Sitting at a table in the front of the bench was an official recorder, taping the proceedings, but also writing in shorthand. These minutes would be copied and produced in the form of a daily transcript for the record, though these were often in need of correction. This official was changed several times throughout the case.

Coughing to clear his throat, Sir Stephen made his opening address, saying he hoped that with the discovery of the wreck, and subsequent exploration by the research vessel, the new inquiry would be able to shed more light on this tragic case. The Court was to assess the report of the survey and the subsequent findings of the JPE, and these were to be tested by the reopened, Board of Inquiry.

It had been an extraordinary circumstance in which *Trident III* had been lost. The vessel, with seven hands on board, had left Troon on the Ayrshire coast just after midnight on 2nd October 1974. She was to escort *Faithful II*, which had a suspected gearbox problem, on the passage to Peterhead on the north east coast of Scotland, via the notorious Pentland Firth. The tide through these narrows between mainland Scotland and Orkney flows at a tremendous rate.

Both *Trident* and *Faithful* were part of a four-vessel, herring trawling partnership. The others being *Accord* and *Starcrest*. The pair on passage were to stay in frequent radio contact throughout their passage home.

At 12.15 the following day, someone, presumably the temporary Skipper of *Trident*, spoke to the 80 foot Aberdeen trawler, *Glenesk*, sheltering from the weather in the lee of Copinsay, a small isle on the eastern side of Orkney. The wind was NNE force 7-8 with *Glenesk* at the time. The caller on *Trident* was asking about tide times in the Pentlands. She was in a position six or seven miles to the west of Dunnett Head, the northernmost point of mainland Britain, fifteen miles from John o' Groats.

It was slack water at the time of the call and she would just get through the Firth before the ebb came away too strongly. There were exceptional, Spring Tides during the first few days of October, which would have slowed the vessel to a standstill, had she been any later.

Ahead of her, *Faithful,* having rounded Duncansby Head and entered the North Sea, stopped her engine three miles beyond the promontory, to repair a damaged seacock inlet pipe. The weather was still poor, with the wind blowing gale force from north to north east.

Trident, catching up with *Faithful,* had some special, waterproof, adhesive tape on board, but she couldn't go too close to her partner in the poor weather, so had floated this compound across to *Faithful,* attached to a buoy. Having assisted her consort, *Trident* continued her passage south east. The deep swell was on her port quarter. The strengthening ebb tide was running against the strong wind.

When the repair was completed about 1430, *Faithful* also continued on her passage. Being the faster of the two vessels, it was expected she would catch up with her companion at some point. Radio contact was re-established and *Trident* was spotted on *Faithful's* radar between 1520 and 1545 at a distance of 5.5 miles and was a compass point to starboard.

At 1554 *Trident* contacted Wick radio, wanting to make a ship to shore link call. The operator told the caller to stand by and await his turn in the busy radio traffic. This was the last communication heard from *Trident III*.

At 1644 when the shore station tried to contact the vessel to patch though her message, there was no response. Neither could *Trident* be raised by *Faithful* on the VHF radio. Continuous calls to the ship met with no response. The weather was still poor and *Faithful's* radar was full of clutter from the spray and swell. It was a possibility that *Trident's* radio aerial had been damaged in the bad weather. She was a large, new vessel and should not have come to harm in these conditions.

It wasn't until *Faithful II* arrived into Peterhead after midnight that it was realised *Trident* had not arrived into her homeport. Her Skipper, David Tait and families of her crewmen were waiting, in vain.

HM Coastguard was immediately informed. The ports of Wick, Buckie and Fraserburgh were contacted for possible sightings, but to no avail. A Nimrod surveillance aircraft was diverted to search the area, and at daylight, lifeboats and a pair of Shackleton aircraft were launched to search. Fish boxes and floating oil were found, but no rafts, and crucially, no survivors.

Of course, all this information was known from the original inquiry and was available to read in the first few pages of the report from the JPE.

Now, at the reopened inquiry, it was time for introductions, and the Judge went around the table, allowing each barrister, seated at the front of his party, to give their name, to say which law firm they were representing, and who they were acting on behalf of, at the hearing.

Next Sir Stephen introduced Nick and myself and gave an outline of our credentials before handing over to Miss Wilson, representing the Advocate General for Scotland.

Miss Wilson was a formidable, no nonsense, though attractive lady, probably in her early forties. Small, sturdy, round of face, her hair mostly hidden by a white curled wig, Miss Wilson had an amazing grasp of words. In her barristers' gown, this lady commanded attention.

Addressing the court, the Advocate's representative said, "there are ten points that this inquiry should have regard to during its proceedings."

We on the bench were presented with our first production, listed, 1/1. There would be many more documents to follow during the proceedings. The room was silent, taking in her every word. Miss Wilson read from her script.

"1/ What was the cause or causes for the loss of *Trident*?

2/ What can be eliminated?

3/ What causes remain open?

4/ Has any new evidence come to light?

5/ Was the vessel unseaworthy when she sailed?

6/ What was the position?

7/ What were the weather conditions?

8a/ What was her condition of loading?

8b/ Was the vessel's stability intact?

9/ Was there a wrongful act?

10/ What beneficial, can be learned for the modern industry?"

The next barrister, representing most of the families of the lost crew, including one poor lady, who'd lost both her husband and father said, "my clients wish particularly to know about the vessel's stability and the weather at the time of the loss. Apparently, there is new evidence from a scientific, 'hindcast' showing a different weather scenario to the one given in the original inquiry."

These statements made, the major participants went into a procedural discussion that went on for most of the morning. This, about various legal matters which the lawyers couldn't agree on, and on which the Judge had to rule.

We finally started the proceedings near to lunchtime.

The general arrangement plans of the vessel, which had been built by Tees Marine, Middlesbrough between 1971-73, had been distributed previously and agreed to be correct by all parties. This would save some time, but then the first witness, from Marine and Offshore Services Company took the stand.

He began answering questions from the first barrister relating to the layout of the deck equipment, the winches, hatches, doors, windows, accommodation, focs'le and all the many component parts of the vessel and its purpose. These were details that I'd taken for granted, and I found this process mind-numbingly slow, but it did highlight why I was there as a special advisor.

I spent the evening and most subsequent nights alone in the hotel, sometimes going out for an early run, then eating in the dining room and watching television. Aberdeen harbour and its foreshore are great places for running. The area is flat to the harbour entrance and north pier, as is the promenade by the beach, which extends for miles. I needed the exercise after sitting in a chair all day, every day. I'd ring Dotty each evening, telling her about my day and would also ring anyone I could think of to chat to, though not divulging sensitive information. I wasn't used to being, 'Billy No-mates'. By nature, I'm a gregarious person and also enjoy humour. There hadn't been much amusement so far.

The familiarisation of the vessel by all parties continued the following day and brought more questions and productions. This first witness continued to be challenged in turn by each of the barristers throughout the following day. There were some pertinent, searching questions, which I noted. There were others that seemed irrelevant, though had to be played out and which consumed considerable time.

This same line of enquiry relating to the vessel, its deck equipment and every detail of her would continue for the remainder of the week. At the end of the cross examination of this witness by the barristers, the Sheriff asked Nick and myself if we had any questions. Nick had some relevant queries relating to the vessel's lightship status, which were crucial and his answers recorded. This would be discussed again later in the case. Now it was my turn.

Turning to me, Sir Stephen said, "do you have any questions for this witness, Mr Normandale?"

"Yes, my lord," I answered formally.

A couple of days earlier the witness had said the crew of *Trident* would stop the main engine when alongside the quay discharging the catch, and would use the vessel's auxiliary motor. I wanted to challenge him on this statement.

I addressed the witness. "Sir, earlier in the proceedings, you said the crew would stop the main engine when they began to land the catch. Is that correct?"

"Yes sir, that is correct." he replied. "They would do this to save fuel."

"Well Sir", I went on, "with your Merchant Navy background, I think you'll be unfamiliar with fishing procedures. It is my contention that the main engine would have to be used for landing the catch. I've looked at the hydraulic arrangement of the vessel and the auxiliary engine was not capable of driving the main winch. This winch was essential for discharging the catch. The auxiliary engine would only be used for driving the power-block at the stern of the vessel, and for charging *Trident's* banks of batteries." I paused for effect, then said, "unless of course you are suggesting they used the power block to land the catch."

I heard a few muttered comments and little chuckles, but daren't look round. I hadn't finished. "I'm sure you'll now agree that the main engine was running when the vessel landed her catch, and that the power-block was only used when the trawl net was on the surface, prior to taking the catch on board, on to the foredeck."

"You may be right," the witness conceded.

"May be right?" the Judge interjected.

"I'm sure Mr Normandale is correct," the witness grudgingly admitted.

I continued, for the record. "At the present time, the international price of crude oil is nearing record highs, but at the time of the loss of *Trident*, the cost of marine diesel was not much more than ten new pence a gallon. A gallon," I emphasised. "We were not using litres at that point. Fuel was extremely cheap and wasn't a major consideration for fishermen."

The witness looked disconsolate, but, having finished making my point, I said, "no further questions, my Lord."

I looked round. Two or three of the advocates acknowledged, slightly nodding in approval and Mr Tait, the former Skipper/owner of the vessel gave me a weary smile. I felt my presence in the proceedings was justified.

Once we were through the door and into the robing room, the Sheriff turned and beamed. "You've lost your way my boy. You should have been a lawyer." Where had I heard that before?

It was Friday, and thanks to the kindness of the Judge, who ended the hearing mid-afternoon, I was able to get an earlier flight back to Humberside. Sir Stephen said the barristers would be pleased to get back to Edinburgh in good time. The Judge lived in Inverness.

I had my first laugh of the week when, arriving home, I opened the door of the room where Dotty was sitting, knitting in hand. I called out, "all rise."

I didn't hear her reply as I was still laughing. Needless to say, my wife didn't rise. (to my joke)

The weekend went swiftly, though was fun. It was good to be home and I told the 'all rise' story several times. I could also relate the story of the last tragic hours of *Trident's* loss, as this information was already in the public domain and was fascinating to my maritime friends, some of whom could recall the tragedy. I would 'shut up' on all other matters.

Soon it was Monday again and I was back on the road early and into Aberdeen for the second week of proceedings. The hotel receptionist had allowed me to keep the same room, which was helpful, and I was soon changed into my 'office wear', before departing for the Council Chamber. On the right, on Union Street, before I crossed the road to the huge gothic, granite edifice, was a newsagent/general store. I'd make this a stop on the way to the court house each morning, where I'd buy a bag of mints or fruit gums. These would be pre-opened and hidden in my left-hand pocket, so I could surreptitiously pop one into my mouth from time to time without the Judge noticing.

The inquiry began again, but the morning session was completely bogged down with technicalities and legal points of order, all of which, initially the Sheriff seemed to bear with tolerance, though when the delays continued into other sessions throughout the week, these became an issue and a source of irritation to the Beak. Both Nick and I felt the players were stringing out the proceedings.

Eventually, after more hold ups, the Sheriff Principal announced that in future the court would commence at 09.45 not 10.00 and he would allow only one hour for lunch, a reduction of thirty minutes. This edict clearly didn't find favour with the participants, but the Judge was making his point.

Lunch was always soup and a bread roll, taken in the council canteen, so it was no problem for we on the bench. There was even time to catch up on any missed calls on my phone, which was always left in the dressing room, by order.

Next morning, a witness from the original inquiry was called to give evidence again. Now an old man, the gentleman was brought by taxi from Caithness, which must have cost a huge amount. The cab driver had parked up for most of the day, awaiting the return of his fare.

The witness, Hector Sutherland was an agricultural worker who, around midday on the day of the loss, had stopped working on the fence he was erecting, to enjoy his sandwich and flask of tea. The man was adamant that he'd seen a boat out at sea. His question and answer session took a considerable amount of time, but it quickly became clear that from his vantage point, Mr Sutherland may well have seen a boat, but it was highly improbable that he could have seen *Trident*. She would have been too far off shore and the visibility was poor. Even the timing was wrong. It was several hours after the man's lunch that *Trident* had foundered. Two of the barristers had no questions for the witness.

"He must be heard," the wise Judge said later, when I questioned the man's appearance in the court. "He may have had something of importance to add to the proceedings. We had to find out."

The remainder of this week and some of the following week was spent with questions to the experts relating to the technical design of the vessel from her drawings. This consumed a huge amount of time.

Next the fishing gear on board *Trident*, the size of the openings at the mouth of her midwater trawls, the location on board of various nets and weights and the description of the fishing operations was disseminated. The size and weight of her nets was important. Also, as part of this section of the inquiry, the weight of the trawl winch and the wires on the machine were discussed.

It was revealed that the group of vessels were trawling with their smaller nets, for shallow water use, and this gear was stored in wooden pounds aft, and worked from the stern of each boat.

A large net was also carried on board *Trident* for use in deeper water, but as this trawl was of no use on the West Coast, the net was stored out of the way on a pallet on the foredeck, in front of, but unseen from the wheelhouse. This large net was due to be put ashore in Peterhead.

Comparisons were made between the fishing gear on *Trident* and on her sistership, the subsequently built, *Silver Lining* and the difference in top weight of the fishing equipment on the two vessels' decks.

There was a huge amount of questioning and conjecture by all the barristers relating to *Trident's* stability, which continued all week.

Much comparison was made of the deck layout of *Trident* and *Silver Lining*. The latter had been built to fish demersal (bottom feeding fish) with the Danish seine net, in the northern North Sea.

Trident had a big trawl winch with hundreds of fathoms of heavy wire warp, spooled forward under her whaleback. Her nets were large, and being nylon, would absorb a significant weight of water. At the time of her loss the vessel was extremely light, with little fuel or water and no ice or fish on board.

Silver Lining had a small seine winch and her nets were lighter and of polyester construction that didn't absorb water. Her twenty-four coils, each of one hundred and twenty fathoms of lead-cored fishing ropes were heavy, but stowed in two lockers below deck level. She would have several tons of ice below in the fish hold.

The two vessels were being compared, though only the hulls were comparable.

What I did find extremely disturbing, and thought very relevant was the freeing ports on *Trident,* that were supposed to allow water to flow back overboard from the deck. These were very narrow openings, and to compound this, a half-inch round bar had been welded along all these scuppers. This made the gaps extremely small, presumably to prevent herring passing through. I made a note to say I thought this was an act of unbelievable lunacy, possibly by the Skipper.

Three weeks had now passed and the inquiry was supposed to be ending. Dotty and I were due to go on holiday at the end of the following week. I'd informed the court of this when first joining the inquiry. Apologetically, I mentioned this to the judge again on the Friday morning. "Dotty and I are due to go on holiday a week from today, Sir. I'm afraid you'll have to carry on the procedure without me. I'm free most of next week, then I'll be away for three weeks."

I was surprised when Sir Stephen replied, "we can't continue without you, Mr Normandale. You're an integral part of the proceedings. These people will find other things to do in your absence. I know I can."

We did two more days the following week and concluded the part relating to the comparison of the vessels. His Lordship said we would meet again four weeks hence. In the event, for various reasons, it would be February of the following year before we met again.

The inquiry was resumed in the third week of February after I'd spent a week on board *Tenacious,* sailing from Malta into the Mediterranean, then returning to Valetta. The highlight of the voyage was seeing Mount Etna at night: the volcano glowing menacingly. Dad had seen this same wonderous phenomena frequently during his wartime service in the Mediterranean.

This new phase of the proceedings related to the survey of the wreck by the oil-related vessel, *Fennica.* In the centre of the floor space was a table, displaying various items recovered from the wreck, including samples of netting, a section of the fish hold combing with buckled lug, the outer ring of a deck scuttle, a piece of steel from the fore part of the vessel and her masthead light, found on the seabed. These items would be discussed in turn during questions to the assembled bodies.

We began to watch the extensive underwater video footage, taken from an ROV, (remotely operated vehicle) with comments throughout, by another member of the same offshore survey company. The entire film had date and time in seconds imprinted, and was frequently stopped and re run to satisfy the many questions which were asked for clarification.

Much loose netting had been festooned around the masts, wheelhouse and rigging and had to be removed remotely before the cameras could operate. This was nylon net, and could only have been *Trident's* own. Other fishing gear, lower down around the hull had been lost by an unknown trawler, hitting the uncharted wreck while fishing. This was doubly expensive for the fishermen. The gear had to be replaced and lost fishing time was incurred while doing so, either on board or back in port.

There were many hours of footage to be viewed, and the screening continued throughout the week, showing the vessel lying to starboard. Doors, windows, the fish hold hatch, which was open, and all the aspects mentioned in the first witness's question and answer session, were to be seen. I realised that everyone in the courtroom was now familiar with what they were seeing on this underwater footage, having intensely studied the layout of *Trident* during the previous session.

There was a significant moment when we saw the transom stern, where all the plating below deck level was buckled inwards and we viewed footage of the rudder, jammed hard to starboard, way past the 'stops'. *Trident* must have sunk by the stern, having listed to starboard, then landed on her rudder, forcing the blade to the maximum distance possible.

The filming with the ROV's camera could only be done at slack water, between the tides, and no divers were put in the water at all, due to the strength of tide in the area.

At the original inquiry, Norrie Bremner, a greatly respected and successful Skipper, who'd fished the North Sea from Wick his entire career, had said there was far more tide running in this area, than the navigation chart for the region stated. I could certainly believe this. The huge rush of flood tide passing through the Pentland Firth was well known, and the wreck site wasn't too distant. This was borne out by the reluctance of the surveyors on *Fennica* to put divers in the water.

The visibility was only about six to ten feet and there was a mass of plankton particles in the water. There was a poignant moment when the camera looked into the galley and showed footage of white mugs, plates and cutlery in the sink and on the floor, half buried in silt. These utensils would have been used by the crew, not long before *Trident* foundered.

The JPE member, following his commentary, stated that in his opinion the vessel sank stern first vertically, landing on her transom. This, he said would have caused the damage to her stern plating.

In our next recess, both Nick and I disputed this statement, simultaneously saying this damage was caused by implosion, when internal air was compressed by the depth of water. I also pointed out that, had the ship sunk vertically, the crockery and cutlery would be at the back of the galley, not in the sink, on the floor and doorway. Also, had the vessel landed on her transom, the rudder, under the transom, would not have been jammed hard over.

I was amazed throughout the entire process at the depth of questioning into sometimes intricate, and occasionally irrelevant details. No stone was left unturned.

The members of the JPE had been on board *Fennica* and had expressed their dissatisfaction with the entire enterprise, which had cost an exorbitant sum. I could understand their frustration. I'd have liked to have been involved in the survey too. My presence would have enhanced my knowledge of the case but this had occurred long before I was invited to take part in the inquiry.

We'd now reached the end of March and were faced with another break.

It was late May before we reconvened and were now to concentrate on the principle of stability in general and *Trident's* in particular.

The vessel had been late in her delivery from the builder's yard. She was due to be signed for, and handed over on the Isle of Bute by the contractors, following an inclining and stability test. This survey was supposed to happen on the Friday, but due to the difficulty in getting a White Fish Authority representative to this isolated location, the survey was postponed.

Skipper Tait must have been extremely annoyed at not being able to get his vessel to sea, fishing. She was already overdue for delivery by many months, and I could understand his frustrations. I'm sure I would have felt the same. Even had the inclining test been undertaken, the surveyor would have had to take his data away to work up the figures. It would be at some unknown point in the future when the calculations would be completed.

Skipper Tait and his crew took *Trident* to sea.

I advised the court that when my vessel *Independence* was built in Fraserburgh, the stability book arrived in the post several months later. It would have been impractical to wait for the document before sailing.

* * *

The next period of the proceedings concerned the weather and tides. There were scientific hindcasts presented, giving historic evidence of the actual weather at the time of *Trident's* loss, which I found fascinating.

The first thing I noticed on entering the council chamber, standing on a table in the centre of the room, mounted on small chocks, was a scale model of *Trident*, made from her original plans.

The model was the product of a company from the Netherlands, commissioned to build the 1-14.5 model and to tank-test this vessel. The small boat would feature greatly in the following proceedings.

Companies from North America and Europe had tendered for this work, but the huge tank in Wageningen, operated by the Marin Co. had been selected, and was amazing. This company could simulate the swell from nearly all aspects of the wind.

The scientists operating the simulator tank had made hundreds of test-runs in different scenarios, all filmed, and on several of these runs in steeper waves, the model had capsized. This was fascinating, and very convincing.

What the tank-tests couldn't simulate, was the weight of wind and tide. I could imagine the strength of wind that would cause these big swells. Even more so, the amount of heavy spray this force of wind and wave would create. In my mind's eye, I could see the build-up of water on *Trident's* deck, and her inability to clear this deluge.

In tandem with the tank testing, a computerised simulation had also been run, with many variable scenarios. These calculations also predicted the vessel's capsize at critical points. According to the ship's stability data, even if *Trident* was intact, she would only heel to 47 degrees, before reaching the point of no return. This wasn't a massive margin of safety, and wouldn't be acceptable on modern vessels.

Trident also had a mini shelter from the top of her bulwark on her starboard side, to protect her accommodation doorway from weather. If the vessel had lain over on her starboard side at a critical angle, this structure would be partly under water and would act as a drogue, preventing her from righting.

I was captivated watching these many runs, and realised this was probably the scenario in which the seven crewmen had been lost, and what they must have encountered. The thought made me shiver.

I'd got the vision in my mind of *Trident* taking a big roll to starboard, causing the large spare net in front of the wheelhouse to wash across the deck into the scuppers, unravelling and blocking the already inadequate vents, causing her to list. The next sea, only a few seconds later would take her over. The crew would have been helpless to prevent the capsize.

The large net was never found, but there had been loose nylon netting in the rigging, and I could envisage this huge trawl deploying like a parachute as the vessel submerged.

While not being fully conversant with the scientific aspects, this was, in my opinion the cause of *Trident's* loss, and I reported this to the Judge and Mr MacWhirter at the first opportunity.

Both were interested in my potential scenario and the theory would be mentioned as part of the Sheriff Principal's final report.

* * *

I found Skipper Peter Johnson to be an extremely reliable witness from my perspective. He related how he'd steamed his new vessel, *Silver Lining* down to nor'ard from Peterhead, overnight in poor weather and the vessel had performed abysmally.

The judge interjected, saying, "don't you mean 'up' to nor'ard, Mr Johnson?"

"Down to nor'ard, m' Lord," the Skipper re stated.

I took the opportunity to explain to the Judge and the court that in fishing parlance, the Skipper was correct, and that in the North Sea, we went 'up' with the flood tide, or 'up to London' in a southerly direction and down with the ebb.

This did rather perplex the Sheriff briefly, but he accepted my explanation and allowed the witness to continue.

Skipper Johnson said *Silver Lining* had been carrying a large quantity of new, wooden fish boxes on her deck. When daylight came, there was hardly an intact box remaining. They'd been smashed to matchwood with the weight of water shipped on board. This was graphic evidence, and left me wondering what might have happened, had the vessel not had tons of ice and boxes below and the heavy seine rope, coiled below deck level. I dismissed this potential scenario with another shiver.

Following *Trident's* loss, *Silver Lining* had been compulsorily tied up and had lain in port for over a year before being lengthened by ten feet. She'd also had an additional ten tons of ballast added, which made her a much safer vessel with greater intact stability. This lay-up was a massive loss to Skipper/owner Johnson, but it was a financial loss. No further lives had been lost.

* * *

During a very long session lasting many days, relating to the principles of stability, The Torremolinos Convention was initially mentioned, then referred to several times subsequently. This international conference, held in 1977 related to fishing vessel stability and safety. Originally for vessels over 24 metres in length, nevertheless, the principle was acknowledged that fishing vessels of all sizes would benefit from the fitting of watertight shelter-decks. It was established that vessels could list up to 90 degrees and slightly more in some cases, without foundering, then come upright again.

This was revolutionary stuff and would save the lives of an unquantifiable number of fishermen throughout the world. The UK didn't initially sign up to this charter, but the use of shelter-decks, both for safety and comfort in smaller vessels would eventually become the norm. It was essential however, to keep water out of the enclosure, as Iain had learned the hard way.

Many vessels had been lost when water became trapped inside a confined space. A classic case was the loss of the cross-channel ferry, *Herald of Free Enterprise,* when she'd sailed from Zeebrugge with her car deck doors open. It had taken only a small quantity of water to flow through the bow doors for the vessel to founder, close to the Belgian port.

In Aberdeen the following week, a well-known ships' architect was being questioned by the barristers on his knowledge of steel fishing vessels and their stability. After listening to many of his answers over a prolonged period, I could tell he was bamboozling the court with his apparent knowledge. This expert had listed two and a half, A4, typed sheets with the names of the many vessels he'd designed.

On a day when the court had finished at lunchtime, I hired a car, driving along the Moray Firth to Rosehearty, where the son of the builder of *Emulator* lived. His father, Derry had passed away some years earlier, but I was able to chat to Rory Forbes, who'd been the shipyard foreman when she was built.

Rory confirmed information that I'd thought correct, relating to two vessels, *Coronella* and *Brenaline,* which the witness stated he'd designed, and Forbes yard had fitted out at the time of *Trident's* loss.

Next day at the end of the questioning, and given the opportunity, I addressed the witness. Holding up the A4 list, I said, "this is an impressive list of vessels, sir," then pausing for effect, went on, "how many of these vessels listed are of traditional wooden design, and how many are built of steel?"

I'd already confirmed that the boats listed were almost all of wooden construction. Only three vessels from the pages were built of steel and the witness reluctantly confirmed this.

I was now able to prove to the court with confidence that two of these steel vessels, *Coronella* and *Brenaline,* were berthed side by side in Fraserburgh harbour in May 1977, when I'd taken delivery of *Independence*. The pair of steel hulls had newly arrived from the fabricators and were awaiting fitting out. It would be the following year before the two would be ready for sea. At the time of the loss of *Trident* this witness had never been involved in steel vessels. My efforts had undermined the witness's credibility and I gained more nods of approval from the barristers.

Addressing the matter of the third steel vessel listed, I was able to add for the record, that this was *Guiding Light*. I'd towed the fabricated shell of this boat to Scotland with *Emulator* in 1984, from a yard on the River Hull, a tributary of the Humber. This was more than ten years after the loss of *Trident*.

* * *

I'd always flown north from Humberside Airport, but on one occasion the small plane was fully booked, so I was compelled to fly from Teesside to Aberdeen. It wasn't much of a problem. The flight went a little earlier and the distance to the airport was ten minutes longer, so this meant an earlier start.

It was still dark when I left home and the streets were quiet when I headed out of town. Between Scarborough and Burniston, the first village north, I approached two cars going quite slowly. I waited a while then, on what I knew to be a straight stretch, overtook both vehicles. The first was a small Peugeot car and the second, a green van with the word 'Arrow' on the side. A mile further on, in the village, I was stopped by a police car, manned by a friendly, smiling policewoman, who requested I waited until the Peugeot arrived.

It transpired this vehicle was an unmarked police car and had been shadowing the van as part of an operation, looking for sheep rustlers.

When the vehicle arrived, the Officer stepped out. Overweight, with a round, red face, he was quite overbearing and aggressive, saying I was driving at an excessive speed, and there could have been a milkman or a paperboy on the road.

I was most indignant and in reply, disagreed with his statement. I wasn't driving excessively fast and I was in the countryside. The cars in front of me were going too slow. The road wasn't in a built-up area. I explained that I had a flight to catch, and was involved in an important case in Aberdeen.

At this point the copper gave a nasty grin and said I had two choices. I could go to the police station with him and be interviewed, or accept a warning that involved me signing a form saying I wouldn't transgress speeding laws for the next twelve months, or would be penalised.

Given that I needed to get to the airport urgently, I signed the paper, leaving the unpleasant man behind, and was able to make my flight.

Totally incensed at the high-handed treatment, at the first opportunity I wrote to the Superintendent of Scarborough Police, naming the Officer and complaining of his attitude and unwarranted actions.

The official reply, when it arrived, offered me the options of accepting the warning, or my day in court. As there was no sign of an end to the *Trident* inquiry, and I probably wouldn't be free to attend court, I was left with no choice but to accept the former.

Unofficially, I heard from a policeman friend that the Officer in question had been spoken to by the Superintendent, and had been given a warning for his offhand manner, which would also last for twelve months.

"Good," I said. "He was a tosser."

My copper friend laughed and said, "that's funny, that's what he said about you."

I booked early for the Humberside flight the following week.

A few months later, while driving to Heathrow Airport with Dotty to collect a home-coming Sarah, our younger daughter, I passed a police car on the M1. Aware that my speed warning was still current, I was doing exactly seventy miles an hour. Despite this, I was flagged down by the speed cops and, worried about the order I was bound by, immediately protested that I wasn't speeding.

"No sir, you weren't," the first cop said. "We've noted you have a twelve-month marker against you on our computer, but could you tell me who you're insured with? We can't find any evidence of cover for this vehicle."

I was adamant I was insured, but couldn't remember who with. It was Saturday, so I couldn't ring the company I thought I might be with, or to get cover in the unlikely event I wasn't insured.

In answer to the "where are you going" question, I explained we were going to Heathrow to collect our daughter, inbound from Australia.

The second Officer, who was quite matter of fact and dispassionate said, "legally, we could seize this vehicle and take it to a compound until we establish your insurance circumstances.

Do you drive, Mrs Normandale?" the first policeman asked of Dotty.

Dotty affirmed and gave her car registration, which was checked on their computer.

"We'll allow you to continue your journey, Mrs Normandale, as long as you drive, and it's on your insurance."

Turning to me he said, "sort your cover out sir. Have a safe journey."

"Phew!" I said, sweating, as we left the scene. "That was close. We nearly didn't get to London," though I was still adamant the car was insured.

We made it to the airport in good time and it was wonderful to welcome our little girl back. There were lots of hugs and tears. The journey home was faultless. I did briefly wonder what Sarah would have done, had we not been there.

The following day, I checked the car's insurance policy, which I'd taken out online with a company called Simple Cover. I'd missed the renewal reminder, sent on line, by five months!

The fat cop who'd pulled me on the road to Teesside would have been delighted, had he known I wasn't insured when he stopped me. I've used a broker ever since, and get annual reminders by post and email.

* * *

The inquiry just seemed to go on and on, and though not sitting every week, the months passed.

A considerable amount of time was lost when the formidable, Ms Wilson, the Advocate General's barrister was laid low with an extremely serious illness. Much to everyone's relief, the lady did make a full recovery. During this break Dotty and I managed a trip to the West of Scotland, one of our favourite parts of the UK.

The proceedings were eventually completed in four separate sessions. It was almost mid-July before the inquiry was finally wound up. There'd been much summing up and thanks to and from each of the barristers. I was pleasantly surprised to be included in the thanks for my contributions on specific points.

The Sheriff Principal would subsequently issue his findings the following January, in a fifty-page document addressing all the points the inquiry had been set to examine. Both Nick MacWhirter and I, if satisfied, were required to countersign, saying we concurred with the Judge's findings. I was happy to concur with the report. Mr MacWhiter would add annotations to the document.

Pleasingly, we were commended by Sir Stephen for our contribution to the case.[13]

* * *

---

13 A shortened version of the official report can be found at the back of this
    book.

Not long after the case had started, I'd rung Dotty and she'd said, "you know we've always rented a chalet in Summer on the North Bay promenade, where we take the grandkids? Well there's an article in the local paper saying the Council are going to build new ones, and they're for sale. I've put £1000 down as a deposit."

Initially I thought this was good news. Our kids and grandkids had spent many Summers of pleasure on the beach, playing on the sands, in rockpools, and with body boards in the waves. The location of the chalet was very safe with no distractions, and there was a commanding view from the promenade to watch the youngsters. Then it occurred to me that this was, the deposit.

"'Ow much are they?" I asked in trepidation.

"Thirty-five thousand," came the unconcerned answer.

"Thirty-five thousand," I choked, "where are we gonna find that sort o' money?"

At the end of the case, the fee for my part in the nine-month, on and off, *Trident* Inquiry, including travel, accommodation and food expenses, within a couple of hundred pounds, came to this amount. The new chalet has since given many years of pleasure to family and friends, and has already been passed on to the next generation.

* * *

Soon after the case, I was back on board, *Lord Nelson,* sailing from Oban to Aberdeen, one of my favourite voyages. I loved the wild ruggedness of the Western Isles, Orkney and the Pentlands, though it was quite poignant when we passed a couple miles from the site of the lost *Trident.*

I'd identified the position of the wreck on the ship's chart, an hour earlier. The weather was fine and I found it difficult to believe a ship like *Trident* and her crew could be lost in foul conditions in this very place.

I thought it would be a good idea to invite Janie & Melody on board for a tour of Lord Nelson and a drink when we got to Aberdeen. I'd mentioned such a visit to the two ladies before the case had closed, suggesting they might want to have a look around the ship that had delayed the court proceedings so often.

The Granite City would be the end of the voyage and the fine weather meant there'd be a barbeque on the stern platform for all hands in the evening. These ladies had been a pair of angels throughout the court case, so it would be a great opportunity for me to repay them for their help and kindness.

It was a Friday and having texted Janie the evening before, she'd replied that they would both turn up at the ship, a few minutes from the court house, when they'd finished their work at 1700 hours.

I wasn't watching the time and was working for'ard when a message came over the speakers. "Can 'Fred the Fish' come to the bridge please. You have visitors."

Looking at my watch and realising my guests must have arrived, I headed for the gangway. I was wearing a pair of old trainers, baggy, work worn shorts, a dirty tee shirt, had unkempt hair and hadn't shaved for at least a week.

I hurried through the chartroom and met my young friends on the bridge, talking to Captain Barbara. Hearing me approach, the group looked in my direction.

"Good afternoon ladies," I called, smiling widely.

Hardly recognising me, in unison, the Scottish girls both exclaimed, "Mister Normandale!"

It was only then it occurred to me that throughout the past nine months of my intermittent visits to Aberdeen, these sweet young court officials had only seen me clean-shaven, suited and booted with a briefcase. My appearance must have been quite a shock.

Giving the pair a tour of the ship, which they thoroughly enjoyed, we ended at the stern platform, where the huge barbeque, newly lit, was filling the air with grey smoke. Upwind, the two Engineers, Marco and his second, Chips, each with a beer in hand, were not ready for cooking, and were in no hurry for Dave the Cook to bring the several trays of meats for the grill. Their speakers were blasting out music, none of which I recognised, but the sound seemed to find favour with the guests.

I made my apologies, and leaving the ladies in bad company, headed for the shower, razor and a change of clothes. I turned to see the new arrivals, already holding bottles, were chatting amiably to the engine boys.

Feeling a little more presentable, while taking no more than twenty minutes, I returned to find more bottles had been opened and all the secrets were out. The Engineers didn't recognise the 'Mr Normandale' from the court house, described by the girls. In turn, 'Fred the Fish', the clown who constantly made people laugh with his daft jokes, wasn't someone they could envisage.

"Hello, Fred the Fish," Janie said, grinning.

I returned a smile.

The voyage crew had now mostly returned to the ship after exploring and shopping in Aberdeen and were gathering by the mainmast, where the portable table was stacked high with plates, numerous salads, sauces and bread.

An announcement from the speakers requested all hands make their way to the bridge, where sundowners were being dispensed. "Sundowners? July? Aberdeen?" I thought. "That should be about ten o'clock tonight."

I escorted my guests to the bridge. The drink on offer was punch, but the liquid wasn't in a bowl. Earlier in the afternoon, the Engineers had found the biggest pan in the galley, then concocted an evil brew, which had been chilled with ice then stored in the vegetable locker. There were lots of bits of fruit floating in the mix, which helped to disguise the several bottles of spirits, thinned with juice and soda, plus anything alcoholic in part bottles that came to hand.

A rumour was spread that the pan also contained bilge water and old engine oil, which the grinning Engineers didn't deny.

An endless line of white plastic cups ensured a constant supply of drink for all, so the evening got off to a successful start as the punch did its work. By the time the vat was empty, the food was prepared and everyone in turn made the passage aft with an empty plate for something from the barbecue, then back midships to the table for the accompaniments.

People were sitting or standing all around the main deck and there was a wonderful camaraderie amongst the sailors from the voyage. The pair of Scottish lassies entered into the spirit, in more ways than one.

By 2100 hours my guests were ready for home, and with a taxi waiting at the quayside, I escorted the lovely ladies to the shore. I was the lucky recipient of a hug and kiss from each, they having thoroughly enjoyed the ship's hospitality.

* * *

Sometime later, I was on my way to Aberdeen once more to join *Lord Nelson* for a short trip, sailing to Douglas in the Isle of Man, on a leg of a Round Britain challenge. The ship had done more than half of the circumnavigation and we were to do another twenty-five percent, though the weather outlook was decidedly unsettled. It was Springtime, but a late and severe storm was growing, blowing in from the Arctic.

It was a pleasant journey to Aberdeen by train. My previous, frequent passages had, by necessity been air travel. The scenery throughout this rail trip was spectacular and from Newcastle north, a significant amount to the east is coastal. Alnmouth, Holy Island and Berwick in England, then, leaving Edinburgh, the huge Firth of Forth and Bridge, with great views of the parallel road bridge, shipping and little harbours and islands below.

We crossed the Tay Bridge, then further north, passing lots of stunning little coves and historic ruins. Drawing into Aberdeen from the south, there was endless evidence of the city's links with the oil industry with acres of hardware, destined for the North Sea.

I arrived at the ship, only a few minutes walking distance from the station to find the voyage crew from the previous voyage leaving. A hired coach was on the quay, awaiting many of those departing for the return journey to Tyneside.

Graham, a wheelchair bound watch-leader was one of the first down the gangway. He was lowered backwards, a heaving line around the front wheels of the chair, which was slackened as required by willing hands, the Bosun holding the chair handles. Graham's passage ashore was well practised, smooth and easy.

Greeting the old shipmate from South Shields, we chatted about the voyage for a while and our recent and future planned trips, then I looked towards the gangway, to see Naomi about to step on at the top. Rushing to the bottom of the aluminium access, I timed my ascent to meet 'Nomes' mid-way, but of course, Naomi couldn't see me.

This adventurous lady had only vague, peripheral, dim vision, but had a great sense of spatial awareness. She had a perplexed look on her face, knowing there was someone coming in the other direction and she stopped, holding onto the manropes as I drew close. We met in the middle.

Putting my arms around her waist, I whispered, "hello, Lovely Lady," and saw a huge smile of recognition come to her face.

"Fred the Fish, you're just joining. That's dreadful timing, I'm just leaving."

Fred & Naomi – unknown

I squeezed past her to grab her bag from the bridge, then turned to follow her to the quay, where we could talk. We'd sailed together many times and Naomi, despite her lack of sight loved nothing better than to be aloft, out on the yards, working on the rigging or stowing sails.

I reminded her of a time awhile back, when the ship had recently changed a tops'l. The 'head' of the sail, with brass eyelets equally spaced a short distance apart, was fastened on to the rail running the length of the yard with short nylon strops, 'rail bands'. Though the sail was secure, the rail band ends required stitching to prevent the lashings from working free.

My job for the afternoon was to stitch the rail bands and Nomes had volunteered to help. The plan was that, starting in the middle of the yard, we'd work outwards. I'd make the first stitch then, with another needle, move out to the next band. Nomes would follow up, finishing the job. When I heard a little, "ouch," I knew my assistant had found the needle. There were no complaints.

Between us, we accomplished our work on both sides, and Naomi had the bloodied fingers to prove it. She did complain, wrongly, that I'd made the work too easy for her.

* * *

The coach left the quay with much waving, then I boarded the ship, dropping my bag by the main mast. I entered the upper mess to see who I'd be sailing with on this voyage. There was a nucleus of Captains and Officers within the Jubilee Trust, so many permutations were possible and there'd been changes in personnel over the years.

The Captain for this voyage was Darren, who'd originally been Bosun on the ship, prior to my joining the JST. Darren, well-tanned with tousled dark hair and bushy sideburns was small in stature, though stocky and powerful. This was an extremely competent Captain, confident and being approachable, was a good man to sail with.

At the morning meeting, prior to the voyage crew arriving, Darren explained the dilemma the forecasted weather was presenting. He also said we were to carry a film crew, who were intending to make a film of the voyage for a television programme. At this point I met Alison, the other Bosun's mate for the next voyage. Ali was a Glasgow lass, about 30, and was really enthusiastic about sailing as a BM.

Tall, thin with dark hair in a ponytail, Ali, I later learned was a free spirit who loved adventure, spending much of the Summer months riding around the country on her bike, carrying her tent, stopping wherever looked interesting.

Unprecedented, the Bosun and his two BMs were called to the Captain's cabin, where we found 'the Old Man' staring at a screen filled with thick, red arrows pointing downwards. "This is what we're faced with folks," Darren said, pointing to the screen. "This massive low is here for at least forty-eight hours. Any thoughts?"

I studied the chart for a while, thinking like a fisherman, then suggested we could get a lee from the worst of the weather if we were to go north round Kinnards Head into the Moray Firth. We could then hug the coast, almost to Duncansby Head, at which point it wasn't far across the Pentland Firth to enter Scapa Flow. We'd be head to wind.

We could exit to the west near Stromness, out into the Atlantic, from where we could head south. The downside was getting into the Moray Firth. We'd be exposed to the weather for many miles, initially.

To his credit, the Captain did consider this option, but dismissed the suggestion, saying he daren't risk breaking the crew or the ship. He spent a short while stepping off the miles roughly with thumb and forefinger then announced, "we're sailing this afternoon as soon as there's sufficient water, and we're going 'south about'."

"Wow!" I said, "we're going t' do 270 degrees." This was a radical, but ingenious solution to the problem. We were to make the passage under engines, and would be a little late arriving, but would get *Nelly* to her destination intact.

All hands were summoned to the lower mess, where our Captain announced his plan. He said the weather forecast was appalling, and the wind was beginning to freshen already. We were leaving in a few hours and going out into bad weather. If anyone didn't wish to sail, they were welcome to leave. He fully understood, and it wouldn't a problem.

Only one person chose not to sail, but unfortunately this big Scotsman was the Cook's assistant. This meant some additional work would likely as not, fall to the Bosun's mates. I looked at Ali and rolled my eyes, but then, luckily for us, an experienced, regular sailor, Mags, volunteered to fill the vacant berth. Wonderful! Mags, from Carlisle, had been sailing for many years and was a good, all round hand.

As we left the lower mess, I overheard one of the newly-joined voyage crew saying loudly, "that's a shame. I love being at sea in bad weather."

I couldn't resist a comment. Turning to the speaker, equally loudly, I said, "if you think yer like being at sea in bad weather, you 'aven't been t' sea in bad weather!"

As *Nelly* motored down the River Dee to the harbour entrance, Ali and I spent useful time securing and lashing down the mooring ropes and anything else that could move on top of the coach house roof.

"There's gonna be a few seasick sailors t' clean up after, this trip, Ali," I said, giving a wry smile.

"Oh no!" she said, grimacing. "I canna dae that. Ah'll hae a go at anythin' else, but I canna clean spew up!"

"Ah well, things'll get sorted," I replied, unconcerned, completing the lashings.

We slipped the pilot before leaving the shelter of the North Pier and once clear, in the freshening gale, *Nelly* began to roll. The fore and aft sails were quickly set, to ease the motion. Once beyond the south breakwater, the ship, still rolling heavily, was brought gradually to starboard on to a quartering sea. Abreast of, and well clear of Girdle Ness, the ship's course was altered more to the south and the effect of the heading change, was immediate. The fore tops'l was set and *Nelly* settled down in a south south-easterly direction and was soon hurtling downhill before the following wind and tide. The next land we would see would be the Norfolk Coast.

We spent the whole of the following day at sea, surging along without mishap, the film crew getting plenty of footage and conducting interviews. By breakfast the following day, with the wind now below gale force, we spied North Norfolk to starboard. Amazingly, we'd averaged well over ten knots. Mid-morning saw us passing Lowestoft, the easternmost point in the UK, and before dark we were in the Dover Straits. What an unbelievable passage!

Another morning and we'd passed St Catherine's Point on the southern end of the Isle of Wight. Sailing across the wind now, we set more sails, though continued to motor. Start Point was the next major landfall and the following morning we handed sail and eased into Falmouth Bay, where we dropped the hook. The film crew had sufficient footage and were keen to leave the ship.

Thousands of sailing ships must have anchored here over the past hundred and fifty years or more, before radio communications. LEFO was a well-known acronym in Merchant Navy parlance of old. Land's End for Orders. Falmouth was the first calling point in the UK, and ships Masters would contact agents or owners for their next port of call. There must have been many a sailor hoping for a UK destination, only to find himself trans-Atlantic again.

A small local boat serviced the trans-shipment, taking the television crew and their heaps of equipment ashore into the famous old port. Falmouth had been on my 'to see' list for some time, but I didn't manage to visit on this occasion.

We picked up the hook early on the following morning. Ali became a 'hooker', which she found greatly amusing. This overnight stay would allow us to arrive at our destination, Douglas, at high water.

South from Falmouth, we rounded, The Lizard, the UK's most southerly point, then headed west towards Land's End. We now had a fair wind and with all sails flying, for the first time during this voyage, the motors were stopped. We were under sail without engines, making good speed, crossing the Bristol Channel.

Lundy Island was out of sight to the east and St David's Head fine on the starboard bow. This course allowed us, overnight, to enter St George's Channel, passing to the west of the Bishops Rock group and the Irish Coast.

Before daylight we were midway between Dublin and Anglesey, with the Isle of Man ahead. It was 60 miles to our destination.

Sails handed and stowed, we entered Douglas, tying up to an old barge; not the best berth, but no one was too bothered. We'd arrived at our destination and were less than 24 hours late. Had we not called into Falmouth, we'd have been on time. What an amazing passage.

Captain Darren had ordered 20 takeaway pizzas to be delivered, which fed all hands before we prepared to leave the ship. Before departing, a hastily produced certificate was handed out to each, showing a map of the UK with the missive, 'The Long Way Round', with an arrow showing 270 degrees, clockwise from port to port. The word 'Long' was crossed out and the word, 'Wrong' was written in.

I was on the next ferry for Liverpool and a short taxi ride found me in Lime St Station. A direct train was waiting, and in less than three hours, I was back in Scarborough. What a trip!

CHAPTER 19

HELICOPTER RIDE

I joined *Nelly* in Whitby again, soon after she docked, saying hello to friends who'd done the recent trip, and who were now leaving the ship. They had great tales to tell of their voyage. Little did I know I'd have a big story to tell of the less than epic passage I was about to undertake.

Meanwhile, tonight there would be a reception on board. In conjunction with Arnold Locker, a former fisherman, now vessel owner and fish merchant, I was taking advantage of the ship being in Whitby to host a fundraising event on board. We'd each invite thirty-five guests to an evening of superb seafood, wine and music. We'd done this before a few years earlier, and the occasion had been a great success, raising a large sum for the JST.

Colin and I spent the afternoon shucking two sacks of king scallops while Arnold provided lobsters, crabs, salmon and quality beef for the cook to prepare. Cookie Dave, on what should have been an easy day, also turned out various salads and lots of home baked bread.

The Co-op store across the road was the source of copious quantities of wine, and there was a well-stocked bar below for other requirements.

The invitations specified the possibility of a mast climb for those who hadn't yet consumed alcohol.

Seven o'clock arrived and so did dozens of guests in mini buses and taxis, plus the Mayor of Scarborough and Whitby, Councillor Tom Fox, a personal friend who arrived in the civic vehicle. As his wife Ros wasn't available, Dotty was an honorary Mayoress for the evening, arriving in the chauffeur-driven car.

Music and singing struck up on the foredeck, performed by a talented young couple with guitars. Some guests gravitated for'ard, having helped themselves to the exceptional seafood, salads, wines and beer from the laden tables at the main mast.

Having established who wished to climb; about a dozen of both sexes, these adventurous folks were fitted with climbing harnesses, checked then safety-briefed. As the yards were braced to port, each in turn made their way up the for'ard starboard rigging towards the futtock shrouds. Col, who was Bosun's mate for the next trip, was on the platform. I positioned myself beneath, encouraging and directing hands and feet, occasionally offering a shoulder to a needy bottom.

All did well to clamber outwards, leaning back before gaining the safety of the platform. Next a few of the volunteers were encouraged to step out onto the tops'l yard, and would later have bruises to prove this. Colin, from the middle of the yard, unhelpfully called out the old favourite, "if you fall off, it'll be splash or splat!"

"We don't need to know that," came a wail from someone on the extreme end of the yard, overhanging the pier.

The climbers all returned to the deck relatively unscathed and quickly joined the party, catching up with the festivities.

The food and drink were almost depleted and the whole evening had gone down a storm. The 2300 hours deadline came and went. "Come on lads an' lasses, it's bed time," I urged the Whitby stragglers, but it was still nearly midnight before the ragged remnants of guests staggered down the gangway.

The Scarborough contingent, with transport arrangements in place had left earlier. I'd given Dotty a kiss and hug before she travelled back home in style with the Mayor.

Next morning, despite hangovers, there was much cleaning of the ship to be done in readiness for the new voyage crew making the passage south.

As it transpired, we couldn't sail on Saturday evening as planned, as there was no pilot available. It seems the Harbour Master, who doubles as pilot, was taking his wife out that evening, so we'd have to wait 12 hours and sail on the morning tide, by which time a fresh easterly breeze had set in.

Late in the morning, pilot on board, *Nelly* cast off from shore and minutes later squeezed through the narrow gap of the opened, swing bridge, where scores of visitors were waving and watching our departure. Passing the new lifeboat shed to starboard then fish market to port, we were soon approaching the iconic Whitby piers, shaped like a whale's jawbone. Once through the narrow mouth, our ship began to roll to the swell as her head pointed north towards the Bell Buoy and safe navigable water. The pilot boat, an ex-Tyne class RNLI lifeboat was soon alongside to take the maritime advisor back ashore.

Col and I, now clad in oilskins against the spray, tightened the bottle-screws, securing the anchors from banging in the hawse pipes, in readiness for the passage to London.

Rounding the buoy and heading into the wind and swell, *Nelly's* head began to lift and drop sharply. Richard the Mate, , ever safety conscious, came forward, directing us to shut the bow doors, which would close off the bowsprit.

Uniquely, *Lord Nelson's* bowsprit was a platform with metal gratings. The structure was wide enough for wheelchair access in fine weather, but not today.

Having previously had squashed fingers and blackened nails; I had good reason to dislike these bow doors, treating them with cautious respect. Little did I know they were about to get me again.

The heavy doors consisted of three, hinged, overlapping parts. The first section was an iron flap, fifteen inches in height when in position, but this piece usually lay flush to the deck, forward onto the bowsprit. Col and I grabbed a side handle each and hauling together, pulled this hinged deadweight upwards, each slotting home a large steel bolt to secure this first section into position, about thirty degrees forward from vertical.

Stepping over this barrier, I went for'ard to un lash the starboard door, which was fastened back to the handrails with light cord. The ship was now ploughing deeply into the seas, water shooting up through the gratings from every wave. Facing forward I felt *Nelly's* head lift to a bigger than average swell and I held on to both handrails, knowing she was about to bury her head.

Her stem went down, ploughing deeply into the next big sea and I braced myself ready for a dousing. The platform went under and I felt icy water shooting up the legs of my oilskins, filling my boots instantly before reaching thighs, then surging to my waist.

I felt myself being lifted from the deck and very briefly was suspended in mid-air/water and my hands slid along the railings. Amazingly, I was still upright. My joy at not being thrown down was exceedingly short lived. Unbelievably, for the brief instant that I was no longer attached to the vessel, she moved forward, and I felt an agonising pain as the iron flap we'd, only a minute earlier fixed in position, impacted with my left calf. The pain was indescribable.

I looked to Colin for help, but he was down on the deck, his glasses hanging from one ear, damaged, fighting to get to his feet.

Somehow, I must have managed to get over the iron flap and back onto the main deck, away from further danger, though have no recollection of how I got there.

Col had now pulled himself upright and was holding onto the windlass, glasses temporarily back in place. He saw me standing on my good leg, hanging on to a brace of belaying pins on the starboard side, close by the flap. I was grimacing and feeling physically sick from the pain.

It must only have been an instinctive question, but Col called, "are you alright?"

Through gritted teeth and in agony I croaked, "do ah fuckin' look alright?"

Poor Colin. He didn't deserve my volley. He's one of the most gentle, caring people I've ever met. I thought I must have upset him, as when I looked again, I was on my own, immobile for what seemed ages, with no one coming to help me. After standing for some minutes, the nausea subsiding slightly, in excruciating pain, I somehow, on one leg, made my way slowly down the starboard side. It was here, Jo, the Medical Purser found me.

Jo, a small, competent, bespectacled, Cornish lass with short, dark hair, asked what had happened and what my injury was.

"Ah think me leg's broke," I croaked.

Leaving me briefly and hurrying below, Jo returned with a wheelchair and now, with assistance from Col, who'd located and summoned the nurse, took me down the disabled access lift, to the sick bay, aft on the port side. This berth also doubled as Jo's cabin.

My oilskins were baggy and with care from the helpers, were not too difficult to remove. Not so my sodden trousers, which were sticking to my legs and were cut away. Amazingly, though lacerated and bleeding at the impact zone, the skin had not opened. The imprint of the flap was clearly indented on my calf.[14] The oilskins and trousers had saved the leg from any cut.

With assistance I transferred from the wheelchair to the bed on the port side. Jo gently cleaned and bandaged the abrasion then fitted an inflatable splint around the entire leg to immobilise the limb, which helped immediately.

Captain Chris entered the little cabin to assess the situation. "What's the problem? What happened?" He enquired, knowing he'd have decisions to make on my behalf.

I explained the circumstances, then Jo gave her assessment of a 'possible broken leg'.

"It's an 'elicopter job ah'm afraid, Captain," I muttered, knowing the ship couldn't get back into Whitby now the tide had turned.

"We'll find a lee and get you into the Whitby lifeboat," he said, thinking out loud.

"T' wind's easterly," I replied. "There's no lee to be 'ad anywhere on this coast. This is ma stompin' ground. It'll 'ave t' be a chopper."

---

14 The impact mark remains to this day and is still numb.

The thought of being transferred by stretcher to a lifeboat with this swell running was a no-no in my book. I could end my days strapped in a straightjacket, trapped between the two vessels, not to mention the embarrassment of being taken off by the Whitby lifeboat. It wasn't long since I'd been the Operations Manager of Scarborough lifeboat and there was always great rivalry between stations.

The Captain left the sickbay in silence to contact the coastguard.

"I've been tryin' t' get in t' this bed fo' years," I croaked at Jo, attempting to lighten the seriousness.

"Only in your dreams," she promptly replied.

It was nearly an hour later when a message came down from the bridge that a helicopter would be over the ship in ten minutes. I was helped into the wheelchair by Jo and Colin, then taken in the lift to the top of the companionway. The chair was halted inside the doorway out of the wind, weather and curious eyes.

I'd only been sitting for a couple of minutes when a wave of warmth came over me and I felt myself fading and weakening. "Ahm goin'," I whispered, then nothing.

With no idea how long I'd been absent from the world, the next thing I sensed was the most amazing feeling of wellbeing and a vivid array of light in my head, brightening to an unbelievable intensity, then I opened my eyes.

I was no longer in the wheelchair but lying on the deck, wrapped in blankets with a pillow under my head. Several concerned faces were looking down on me, including a new, unknown, very pale, young, blond-haired lady.

"Ullo," I said, shakily. "Ah think ah went out."

I later thought, if that's what dying's like, I won't be afraid, when it's my turn to go.

There seemed relief at my emergence from wherever I'd been. The young blond was a paramedic who'd been dropped from the helicopter to check out the casualty, before lifting off.

She was beginning to look like a casualty herself; her complexion ashen. It must have been difficult for her to be dropped onto a pitching deck wearing a personal survival suit in Mid-Summer, but she was attempting to remain professional and reassure me. This rescue must have been one of her first offshore assignments, as the RAF's Sea King, search and rescue helicopters had recently been withdrawn. This service had been taken over by civilian operators with new Sikorsky aircraft, though were still under the direction of the coastguard.

I was lifted into a rigid stretcher that had arrived on the ship with the paramedic, then was strapped securely into position. There was a clatter of helicopter rotors hovering over the ship, then willing hands gathered round, grabbing stretcher handles and strops, carrying me to the ship's stern, where I was gently placed on the platform.

"Please don't let 'em broadcast this, or contact me Missus," I pleaded with Jo. "It'll create panic at 'ome. Ah've got me phone an' will ring 'er when I 'ave definite news."

At my request, Jo assured me the ship would keep an embargo on the incident for the time being. It was the weekend, so there'd only be an emergency contact in the JST office, which I wouldn't need.

I watched helplessly as the chopper's thin wire, weight on the end, dangled in mid-air, drawing closer. The grey and red-painted aircraft with, 'Coastguard' easily visible on the fuselage, was hovering into position. Captain Chris would be keeping a steady course with the wind on the bow. I'd done this several times when fishing, either having a casualty taken off, or assisting the RAF with exercises for this very task.

The chopper's wire drew close, was grabbed, then clipped to my stretcher. As I looked up, I could see a slack bight of wire, which was slowly being hauled in by the winchman, positioned near the opened doorway. The line was drawing tight when the stern of the ship dropped into a deep trough between two waves. The resulting effect was instantaneous. I shot into the air as if on a giant bungy-rope and my purely involuntary reaction was to yell, "fuckin' 'ell!"

There was a dual effect, because, as the ship dropped in the swell, the young, blond medic, who was clipped onto the wire with me, promptly vomited on my chest.

I didn't hear any comments from the deck as we left the ship, but the incident was witnessed by those watching my departure, as I later discovered when the tale was recounted in the ship's bar.

"Is there any chance yer could tek me t' Scarborough Hospital?" I requested, when inside the aircraft. "Ah live there, an' it'd be really 'andy fo' me Missus t' visit."

"Sorry, we're based in Humberside, so we have to take you there," was the apologetic reply from the crewman who'd guided me through the doorway.

The helicopter flew along the coast and over Scarborough's North Bay, though I didn't know this, being horizontal. The aircraft was clearly visible to Dotty and Sarah, who were on the shore on the north side of town. The pair commented on how low the chopper was, not knowing I was inside the machine.

The flight was about half an hour, and on landing I could see an ambulance waiting, through the newly opened door. After profuse thanks to the emerging pilot and crew, I was loaded into the next transport by a couple of cheerful, efficient paramedics, a lovely young lady with brown hair, in a pony tail and a dark-haired young chap. The pair seemed to gel, and enjoy working together.

I was transported across the Humber Bridge to the Hull Royal Infirmary where my swift attention to date, now slowed to a crawl when I was taken through the entry doors into the A&E department.

There were so many people waiting to be registered and attended to, that the queue to the treatment bays lead down the corridor from the entrance.

The wait for registration took about twenty minutes, during which, the paramedics had to remain with me, but the pair continued to chat and seemed really interested in the work of the Jubilee Sailing Trust.

Once in the system my new friends departed to their next pick up, leaving me to wait my turn. The treatment was going to be some time, but I was feeling much happier now I was in the right place, so took the opportunity to ring Dotty.

"Ullo," I said, when Dotty answered the phone. "There's no need t' panic, but ah'm in Hull Royal." This wasn't the first time in our married life I'd rung with bad news, and my lovely wife had taken the situation well.

After I'd explained what had happened, and said it would be a while before I received treatment, Dotty decided to drive to Hull to see me, but to pack an overnight bag and stay with son, Danny and wife, Jane, who lived near the Humber Bridge.

My turn for assessment eventually came, and my leg was examined by one of the doctors, who immediately sent me for an x-ray.

I was wheeled to the Radiology Department by a friendly, volunteer porter, one of many men and women working willingly, for the benefit of the patients in our hospitals.

The x-ray was performed by an extremely efficient, if overworked, young Portuguese radiologist, didn't seem at all concerned by the hustle and bustle of the emergency department's demands.

"Is it like this all the time?" I asked, while he was setting up his 'photo shot'.

"No, sometimes it gets very busy," he replied, eyes twinkling and with a slight smile.

"I guess a sense o' humour is essential in this line o' work," I suggested.

Back to the A&E department, which had a sea of new faces, I spotted my ambulance crew, now waiting with a new customer. I gave them a wave.

My results were through and the good news was, my left leg wasn't broken, though the calf had sustained severe tissue damage. There was a possibility of thrombosis with the compression the leg had sustained on impact. "So far, so good," I thought.

"I'd like to keep you in overnight for observation," said the young, bespectacled Indian doctor, as he assessed my x-ray. "Your leg's not broken, but it has sustained huge muscle damage."

"Well that's a blessin'," I said, greatly relieved. "Ah was 'oping yer'd keep me in."

But then he added, "I'd like to keep you here, but as you can see, we're extremely busy, and we have no room. I'm going to send you home, but if your leg gives you any trouble at all, come straight back in. The nurse will get you some crutches. Do you have transport to get home?"

"Ah live in Scarborough," I replied. "It's fifty miles from 'ere. My Missus will be 'ere shortly, an' will tek me 'ome, but if I 'ave any trouble, it's a long way t' come back."

"Then you must go straight to your local hospital." came the reply.

"That's where ah wanted t' go to in t' first place," I muttered, then Dotty appeared.

Realising I was in one piece, she rolled her eyes and with a wry smile said, "what have you done now?"

"Just a little accident," I replied with a half-smile in return. "I've 'ad a bit of a goin' on with an iron door, an' came second," then added, "but t' good news is, me leg's not broke, an' ah can go 'ome."

This last piece of news, strangely, didn't find favour, then I discovered her plan was to stay overnight. A meal and a bottle of wine had been envisaged following her hospital visit. She would return the following morning to take me home.

I was given a pair of crutches, which I immediately tried to use back to front, until shown otherwise by the porter. I'd never used crutches before.

The journey back was difficult, as I was sitting sideways on the rear seat with my leg elevated. Conversation was difficult as I felt stupid, and couldn't think of anything to say. I'd been going to sea, all my life, in all weathers, working with heavy gear and big catches, then been injured shutting a door in half a gale of wind.

If I thought it was difficult getting from the car into the house, it was doubly so trying to get upstairs. I resorted to shuffling up each step backwards on my bottom, and during the night, after one attempt to get along the landing for a pee, resorted to a bucket for the next week.

Next day the leg was becoming more painful so I asked Dotty to drop me off at Scarborough Hospital, having a concern that I may have a DVT. (deep vein thrombosis)

Reporting to the reception, I subsequently spent a considerable amount of time lying on a bed in A&E with no attention. I was getting a little stressed when a doctor walked past the cubicle, briefcase in hand. He glanced in as he passed, then did a double take and came back.

"Hello, Fred, what are you doing here? What have you been up to?"

This was Andy Volens, an A&E doctor, who was also an author and member of the Scarborough Yacht Club. We'd shared a stall together, along with Alana, my stalwart office manager the previous Summer, selling our books at the Seafest weekend on the West Pier.

"I was on my way home, but I'll sort you out before I go," he kindly offered.

True to his word, the good doctor listened to my story with interest, then examined my leg, which was starting to blacken with bruising. He said, "You did quite right to come in. I think you're ok. It's probably the bruising coming out, and the body's defences kicking in, causing you discomfort. You've had a hell of a bang. Come back tomorrow and I'll get you an appointment for a DVT scan."

How good was that? This news was just so reassuring, and an early appointment to boot!

Back at the hospital next day, I hobbled into the A& E department on the sticks, which I was now getting used to, and received another examination by the good doctor, then was sent for a thorough DVT scan. This screening was conducted by a very competent nurse, who, after the smearing of lubricant round the affected limb, ran a probe carefully across the surface while monitoring a laptop computer. After a searching test, the pleasant young lady was pleased to announce the scan had proved negative for any vein blockage.

"Fantastic!" I said with an overwhelming feeling of relief. "Ah've got the all clear. Wonderful."

The nurse also observed and commented on the bruising on the lower limb, around the impact mark.

Had the lady seen the same leg a couple of days later, she may have been surprised. The entire leg was black and blue from my groin to the underside of my foot.

Informed I was discharged, I asked what might be available in the way of physiotherapy. My calf was mostly numb.

"We can put you on the waiting list, but you'll be waiting months," she said. "You need attention now. Try the local rugby club. They have a good treatment room for players and public."

Pleased with the advice, I left the hospital, thanking everyone I'd encountered, returning later with boxes of chocolates to thank the departments I'd passed through. I considered myself the luckiest person in the world. How much worse could this situation have been? My calf had taken the full impact of the ship, and though I was going to be on sticks for some time, I'd survived the accident with no life-changing injury.

I visited the rugby club every couple of days for two weeks, where the programme, based on stretching the foot forwards and backwards, helped to regain some mobility. It was as if the impact had compressed tendons, which were not stretching fully. I continued with the exercises.

Being housebound, I was a dreadful patient and Dotty didn't enjoy being nursemaid, though she did take good care of me and my needs. I suspect she'd thought about what might have been. Had I been facing aft, my shin would have shattered. Had I been further forward on the bowsprit, I might have gone over the side.

Relief came early on Friday evening in the form of Colin, newly home from the ship. He'd turned up to chauffeur me to the Leeds

Arms and touchingly, brought a glossy, lithograph print of *Lord Nelson,* signed on the reverse by everyone who'd been on board. It said, 'Fred the Fish, get well soon'.

Colin was a popular character, a great shipmate and was very thoughtful. I'd felt guilty bawling him out when I'd had the accident, but the pain had been excruciating. We'd sailed together many times, and got on really well, though this was certainly an attraction of opposites. Col was meticulous with everything he did, whether, cleaning, cooking, packing, painting or dressing. He shaved twice a day, and was so full of energy. It was said on the ship that if one of his feet was nailed to the deck, he'd run in circles. He was the best Cook's assistant in the JST, bar none. Being a professional baker, he would also bake bread, cook shortbread for Smoko and would make birthday cakes for anyone lucky enough to have a birthday on board. Normally these were jobs the Cook would do.

It was amusing on the only occasion Colin sailed as watch-leader. It was like watching a mother hen at work. He felt personally responsible for his collective brood and took on all their problems.

I, on the other hand, worked at a steady pace, was scruffy, shaving maybe once a week and didn't so much pack, as throw stuff in a bag and zip it up. I was competent with seamanship, ropes, netting and rigging. We were extremes, but somehow met in the middle and were good pals and shipmates.

Col enjoyed nights ashore but was easily led astray, especially when in the company of Cookie Dave and Marco. I'd be ready for my bunk before midnight and would announce my departure.

"We'll just have one for the road," would be the reply, followed by grins.

Knowing the real significance of what, 'one for the road', meant, I'd make my exit. It would usually be between 0200 and 0300hrs when the party goers returned, and I'd invariably hear them come aboard.

To their credit, no matter what time the bunch arrived back on the ship, the galley team would be 'on parade', ready for a long day, soon after 0600.

* * *

The next five weeks passed slowly, but I was philosophical, and knew I was getting better all the time, and would make a good recovery. I could now get back and forth to the pub under my own steam on crutches, occasionally meeting Col. Dotty and I could go out for the odd meal, though I wasn't able to drive.

Eleven weeks after the accident, I was back on the ship in Southampton, ready for another voyage. I walked into the upper mess at dinner time.

The cheery crew were pleased to see me. Richard, the Mate, (soon to be Captain) said, "Ah! Fred, can you go for'ard and close the bow doors, please."

My answer was in the negative, but with a few expletives included.

CHAPTER 20

FISHING

We'd caught lots of fish over the years on *Lord Nelson* and fed the crew many meals. There'd been times when the line had parted, or we'd hauled a fish close to the ship, only to lose the catch. These were dorado or various types of tuna.

Bound for Malaga and passing through the Straits of Gibraltar, we'd taken eight bluefin tuna, each around 20lbs in two hours. We lost several bigger ones.

On a voyage from Antigua to Bermuda, the shout, "fish on," from someone on the bridge was heard, and both Marco and I dashed to the stern platform. Others gathered to watch the action.

The Engineer was hauling the line and the indications were that this was a big fish. I reached for the gaff, the long wooden pole with a large, unbarbed hook secured on the end.

Looking into the wake, we could see a big fish splashing on the surface as the unknown catch was drawn towards the ship.

"Hey! It's a blue marlin," Marco shouted, enthusiastically.

I was equally excited. The shimmering, translucent blue skin was spectacular as the fish threshed below the platform. The marlin hadn't swallowed the hook. The double-barbed lure was caught in the fish's beak.

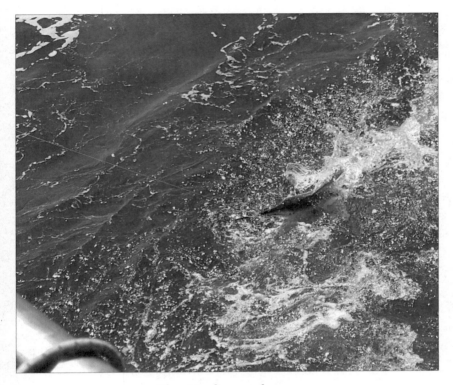

Blue Marlin – unknown

"Gaff it," Marco shouted, and I reached over the top rail with the pole. Leaning out, even at the full extent of my reach, the hook was hardly breaking the surface. When I did get the hook into the water, I couldn't get any leverage, as the movement of the ship through the water, was acting on the gaff.

Had the thought occurred to me at the time, I'd have leaned through the railings to get closer to the thrashing fish. In the excitement, this initiative was lost.

After several frustrating, unsuccessful pulls with the gaff, and worried I was going to tear the hook from the fish, I shouted, "lift the bugger in. The 'ook looks well stuck."

"Are you sure?" Marco asked, doubtfully.

"Yer'll 'ave t'. Ah can't get the bloody gaff in it."

Against his better judgement the Engineer began to haul the shimmering beauty from the water. As he did so, I raised the pole again for another stab at the fish. Before I could draw the gaff towards me, the marlin disgorged the lure and dropped back into the sea, vanishing immediately to a universal, "Oohh!"

I was mortified, as was Marco. I accepted full responsibility and made apologies over and over. It would have been fantastic to have a caught a marlin.

Next day, having slept on the loss, and knowing I'd seen this magnificent creature, I had a change of heart. For the first time in my life I was pleased a fish had got away, but not before I'd been privileged to have viewed the shimmering beauty. "Ah mus' be gettin' soft," I thought to myself.

* * *

On a voyage north from London to Hartlepool, having anchored off Scarborough overnight, *Lord Nelson's* sails were set and she continued her voyage north.

It was late afternoon off the Yorkshire coast and I suspected there'd be mackerel around. I mentioned this to Bill, my Scots Skipper, BM pal. Within minutes Billy had a line with a spinner attached, streaming astern on the surface.

"They'll be deeper than that, Billy," I suggested. "It's bright today. We need t' get down to 'em."

Finding a reel of catgut in the communal tackle box, I attached a swivel and a string of half a dozen feathers on the end, then a six-ounce weight. Pulling at least twenty-five fathoms from the reel, I hitched the line to the railing then, lifting the weight and hooks carefully over the side, let go of the line, allowing the tackle to drop into the wake. The gut snaked out rapidly as the lead weight sank, then began to run astern before coming taught at the knot. Grabbing the line, I felt for movement and could feel the kicking of mackerel.

"Fish on," I called to Billy, laughing. "We're in business." Pulling the line in smoothly, trying not to jerk the fish off, I lifted three, good-sized, threshing mackerel over the rail. Silver-bellied, with olive green and black, zebra-like markings, every fish was different.

The happy Scot quickly hauled in the spinner, switched for feathers and found a weight. While he was re-rigging, I'd brought a bucket from the nearby cleaning locker, dropping the still wriggling fish into the pail. Seconds later my line was dropped back in the water.

"Fish on," I called again.

Fraggle dropped his line to starboard, allowing it to run through his hands as I was pulling in four more fish on the port side.

"Fish on, Mon," the laughing Jock shouted, as he felt the mackerel hit. Fastening the line at the required depth, Billy began to haul his catch in.

We soon had an audience. Others wanted to try their luck, but it wouldn't be sensible to put more lines out. The tangling would be dreadful. We were happy to let the voyage crew pull some fish in, under supervision. It was important to keep the line tight when fish were hooked, and not to drop the wriggling fish on to the line on the deck. We did get occasional tangles and these were time-consuming, but were to be expected. The fish kept coming. We'd started a second bucket for the catch.

A sweet, young, wheelchair bound girl with black, plaited hair was brought to the platform by her buddy. The teenager was really excited to see live fish.

"D' yer want a go?" I asked, offering a line.

Given the opportunity, the enthusiasm of the bonnie girl was palpable. Her buddy was equally excited, and wheeled little Sally to the back of the platform.

"These fish ah comin' up Freddy, they're nae sae deep," Bill called.

I dropped the line over, holding tension as the gut ran through my fingers. The fish struck while I still had about five fathoms of line on the deck. The fish were plentiful and were rising.

Passing the line through the railings, then to Sally, I said, "pull it in."

It was a struggle for the young girl, but she was squealing excitedly as the fish wriggled. I watched overboard as the shimmering catch drew closer. As the first fish reached the surface, I reached over and, taking the line, lifted the string of six mackerel, draping the thrashing fish across her lap. Mackerel were hanging either side. The excited squeal became shrill with excitement as I encouraged little Sally to hold the fish and detach the hook. Others dealt with the remaining catch and I took control of the line. When free of fish, I dropped the unit back over.

I struck when I felt fish, passing the line over to my protégé to repeat the process. Not quite a full string, but Sally didn't notice. The poor girl was exhausted after the second string had been dispatched and her buddy suggested it was time for a rest.

The young girl didn't argue, but her wan grin as she departed told me everything I wanted to know.

"See ya later," I called, waving, and blowing her a fishy kiss. This experience was the highlight of my voyage.

We'd almost filled the third bucket when Triona, our fiery, Irish Cook, having discovered the first two containers of our bonanza catch in her deck refrigerator, came storming on to the platform.

"No more feckin' mackerel!" the red-faced Cook bawled.

Hailing from Cobh, on the southern coast of Ireland, a place I'd visited several times on the ship, Triona was quite a character, and well known in her home town. I got on really well with this force of nature. She was a member of her local inshore lifeboat crew and when we first met I was Operations Manager of Scarborough Lifeboat.

There was fresh mackerel for breakfast and a good supply was split and frozen for future use. We gave a quantity away to the locals in Hartlepool on arrival the next morning.

* * *

Colin and I were to join *Tenacious* for a voyage from Fiji to Sydney. The outward flights, half way round the world, took us almost to the international date line. We flew out via Singapore and Sydney. The flight from Sydney to Fiji took a further four hours. The return voyage, sailing back to Sydney would take nearly four weeks.

Like most of the islands of the Pacific, these had been occupied for at least 4000 years. The first European to sight Fiji was the Dutchman, Abel Tasman in 1643, while looking for the great southern continent. He also discovered Tasmania and New Zealand. Tasmania carries his name.

Captain Cook sighted the islands, stopping for water in 1774 but it was Captain Bligh, of *Bounty* fame, who charted the main islands in 1789.

The first American whaler, one of many that would follow, was *Ann and Hope*, visiting Fiji in 1799.

The islands, of which there are over three hundred, less than a third inhabited, were first settled by Europeans to grow cotton in the wake of the American Civil War, and much of the land was misappropriated. Sadly, workers were brought from many of the Pacific Islands, against their will or by subterfuge to handle the cotton.

The main economy of Fiji now is based on sugar and tourism. Cruise ships are constant visitors.

We enjoyed our few days in friendly, tropical Fiji, though didn't travel far, as there was work for us on the ship. The newly arrived voyage crew had a splendid island experience, before *Tenacious* set sail for Sydney.

As soon as we were at sea and the opportunity arose, I streamed a couple of lines, expecting tuna. We'd been eating huge, fantastic, almost raw, tuna steaks in the restaurants ashore. Strangely, there was nothing doing at all on the lines.

This dearth of fish, continued all the way to Vanuatu, about 500 miles distant. Each morning I'd head up to the bridge, then aft to the stern, paying out the lines. Each evening I'd make the same journey to retrieve the pair. The gear was never left out during the hours of darkness. If the ship went aback the slack line could foul the prop' shaft.

Vanuatu was an idyllic, though poor, tropical island. There was a rickety shack selling soft drinks, beer and snacks on the beach, near the landing stage, where we put the voyage crew ashore. This was the perfect setting to sit with a beer, looking at palm trees, white sand and azure blue sea. Some from the ship would explore the little town on their exotic run ashore, hunting for souvenirs.

The National Bank, in the main street did a roaring trade dispensing the local currency, and with about 150 vatu to £1, everyone felt very rich, though there was little to spend the 100 vatu notes on. The voyage crew would have lots of useless money when they arrived back on the ship, and would be forbidden from spending 'monopoly' money in the bar.

Weighing the anchor next morning, I was in the cable locker on the starboard side. Sadly, no 'hooker' was required, just an assistant with a hand-held radio to communicate with the Mate

Tenacious at anchor – Max Moodie

on the foredeck. Gravity fed, the cable came over the gypsy, down the hawse pipe to the deep cable locker, where, without trimming, the studded links would pile up.

I had to stand outside the locker on a portable wooden box, then open and lower a two-foot square, hinged, watertight door. At this point, at chest height, I was looking into the rust-stained, dimly-lit locker.

To ensure the chain was distributed evenly, the duty BM wore a pair of thick, industrial gloves to pull and flake the cable at the after end of the compartment. A wooden, flat-ended paddle-shaped implement was used to push the chain to the front of the locker. It was quite satisfying to achieve a neat stow, knowing the cable would flow out easily when the anchor was dropped again.

Back underway and with sails set, we were bound for New Caledonia, so named by Captain Cook, who was the first European to sight the group of islands. Cook thought the north eastern part of these islands reminded him of Scotland, though he had been at sea a long time.

This leg of the passage was approximately 350 miles. The fishing lines were soon out again but once more the catch was elusive. The trusted lures, which I'd used for years in the past, were proving useless. My reputation as 'Fred the Fish' was in danger.

We arrived at the island group fishless again, anchoring close inshore in a narrow sound, awaiting instructions from the port. The climate was wonderful and meals were taken alfresco.

On the main deck in the afternoon, we were entertained with a talk from, 'Sir Robin', a small, extremely tanned, sun worshipping watch-leader, in his mid 70s. A retired civil servant and great raconteur, during his career, Robin had spent much of his time in the Diplomatic Service, stationed in embassies around the globe. His final years were spent back in London, where he was part of the unit assessing and awarding the Queen's Honours. Robin was most miffed when, on retiring, due to new regulations, he didn't receive an honour himself, as had previously been the norm.

We'd given him a knighthood on the ship, hence his title. It was surprising how many on board believed he was Sir Robin. The old boy enjoyed the subterfuge and never denied his shipboard award. It wasn't uncommon, before breakfast, to see Sir Robin parading on deck, cup of Earl Grey in hand, clad in a blue silk, dragon embroidered, Chinese dressing gown and carpet slippers.

'Sir' Robin's talk – Fred Normandale

Today's talk was titled, 'Lying for my country' and was most amusing. Robin, if he was to be believed, had been involved in some very dodgy international situations, and had just uttered the words, "I could have been bumped off for that piece of work, had I been caught," when, right on cue, a completely black, two-man helicopter came into the sound, slowed, then hovered overhead. The timing was perfect.

"They're 'ere now, Robin. They've come fo' yer," I called out.

This brought a huge peal of laughter from his audience.

The chopper was probably a Customs plane, assessing our ship before permitting entry to the port. We never found out, but it was a highly amusing incident.

Next morning, we picked up the hook and headed for the capital, Noumea. I was gobsmacked to see French flags flying almost everywhere, but then noticed EU flags too. Being a fervent Brexiteer, I was incensed. We were 11,000 miles from France but this little archipelago was a part of France, and apparently, had representatives in the European parliament.

Sir Robin, looking at the flags, gave his forehead a little thump and said, "of course, it's the 14th of July. It's Bastille Day."

This island is one of the world's major suppliers of wealth producing nickel, though only for the French company and its workers, extracting the ore. The locals profit little and there's a two-tier economy, the Europeans and the locals.

There are Parisian style shops and restaurants for the wealthy.

New Caledonia had been a French penal colony, with over twenty thousand criminals and political prisoners transported during a period of forty years from the 1860s. Prior to this, many of the islanders had been shipped to Fiji to work on the plantations.

Amazingly, the first American whalers from New England had visited these islands in 1793.

Col and I went ashore for the evening, finding a bar in the main street, where we could also get a light meal. We were perusing the menu when the sound of approaching music outside, caught our attention. Taking the beers, we made our way to the door, standing on the boardwalk outside.

We were in time to witness a procession, led by a brass band, with people in period fancy dress, parading behind, celebrating Bastille Day.

"Bastille Day," I coughed, choking on my drink. We're on t' other side o' t' bloody world!" then added, "Ah wonder if they do Bonfire Night as well."

To add insult to injury, our waiter appeared, informing us we couldn't take our drinks outside. Returning indoors we ordered an overpriced burger with 'frites' and another beer then, disillusioned, returned to the ship.

Tenacious was back at sea mid-morning of the following day, and with ropes stowed, the lines were out again, though there was derision from some observers. We now faced a seven hundred and fifty-mile passage to eastern Australia.

A couple of hours later I was called to the bridge by someone shouting, "there's a fish on the line." I rushed aft and could see splashing, but it didn't look authentic. Something wasn't right. I pulled the port line in, only to find a plastic, inflatable 'Nemo' tied on.

Plastic Fish – unknown

Lots of people enjoyed the joke and I couldn't spoil their fun, but I wasn't quite as amused. I was even less amused a few days later when, with still no fish, I discovered a tin of tuna fastened on the starboard line.

The voyage continued fishless, and eventually we sighted Australia. The original plan had been for the ship to sail to Frazer Island, an undisturbed, giant, ecological, sandbank off the coast of Queensland. For administrative reasons, the Australian Government had cancelled this visit, but the change of plan left the ship with two spares days. A huge welcoming party was organised to meet *Tenacious* on her arrival into Sydney, following her passage half way around the globe, but this was date specific.

We were to spend the next two days, slowly dodging north and south off the coast of Queensland, continually passing the same landmarks. Going so slow, there was no possibility of fishing. Fred the Fish's reputation was in tatters.

At least half a dozen times each day, laden colliers with cargo from Newcastle, NSW, passed, heading north to China. An equal number of vessels came south, light ship, their boot-topping, red hulls, high out of the water.

On the two nights we were off the coast, we were privileged to witness the most crimson of sunsets. There were no subtle hues, just pure, vivid red, gravitating to crimson, then maroon, before the black of night took over the western sky.

During the night, the engines speeded up and *Tenacious* headed south to her midday appointment in Sydney's harbour entrance. I was awake before breakfast and as always, went up the starboard bridge companionway, making for the fishing lines.

As I headed aft, I met Ali the Mate, talking to the helmsman. The Officer looked in my direction and said, "I don't know why you're bothering. We've passaged two thousand two hundred miles now, and you haven't caught a thing. We'll be in Sydney this afternoon."

She was right, and I wasn't at all confident at this late point, but it was also my last chance. "If yer don't buy a ticket, yer'll never win a raffle," I muttered as I hurriedly passed by.

After paying the lines out one last time for this trip, I went for breakfast. An hour later, while working on the foredeck, one of the voyage crew, an elderly, serious chap came running to the front of the bridge, excitedly shouting, "Fred, you've got a fish on."

I knew immediately this was no false alarm, and rushed to the stern. Looking aft, I could see the fish on the surface, fighting. "Yesss!" I said, very loudly. "Come to Daddy."

I already had an audience. Quickly donning a pair of rubber gloves with bobbled grip, strategically placed for this wished for occasion, I reached for the line, gently hauling, hand over hand. It

271

was a good-sized tuna and I was praying the fish wouldn't become unhooked.

The last twenty feet of line, before the hook, was a hundred and twenty-pound breaking strain, catgut. Now the fish was close to the stern. Looking down, I could see the hook was well fixed, and began to haul the fish from the water. Without the gloves, the line would have slipped through my hands. I'd lost fish in the past, unable to haul them in.

Gently, until the thrashing fish was almost to hand, with the same momentum, I swung the catch over the railing, inboard. "Yo! it's ours," I shouted euphorically as the fish hit the deck, its tail thrashing violently on the planking.

"Oh! ye of little faith!" I called out to the gathered onlookers; my reputation restored. After grabbing the fish by the gills and unhooking the now bloodied tuna, I punched the air yelling, "Fred the Fish is back!"

I did put the line out again, but didn't catch anything further and didn't care. I was vindicated.

Fish near Sydney – Ronan Ging

A couple of hours later, sails still set, *Tenacious* was approaching Sydney Harbour Bridge, with the famous Opera House on our port bow. Ahead was an orange painted harbour tug, its water cannons spraying jets of vapor high into the blue sky, creating giant rainbows.

Also, close to the bridge to greet our arrival, was *James Craig*, a fully restored barque, usually berthed close to the National Maritime Museum. This fine old ship, built in Sunderland in 1874 as *Clan Macleod* was a magnificent vessel that had rounded Cape Horn twenty-three times in twenty-six years during her working life.

Arrival in Sydney – Fred Normandale

It was a fantastic welcome and there was a multitude of people waving from the sea walls of the Opera House. To port, between the theatre and the bridge, was Circular Quay. This large inlet was the international sea port and ferry terminal. It was here that immigrants first landed in Australia, and from these quays that ANZAC troops departed to fight in the Great, and subsequent wars.

Low Water

Now this natural bay was a cruise ship terminal and little ferries frequently carried passengers to the outlying districts of the city. These ferry boats were named after the ships of the First Fleet, that left Portsmouth in May 1787. The eleven ships consisted of two Royal Navy escort vessels, three store ships carrying supplies, and six convict transports, with in excess of one thousand prisoners on board. The precise number is unknown. The historic fleet arrived in Botany Bay in January 1788.

One of the transport ships, the 411-ton barque, *Scarborough* was built in Scarborough in1782 by Messrs Fowler and Heward. She was the only transport to make the passage to Australia twice, carrying convicts.

Most of the prisoners transported to Botany Bay were guilty of minor offences, but large numbers were needed to populate the new territory.

Flying tops'ls only, we sailed under the famous bridge, from where it was only a short distance to our berth, in a prime location outside the spectacular, National Maritime Museum. Berthed close by, were replicas of the famous ships, *Endeavour* and *Bounty,* and the ex-Royal Australian Navy, Oberon-Class, diesel powered submarine, *Onslow.*

The waterfront was busy and warm, even though it was Winter, but the temperature dropped at night. We had a couple of days free, and along with Col and Ronan, the ship's Medical Purser, I managed a good look around the wonderful city. Ronan, a tall, gangly Irishman was an emergency trauma nurse in a major London hospital, when not on the ships. He was also a talented musician and had the most outrageous, non-PC sense of humour.

We visited Paddy's Market and the Fish Market. Both were amazing venues. The seafood at the fish market was reasonably priced, varied and abundant. Picnic tables, outside in the sunshine, were in constant use. Any unconsumed food was soon devoured by large, scavenging, exotic seabirds at the waters edge and on the grassy shore.

We also discovered the Pyrmont Bridge Hotel, which had a 24-hour licence, though we never put this to the test. This was the first bar I'd ever visited that took credit cards; very useful, but dangerous.

The location for the ship's last night dinner was, coincidentally, in the historic Lord Nelson Inn. This was Sydney's first pub, and was now a hotel and brewery. I'd been here once before, several years previously when on holiday with Dotty.

This gathering was a great event; a celebration of our epic voyage together, with lots of toasts. The voyage crew, as ever, were very generous with their wine.

When Dotty and I had been in Sydney previously, we'd found a wonderful old pub, not far from the Lord Nelson Inn called, 'The Hero of Waterloo'. I couldn't remember the exact location of the establishment, but had mentioned its close proximity to Ronan earlier, and how there had been live music playing on our previous visit.

The Medical Purser had done his research, and led the charge of at least twenty merry crew to this old, atmospheric establishment, where we were greeted royally.

Though it was several years since I'd last been in this dingy old pub, nothing had changed, including the occasional cockroach on the walls. Even the guitar player in the musical duo was the same.

It had been a quiet day when Dotty and I last visited the 'Hero' and we'd been invited down the worn, stone steps to inspect the cellar, after listening to a spooky story told by the barmaid. Down in the dark basement, fixed to the wall, were the original, now heavily rust-flaked, chains and manacles, used to shanghai drunken sailors, back in the days of windjammers.

"These old, broken pieces of furniture and other objects move about inexplicably, down here," the lady said, pointing to a chair. "I daren't come down on my own, or in the dark."

The lady was genuinely disturbed by the haunted cellar. I had goose-bumps and the hairs on the back of my neck were standing on end. The basement was chilled, on a very warm day.

Now, with music playing and a great atmosphere, people were dancing. The locals were joining in and the little place was rocking.

Next, something happened that no one could believe, and I would have bet serious money against. Ronan grabbed Captain Simon's hand and the pair were jiving on the dance floor. Our Captain was the most serious of men, and we were surprised that he'd come along with the crowd. It was certainly a night to remember and a great one to go out on.

Next morning we'd pack our gear, clean the ship, grab a bacon sandwich with a mug of tea then take the Metro to the airport. Another fantastic, unique voyage was over.

CHAPTER 21

SPECIAL LADIES

Betty was a delightful, elderly, larger than life lady in every sense. Due to her age and size, she carried a stout staff to assist with walking.

This lovely volunteer, like many others, had a great affection for *Lord Nelson*. Though living in Margate, whenever the ship was in Southampton, or anywhere close enough, Betty would drive her old banger to the much-loved vessel. On arrival she'd spend her time working in the laundry, stitching bunk curtains or repairing bed linen. This lady felt part of the team and was greatly loved and appreciated by everyone for her dedication. Many volunteers turned up to offer their trade skills for the love of this ship, and to meet up with their mates, but Betty was special.

A battler and fighter of lost causes, she was frequently at war with her local social services with letters and protests, and also wrote to the 'management trustees' of the Jubilee Sailing Trust when unhappy with some of their dubious decisions.

I'd sailed with Betty on several voyages in the past and her enthusiasm, despite her age, was boundless. When going on watch during the night, she would request an early call, as due to her size, more time was required to get into her warm clothes and heavy weather gear.

Now I was sailing with Betty on a voyage to the Canaries and we were to call into Madeira, the island where, historically, sailing

Betty sewing curtains – Alan Fisher

ships had called for fresh food and water from the verdant, volcanic slopes, when bound for distant shores.

Alongside the pier in Funchal, we were berthed astern of a massive, white-hulled cruise liner and, way below her promenade deck, we were organising 'hands aloft', and assisted climbs.

Participating in an assisted climb was another special lady, whom I'd previously met on a day sail on the Thames. Caroline had been a young nurse serving with the Royal Army Nursing Corp during the Falklands conflict. Having seen some of the dreadful burns incurred by the casualties, the young nurse had specialised in the treatment of burns for the remainder of her career until, years later, tragedy struck, in the form of an IED (improvised explosive device) in Afghanistan.

This caring nurse was shortly due to leave the army, when this disaster brought her career, and almost her life to an abrupt halt. Her body was shattered by the explosion. It had taken years and many operations before Caroline was able to walk short distances with the aid of sticks, and had spent much of her time confined to a wheelchair.

Now, for me, it was a privilege to assist this selfless lady attempting the climb to the fighting top. This would be a huge achievement for someone it was thought, would never walk again. I lifted each shoe in turn, placing her foot on a rat-bar until, step by step, we were under the futtocks. The team below took extra weight on the safety gantline, enabling my charge, step by painful step, with encouragement and direction from the Bosun, to achieve her goal, the platform.

We both shed tears and shared a huge, gentle hug, while below, a round of applause and cheers came from the deck, this echoed by a crowd of interested passengers on the stern of the cruise liner.

Funchal is a great run ashore, especially in the month before Christmas, when the entire shore is illuminated with a million light bulbs and there's a carnival atmosphere in the air. The island is a favourite stopover for cruise liners at New Year, when a huge, spectacular firework display takes place at the stroke of midnight.

Located near the end of the promenade is an alpine-type tele-cabin, transporting visitors to the summit of the hill overlooking the port. From here, for many years, a traditional basket run has taken place for tourists. Local men with tyre-soled shoes, steered the enclosed, chair-shaped wicker baskets, fitted with wooden skids, down the narrow street, carrying up to three passengers. It was on this exhilarating ride that the two Engineers, Marco and Alan, known to all as 'Pickles', took Betty. I followed on in the next basket with a couple of other hands.

This was a hair-raising, scary run for us, so I could only imagine how Betty had fared. As we arrived near the finish, I could see the Engineers holding on to Betty, and as we got closer, noticed the large lady was holding a handkerchief to her face.

"Oh bloody 'ell," I said to my fellow travellers. "It's been too much for 'er."

It wasn't until we caught up with the group that we heard Betty laughing. Removing the hankie, this special lady had tears in her eyes and, putting her fleshy arms around the Engineers, pulled the boys to her ample chest. "Boys, I've never had so much fun in years."

The sleds stopped half way down the steep, narrow lane, so we had the remainder of the hill to navigate back to the waterfront, and discovered that Betty, due to her size and proportion, was unable to walk down the slope forwards. A brief discussion ensued, resulting in Betty, hands on hips, walking backwards, an Engineer on each arm, acting as brakes, while I carried the stout stick.

This was warm work for the boys, but fortunately, five minutes down the hill, an open door indicated a small, local bar. Of course, Betty was taken in sideways and had no say in the matter. It was beer o'clock. Our numbers filled the cool, shady little room and we found a similar establishment further down the slope, before we made level ground.

We took taxis back to the ship and later spent a gentle night ashore.

Next morning, leaving Portuguese Madeira, it was a two hundred and seventy nautical mile sail to Spanish, Tenerife. This division of the South Atlantic, by decree of Pope Alexander VI in 1494, split the New World, despite the existing presence and wishes of the indigenous, Incas, Aztecs and many other tribes.

The delineation was supposed to be along the 30-degree South latitude, but a little chicanery was involved. The outcome was that Cape Verde, Madeira and Brazil became Portuguese, the Canaries and other South American countries, including those in the Pacific, became Spanish. This declaration changed the world forever.

* * *

Arriving in the Canaries, we were berthed alongside in Santa Cruz de Tenerife, where, next day the voyage crew departed for home. Betty had stayed on to help with maintenance, and as always at the end of a voyage, there were sheets, pillow cases and quilt covers to wash. She would be in her element being useful and involved. Her assistance meant the Medical Purser could concentrate on planning for the arrival of the next voyage complement and their many needs.

Today the Engineers had another surprise for Betty. Tenerife football team were playing at home in the evening, and the pair had asked her to accompany them to the match. I was going along too. Being a fan of her home town's team, she was delighted at the invitation to a big match. The ship's agent had obliged by acquiring four tickets.

Making an outing of the occasion, we declined dinner on board, to Cookie's delight. Instead we called at a couple of little bars on the way to the match, enjoying tapas and a glass of wine. Arriving at the turnstile a few minutes before kick-off, we helped Betty up the concrete steps to a terrace in the huge open-air stadium. The ground was three-quarters full with many flag waving supporters giving out a great deal of enthusiastic chanting. This was a great atmosphere, though it seemed strange to be watching football in such a warm climate.

Pickles was learning Spanish, and took every opportunity to practice his skill, but during a controversial refereeing decision, he made the mistake of doubting the eyesight and parentage of the referee, though not loudly.

Picking upon his comment, Betty asked, "What were you saying, Mr Pickles?"

Slightly embarrassed that the lady had overheard his expression, he replied, "I said the referee needed glasses, Betty."

In her loudest, booming voice, Betty repeated Pickles' rude comment.

All the fans in earshot went quiet and looked in our direction. As Betty inhaled, ready to repeat her chant, a hand was placed over her mouth, stifling the words.

This was a source of huge entertainment for the locals.

It was an entertaining match and though neutral, we cheered for Tenerife, who won the match, two goals to one.

Leaving the ground, another gentle stroll, via a small hostelry, found us back at the ship. It had been a great run ashore, a good result, and a quiet, "thank you boys, I've had a wonderful evening," was a great reward.

I spent several days helping to get *Nelly* ready for her busy Christmas period, then flew home to Leeds Bradford Airport then bus and a train home. I'd missed much of the commercial, pre-Christmas hype but still had plenty of time to readjust to Scarborough life before the festivities proper, began.

CHAPTER 22

FAMILY MATTERS

Dotty's Mum had recently passed away, but it was near Christmas and there was as yet, no funeral arranged for her.

A few days later my Mum rang and through tears said, "can you come and see to your Dad. He's half in and half out of bed and I can't move him and he's not answering."

I rushed down the hill and found Dad as Mum had described. I managed to get him back into bed then dialled 999. The ambulance was quickly on its way.

Dad was now 94 and had recently completed a course of antibiotics to shift a constant deep cough, but the medication had not touched the problem.

When asked for an alternative antibiotic, the doctor had said, "let's see how he gets on."

On reflection, it was obvious how he would get on. Pneumonia set in.

I went with Dad in the ambulance. The paramedics were fantastic, immediately putting an oxygen mask on his face, they sounded the siren to speed us through traffic for the three miles to the hospital.

Jumping the queue, the two men registered Dad and he was taken to an acute ward and fitted with a drip. I sat with him, as he drifted in and out of consciousness, aware of my presence, but he was weak and struggling for breath. I think the orderly must have been expecting Dad to expire, as he left us alone together, but Dad rallied a little and was taken to an acute respiratory ward.

It was almost Christmas, and Dad was seriously ill with pneumonia, though was in no pain. He had a constant stream of concerned family visitors, but he was failing. Frederick William Normandale died late on Boxing Day night 2016, quietly with family round him.

* * *

We now had a date for Dotty's Mum's service, and in the second week of January we attended two funerals in two days, in Hull then Scarborough.

Our extended family had set a date in May of that year, when everyone would be available to scatter Dad's ashes at sea. He'd requested to be strewn in Hayburn Wyke, a beautiful little bay to the north of Scarborough. When lobster fishing, he'd worked close inshore here, with pots on rock, then, when trawling for sole and plaice, he'd tow north and south in the sand, further off shore.

On the day before the planned service, Dotty and I were driving back from Scotland when I received a phone call from Marco, on board *Lord Nelson*.

"Hey Freddy, we're coming past Scarborough tomorrow morning about 0800 on our way to Canada. We're off the Norfolk Coast just now. Can you get us some fishing tackle, and maybe some fish for tomorrow's evening meal."

I knew the ship was going to Canada but didn't know when she was departing. *Lord Nelson* was to be part of the 150th celebrations in Quebec and various other places in Canada. Along with Colin and Dave, my regular shipmates, I was due to join her in July in Newfoundland, then sail to Nova Scotia.

"We're due t' scatter me Dad's ashes tomorro' mornin', off Hayburn Wyke at ten o'clock. Ah'll get yer some fish an' some tackle. We'll meet yer there. I'll give yer the lat' an' long' later."

"We're due off Scarborough at 0800," he said again.

"Well slow down then," I said. "Yer've plenty o' time t' spare. Yer goin' thousands o' miles."

I rang Tony, a fish merchant based on the West Pier, requesting fifty fillets of haddock for collection the following morning. I knew he'd have top quality stuff for his discerning clients, and he delivered daily.

There was a slight confusion when, having supplied the ship with the latitude and longitude of Hayburn Wyke, I later received a call saying the position I'd given was miles out to sea. The navigator had taken the longitude as east of Greenwich Meridian instead of west.

Next morning at 0930, about twenty of our extended family and close friends gathered at the Golden Ball Slipway, from where the two commercial speedboats operated. Dotty would stay ashore with Mum and we'd meet them on our return.

I'd previously arranged with Rudi, the operator of the boats to charter his craft for the occasion. It was almost 10.00 when Tony brought the fish. I had a bag of mackerel hooks and feathers for the ship.

My phone rang. It was Steve, the current Mate, the stocky ex Royal Marine.

"Hey Freddy, we're here in position. Where are you? There isn't a boat in sight."

"We're just leavin', Steve. We're runnin' a bit late, sorry. We'll be with yer in ten minutes," I laughed.

I was one of ten passengers in the first boat with our consort close behind. We turned to port at the pier-end and, looking north, could see *Lord Nelson*, under full sail, not far from land, about four miles distant. Rudi opened the throttle and we shot forth at about twenty knots. There was a fresh breeze off the land but the spray was missing us and blowing behind the boat.

As we approached *Nelly*, I realized that though all her sails were set, Captain Richard Cruse, the former Mate, a young, but now accomplished Master, had boxed the yards. The main yards were braced to starboard to the wind but the fore yards were aback, braced to port. The ship was making no headway, but was blowing slowly downwind with the breeze.

We drew alongside the old girl, to find the entire crew standing along the starboard bulwarks to watch the proceedings.

Steve had opened a gangway gate in the side of the ship and I easily slid the box of fish onto her deck, followed by the bag of tackle. In return, the Engineer and bar stock manager, passed over two bottles of 'Goslings', Bermuda rum.

Rudi stood off a few boat-lengths and killed the engine. Our consort craft with my sisters and their children, stood close by. It was a very moving eulogy that son Danny read for his Grandad, and I and others were tearful. The many familiar faces along *Nelly's* starboard side stood in dignified silence.

I held the plastic tub containing Dad's ashes over the side, very close to the water and gently shook out the contents. I'd seen ashes fly high in windy conditions in the past.

The short but moving service over, I took the top from one of the bottles and poured the first drop into the sea for Dad, then swiftly took a good swig before passing the bottle round. No one declined.

We'd blown a good way offshore during our time with *Nelly*, so with constant waving, I bade farewell and good sailing to shipmates and we headed inshore for a lee under the land.

Looking back, *Lord Nelson's* fore yards had been braced back to starboard and she was already making good speed across the wind. I'd next see her in July in Corner Brook, Newfoundland.

A gentle, half-speed cruise back to Scarborough and we were soon alongside the slipway once more. There were customers waiting for speedboat trips.

Approaching Rudi, I expressed grateful thanks for his kindness, enabling our family to give Dad this send off. I had several hundred pounds in my pocket and said, "what do I owe yer, Rudi?"

"Nothing," was his reply. "It was a privilege to take your Dad's ashes, and wonderful to see the ship."

Lord Nelson's yards boxed when scattering Dad's ashes
– Jonathan Rhodes

I couldn't speak. I was already emotionally drained and this was just such an amazing act of kindness.

We made our way round to the West Pier to the fishermen's café where we met Dotty and Mum. Debbie, the cheery proprietor, supplied everyone with teas, coffees and breakfasts at hugely discounted prices. More rum fortified the teas and coffees. The balance of the bottle was left with Debbie for her fishermen customers to raise a glass (mug) to 'Absent Freds.'

Rudi was given the intact bottle and I paid for five pints of lager in the bar of the Golden Ball opposite his base and another five in the Leeds Arms, which he visited occasionally. Sadly, with a new baby at home, Rudi wasn't getting into the pub much, but his Dad made sure these drinks didn't go to waste.

I spoke to many people following the occasion of Dad's ashes, both at home and later with shipmates on *Nelly*. To all I said, "that day was meant t' be." I had no idea *Lord Nelson* would be passing to coincide with this special day. Had I had a million pounds to spend, I couldn't have arranged the timing of that coming together. It was meant to be.

Dad had enjoyed, and often recalled his voyage on this unique ship and now she had assisted in his final passage.

Following Dad's passing, a family bench overlooking the harbour and sea was placed to his memory. The words on the plaque are from Psalm 109 v 23-24.

²³ They that go down to the sea in ships' that do business in great waters;

²⁴ These see the works of the Lord, and his wonders in the deep.

* * *

It was exactly six months to the day after Dad died when my old pal, George McLean passed away in Gardenstown, North East Scotland.

We'd travel north to the funeral by car and stay not too far away.

Meeting Iain on arrival in the village, we went with him to see his Mum, Hazel. Small, bespectacled and always extremely well attired, her accent was a very strong regional Doric. I'd first met Hazel while still at school. With friends she'd visited Scarborough to see their menfolk, when they were herring fishing. This became an annual holiday in August. Even when the boats ceased drifting, George and Hazel would bring their family to Scarborough in Summer.

Hazel had asked previously if I'd speak at her man's funeral, which I'd thought a privilege. While we were drinking tea and chatting, Iain said, "you've got a chord tomorrow, Fred."

Confused, I looked to him for an explanation.

"You've got a chord," he repeated.

I still didn't grasp what Iain was saying and he explained that six family members or friends were chosen to lower the casket into the ground, and each man held a thin rope chord attached to the box. I was to be one of these six. This was another privilege.

"Don't wrap the line round your hand," was a good tip.

I'd been to (too) many funerals, but few interments. The lowering of the casket fell to the Funeral Director's pall bearers at others I'd attended.

288

I was pleased with the tip Iain had given me, for I would surely have finished up in the hole, had I got a riding-turn around my hand.

When the coffin was settled in the grave, we dropped our chords in also. This was goodbye to a lifelong friend.

CHAPTER 23

BACK FROM THE AZORES

"Whale alongside, to port," came the call from the speaker.

A mad panic ensued as people scrambled to the deck. Frequently, whale watchers would be too late, but not on this occasion.

The leviathan was alongside, less than fifty yards from the ship and moving gently, slightly faster than *Nelly*, under easy sail. The big whale, about forty feet in length, was slowly overtaking the ship, its right eye scanning our deck.

All hands moved forward to follow the creature until, beyond the bowsprit, the black beast sounded. Some went below, attempting to identify the whale from a wall chart in the lower mess, others departed about their business.

"Whale on the port quarter," came the call, fifteen minutes later. Speculation was, this was the same creature, and it was possibly a 'right whale'; extremely rare now, but this was the 'right' whale to harpoon at the onset of whale hunting.

The great mammal took at least ten minutes to run down our side, but then repeated this performance, twice more. It seemed we were mutually curious. We were two days out from Ponta Delgada when our visitor came along. Never before or since have I see a whale so close, for so long. This visit was unique.

The wind freshened after lunch, and soon *Lord Nelson* was making an exhilarating passage towards home. It was March and the wind and seas continued to grow, with winds soon gusting 60 to 70 knots. The old gal was heeling to starboard and stonking along, now under tops'ls only. She continued to hold her course and speed wonderfully.

It was almost 1800hrs and dinner was ready. Sitting with the crew at the table in the mess, food was about to be served when an urgent message came over the speaker.

Captain Richard shouted, "all hands' on deck, quickly. The main tops'l's blown out. Bosun and Bosun's mates only, to go aloft."

"Great timing," I thought. "Right on dinner time."

I was one of three BMs on the voyage, and the Bosun was Beth. This was the same Beth who'd sailed as a teenager a few years earlier and had shown great aptitude. The tall, blond, attractive young lady had continued sailing and was now part of the permanent crew. Despite her lack of years and a probable forty-plus year difference in our ages, Beth was extremely competent, and I was quite happy to work under her direction.

Leaving the other BM's on deck, Beth and I, in oilskins and harnesses, made our way up the weather shrouds and, above the platform, she stepped onto the port cranline, then footrope, and I followed. *Nelly* was heeling to starboard and the howling gale made communications almost impossible. It was going to be uphill and into the weather, where the shredded sail was flogging and whipping viciously.

Meanwhile on deck, the voyage crew and other BMs, supervised by the Mate, had dropped the yard, hauled on buntlines and carefully slackened bar-tight sheets. The damaged port side of the sail was still flogging violently, but the starboard side was snug home, though would need a sea stow later.

The seamanlike way of controlling a rogue sail is, if possible, to get a gasket or two in the middle, where the sail is at its narrowest and lightest. Beth, with long, strong arms, and with my assistance, wrestled the canvas and, while she contained this section with her arms and upper body, I was able to reach over, grab a gasket, haul the line over the sail and work some purchase around the back jackstay, hardening the line tight, then making the short strop fast.

"Well done gall," I bawled in her ear. It took more fighting; the shredded sail whipping viciously, but we managed another couple of gaskets. "Take a breather lass, it's ours now."

I received a happy grin in reply.

There was more flogging sail to control yet, and gaskets to fasten, but we'd broken the back of the job and could now work our way out in sections, each would get easier.

Before we could go further with our work, there was a loud 'crack', heard above the wind, and the port, fore tops'l brace on the yard ahead, leading to our mast, dropped, and was now dangling below where we were working. A short, immensely strong, but worn, Dynema grommet had parted at the outer edge of the fore tops'l yard, allowing the block and purchase, shackled in to the grommet eye, to drop, leaving the yard unstable. Fortunately, the lee brace was taught, preventing the yard from swinging too wildly.

Beth didn't need telling that she'd be required on deck, but I was between her and the platform. Not standing on ceremony, the long-legged young lady passed her long safety tether behind my back, clipping it smartly onto the thin silver wire, then unclipped her short stay. Reaching round my back, the blond Bosun grabbed the jackstay then swung her right leg round behind me and on to the footrope.

I was straddled by Beth as she waited for the right moment to haul herself round.

"We 'ave t' stop meetin' like this," I shouted loudly. "We 'aven't been introduced. We'll 'ave t' get married now."

I heard her snigger in my ear at the corny line, then she was round and moving down towards the mast.

Below, crew were dashing forward to hand the sail on the loose yard, then the main engine roared into life, allowing the ship to continue on her course and speed. I continued to secure the sail before me, which took some time, the flogging cloth still cracking in the wind. Someone would be required on the main mast before long to assist in coming operations.

On deck a plan was in operation to rectify the rogue yard. This involved a new coil of Dynema from the sail locker below, with an eye spliced in the end. This splice, made in multi-stranded, plaited rope, was beyond my grasp, but the Bosun had mastered the skill and was getting stuck in to the job, deploying a two-foot, thin, stainless rod. This splicing was a lengthy process. The strength of the rope lay in the centre core. The thick, surrounding plaid was for protection.

Amy, a young Canadian BM brought a heaving line to the fighting top, with instruction that we were to recover the dangling brace and block, secure them to the platform, then standby for the new rope, when ready.

While Beth was making the eye, several of the crew, including the Engineers, were flaking the remainder of the new rope up and down the deck.

With the eye complete, young Beth made short work of getting up the for'ard shrouds, heaving line fastened to her harness. The third BM followed in her wake. The pair put a lashing from the rogue yard around the mast to reduce the motion. The Bosun then steadily made her way out to the end of the, still moving yard with BM in pursuit.

Beth threw her heaving line out into the teeth of the gale, the heavy monkey's fist in the end, countering the wind. The rope dropped to the deck inboard, where the line was recovered and her new splice hitched on. It was a struggle for Beth and assistant to haul the new rope up, as, below someone was keeping the line under tension, preventing the Dynema from blowing wildly across the ship out of control.

After hooking the new eye over the yard-end and unhitching the heaving line, their work was done. Exhausted, the pair made their way down to the deck.

Now it was our turn. Amy threw her heaving line down and to windward, expecting the line to land near the deck. In the event, with a lighter line, the wind took the rope across the ship, but it was recoverable and transferred back across to the port side.

The other end of the new rope had been passed through a metal block to approximately the required length and with a shackle attached, we hauled the block and bight of new rope aloft, again under tension.

It was a hard pull, but we got the block and shackle onto the platform.

"We'll need more slack yet," I bawled to Amy, and we heaved another twenty feet upwards.

At this point, with Amy holding the weight I, hitched the rope around the platform handrail. Now we had enough slack rope to work with and the block with shackle attached, was free to be fixed in place.

The pad-eye which the block was to be shackled to, was on the mast, above the tops'l yard, meaning I had to stand on the yard to fix the block in position. This was going to be challenging but, going up the windward side of the rigging, it would have been almost impossible to fall off, with the gale at my back. Clipping on as I climbed, I stepped onto the top of the yard. Reaching up, I snapped my long clip into the adjacent pad-eye then, reaching down to the extent of my harness, took the block and shackle from Amy, who was now in the rigging holding up the working end.

Up on the yard again, with short harness tethered tight, feet braced against the rolling of the ship and gale, reaching up, I was able to use both hands to shackle the block into the required pad-eye, being ultra-careful not to drop the pin. Job done!

Looking around, I was overcome with a great feeling of euphoria. I had never felt more alive. I realised for the first time that it had grown dark. I couldn't see the sea. The ship's downlights were illuminating our working area.

Back on the platform the new rope was unhitched from the railing and the line from the fore tops'l to the block above our head became taught. Keeping the tension, we could now pull the remainder of the coil onto the platform then pass the end down between the mast and the grating. Amy climbed down from the platform, reaching for and grabbing the dangling line, then hitched the end to her harness, leading the line down to deck level. When all the Dynema was back on deck, I followed, discovering the Mate and his team had taken a turn on a belaying pin at the fife rail, hauling the makeshift brace tight. The fore tops'l yard was secure again.

Discarding oilskins in the alleyway of the upper mess, it seemed very quiet and warm, out of the wind. I looked at the galley clock and was astonished to see it was almost 2200hrs. We'd been up the mast nearly four hours. I was ravenous and looking to get a mug of tea and a sandwich. Surprisingly and very welcoming, Dave the Cook was still in the galley, patiently waiting our return.

"If you lads and lasses are working, I'm working," said the jolly Cook, lifting a big pan of steaming savoury mince onto the counter, to be accompanied by mashed potato. Dinner was quickly served for the hands, newly in from the rolling deck. At this point I was extremely pleased not to have eaten a portion of this rib-sticker before going aloft.

Warm, and full of food, I could feel my eyes closing. It was going to be an early night.

Next day, at the morning meeting, with the weather easing, Captain Richard announced that we'd be bringing the damaged sail down. This came as no surprise, but then he went on to say we'd be putting the spare tops'l in place before lunch. "The tops'ls are our main drivers," he said. "We need their input if we're to continue sailing," he added, emphatically.

The Captain then announced he'd be assisting in the process. That 'was' new, though not necessary.

Each mast on the ship was fitted with two gantlines, one on each side. These heavy-duty, inch-diameter, plaited nylon ropes, with both ends fastened at deck level, abaft the mast, each led to the top of the mast and was reeved through a large, heavy-duty metal block. The gantlines were multi-use but were positioned for 'rescue from aloft'. We'd need the main, port gantline to lower the damaged tops'l to the deck, then to haul the replacement aloft.

This operation was to take place over the front of the yards, so a volunteer was required to climb to the top of the main mast then, with an assistant below to release one end, haul the gantline aloft, before running the long rope over the top of royal yard and its lift, then down in front of the yards to the tops'l. This was a physically tough job, and the ship's rolling was accentuated hugely at the top of the mast. I'd re lead gantlines many times, but on this occasion was pleased when Amy volunteered.

Meanwhile Beth and I were on the yard, one each side, with a couple of willing helpers, working from the middle outwards. On the arrival of the gantline end, the Bosun hitched the rope near the mast, ready for use. We began cutting the stitching on the rail-bands then, releasing these short lines from the jackstay, passing each around the sail then back though its eyelet, hitching each, to keep the sail sausage-shaped. Most gaskets were released, leave occasional ones to support the weight of the sail on the yard. Hands on deck released the buntlines, enabling us to detach these from the foot of the sail, hitching the slack lines to the jackstay, ready for the next sail.

At the end of the yard, out on the flemish horse, the head of the sail had been hauled taut, with many turns between the stainless ring in the top corner of the sail and the metal lug on the yard end. This line was also stitched. Five minutes saw its release.

The heavy bottom corner of the sail, with metal clew ring sewn into the corner, was shackled into the slack wire sheet, leading up from the course yard below. The eye in the shackle pin was moused with stainless wire, ensuring safety. Cutting the seizing wire with pliers and unshackling the pin, I allowed the corner of the sail to fall. The first gasket arrested the drop. The sheet wire was lightly shackled to the jackstay, again awaiting the replacement sail.

Beth had retrieved the end of the gantline and I helped her take a round turn around the middle of the sail, then, make a bowline in the standing part of the rope, shouted, "below, on deck, take the weight," to the team on the gantline.

The group began to haul on the nylon rope, pulling the doubled sail upwards. This was heavy work, with someone taking up the slack on a belaying pin. On each side, we let gaskets go until the sail was free, doubled and dangling from the mast top. The Bosun fastened a heaving line through the two clew rings then dropped the heavy end of the line to the deck; our work was done for now. The team on the gantline lowered away and the folks on the heaving line pulled the doubled sausage onto the deckhouse roof. That was the easy bit, and gravity had done most of the work. Now it was time for an early Smoko, then the harder part.

The replacement sail had been stretched along the deck with the 'head' on top. Front, port and starboard were marked with black ink. The rail bands and long head-lines had been transferred from the damaged sail and the gantline hitched round the centre.

We now needed more hands on the yard to replace the spare sail. With a few useful volunteers and the Captain, we had three each side and the Old Man in the middle. Beth and I would each take an end.

On the Bosun's call, the team on deck hauled on the gantline, reversing the earlier process, hauling the middle of the new tops'l to the top of the mast; a heaving line keeping the now swinging, doubled sail steady. With the middle of the sail high enough, the ends were within reach and could be spread along the yard as the heavy sail was slowly lowered again. It was critical to ensure the sail was facing the correct way and had no twists. Slack gaskets would help support the weight, as the bulk was handed along the yard.

I was given the long headline, Beth received the other, and I passed this line through the head eye at the end of the yard then, with assistance, back through the stainless ring in the sail, giving me some purchase to help stretch and draw the bulk of the tops'l along the yard. The middle of the sail was now in its approximate position, indicated by an arrow, marked in felt tip on the centre line.

This gave Captain Richard the opportunity to fasten a couple of rail bands to hold the weight, then release the gantline from the sail, hitching the loose end.

On my side, with assistance, we hauled the sail as tight as possible, fastening an occasional rail-band and slack gasket. I took several more turns between the two eyes and hauled tight, knowing we'd now pulled the centre arrow several inches in our direction.

Beth and her team had also drawn the starboard side tight, then to get the head of the sail even tighter, they'd attached a small, 'handy billy', a two to one block and tackle on the end. As the Bosun and her team hauled on the purchase, I gently eased my line till the Captain yelled, "OK, that's back on the centreline."

Now everyone began fixing the rail bands, while the Bosun and I, at opposite ends, re-shackled the clews to the sheet wires. On our way back off the yard we re-fastened the buntlines. The mousings and stitching could wait till later.

No sooner were we off the yard than the Mate was rounding up volunteers to set the sail. It was almost lunchtime, but there was still one job left to do. Someone had to climb to the top of the mast to re lead the gantline.

I rolled my eyes, dreading the request, but to her credit, Bosun Beth said, "get cleaned up for lunch all of you. I'll re lead the gantline."

"Oh! to be young and fit," I thought.

There was a great sense of achievement at lunch and to add to the atmosphere, Captain Richard announced he would treat all hands to a Devon cream tea when we arrived in Dartmouth; our first landfall.

No one was impressed when I said the old clipper ships changed their entire suit of sails twice outward bound, and again on the homeward passage. Old, worn, thinner sails were flown in the tropics where the sun's harmful rays would rot the canvas.

The Captain was as good as his word, and when the voyage crew had left the ship in Dartmouth, all hands were taken to a quaint, seventeenth century, converted, two story building, which was now a café/restaurant. The dozen people that trooped up the rickety stairs must have been the most unlikely group of customers the establishment had served for some time.

* * *

Sailing on *Lord Nelson* had been life changing for me, and whenever I left the ship, I always looked to the programme for more passages. I'd sometimes have four or more trips lined up in a season.

The Jubilee Sailing Trust was inspirational. There are few places in life where people turn up constantly, at their own expense, giving time, seeking no reward, yet gaining so much. To be able to use lifelong skills that would otherwise remain dormant is a great feeling. To help change lives, encourage those less able to reach personal goals is a wonderful feeling. I'd never found so much good will and camaraderie anywhere.

While volunteering on the ships I'd made about ninety voyages, plus many maintenance journeys, near and far. I'd sailed as far afield as Fiji, Australia, North and South America, Ireland, the Baltic and European ports, the Mediterranean and North and South Atlantic, yet my favourite region was the Scottish Western Isles, Orkney and Shetland.

I'd worked willingly and for free, the rewards far greater than my input and I'd gained many lifelong friends. I'd sailed with thousands of voyage crew and had dozens of regular shipmate friends, whom I sailed with frequently.

During my years of sailing I'd met many Captains, none finer than Captain John Etheridge. Short in stature, bearded, dark, but greying hair and twinkling eyes, 'Ethel' wore his authority lightly. His interaction with the voyage crew made everyone feel special and involved.

It was amusing to watch him on his rounds. Captain John always carried a clipboard, making notes and stopping to talk with everyone. "People think I'm working when I carry this," he'd say, pointing to the board. On departing, he'd add, "carry on with, err, whatever it is you're doing?"

In addition to his Master's certificate, Ethel also had a pilotage licence for the Solent, which meant he could take the ship from the English Channel all the way to her berth in Southampton. It was very convenient not having to wait for a pilot, but the qualification also saved significant expense to the JST in pilotage fees.

* * *

Alan Bishop came to the Jubilee Sailing Trust late, not being aware the organisation existed. I first sailed with Alan in the

Canaries. A retired Chief Petty Officer in the Royal Navy, he was immediately inspired by the company and ethos the ships gave, and subsequently spent as much time as possible on board. With his age, grey beard and being ex RN, he was quickly dubbed, 'Uncle Albert', a character from the well-known television series, 'Only Fools and Horses'.

The old boy was a tireless worker and would always find a job, whether sweeping up, peeling spuds or wiping plates, when not on watch. During his time in the RN, Alan had been part of one of the navy's Field Gun teams.

These amazing, tough men could strip a field gun down to its component parts, haul these parts over two walls using a pair of tripods, (sheer-legs) then re-assemble the gun and fire a blank round. Alan's role was to swing across from wall to wall with an eight-stone, gun carriage wheel on each shoulder.

Competition between the UK's naval bases in the annual tournament at Earls Court was fierce, and against the clock. The prestige gained by the winning team was enormous, and the participants were legends.

* * *

It was so dreadfully sad, and the end of an era when, due to lack of funds, in October 2019, *Lord Nelson* was decommissioned and laid up in Bristol. All her electronics, furnishings, awards and nautical trophies were stripped out, and the ship left to rot. No funds were available for maintenance and throughout the Winter and following Summer, her plating rusted and her decks turned green.

I found it heart-breaking that this wonderful old lady, that had changed so many lives and carried thousands of people's happy memories, should meet such an ignominious demise.

In Spring 2020 *Tenacious* returned from the Caribbean and was due for a massive, costly, twenty-year refit with sticks (masts) drawn. Due to the Covid19 pandemic the ship was laid up in Barrie Docks for six months. At the time of writing the refit is due to be completed early in December 2020. She'll then passage to Portland where, funds permitting, will await the post-pandemic summer season.

Had *Lord Nelson* been sold as a going concern, as some suggested, the funds generated could have paid for the *Tenacious* refit, and the old lady would have continued sailing, keeping her stately dignity.

There is much I could write about the past six years of management of the ships by the CEO and Trustees, but this would tarnish all the wonderful, happy times I'd experienced. I pray the Jubilee Sailing Trust survives to continue changing lives.

* * *

Much has changed in Scarborough Harbour during my lifetime. The successful trawler fleet is no more. The port is now predominantly a shellfish landing base. Local and visiting boats discharge lobster, crab, scallops and langoustine, mostly for export.

There are few of the original families of my youth making a living from the port. Fishermen no longer live close to their place of work. The character and characters have gone. It has been a privilege to have known and recorded these special times and to have been part of the Scarborough fishing community.

During a career at sea fishing, and on many voyages on tall ships, I've seen nature in all its glory; storms, calms, fabulous sunrises and sunsets, and the heavens as they are seldom seen on shore. There have been sightings of all manner of sea creatures, from turtles to whales, with a myriad of creatures in between. I am profoundly grateful.

Fred Normandale

January 2021

Gone but not forgotten

Denk Mainprize

Rory Railton

Harry Sheader

'Young' Bill Pashby

Ron 'Bonzo' Smalley

Pete Exley

Kenny Leader

Marina Drydale nee Crawford

Dennis Crawford

John Crawford

Fred Normandale 'Dad'

Doris Smith – Mother in Law

Mick Bayes – Diver/Engineer

Colin Bell – Diver

Shirley Oakes

Larry Mainprize

Alan Kitto

Alana Parker – Accountant and friend

Bill 'Biscuit' Jenkinson

Pete Ibbotson – Bridlington Skipper

George & Hazel McLean

Wilton Jones – Watch-leader/Teacher

Keith Bacon – Watch-leader/Marine artist

Fiona Spears – Ships Cook

Dot Arnold

Patsy Crawford

Jim Sheader

Dave Bevan

Bruce Temple

Michael Anderson (Big Andy)

Appendix I

I'd found the life and stories of whaling from New England fascinating and have reproduced the following, copied from the website of the New Bedford Whaling Museum, with grateful thanks for their permission.

Life on a Whaleship

Although the crew's rations ranged from unpleasant to revolting, hard work gave them good appetites, even for greasy pork, hard biscuits, and cockroach-laden molasses.

An isolated society: The whaleship was an isolated community that roamed the oceans of the world on journeys that lasted for years. In Etchings of a Whaling Cruise (New York, 1846), J. Ross Browne describes the crew's quarters called the forecastle, or, in sailor's parlance, the fo'c'sle:

"The forecastle was black and slimy with filth, very small and hot as an oven. It was filled with a compound of foul air, smoke, sea-chests, soap-kegs, greasy pans, tainted meat," sea-sick Americans and foreign ruffians. The ruffians were "smoking, laughing, chattering and cursing the green hands who were sick. With groans on one side, and yells, oaths, laughter and smoke on the other, it altogether did not impress [me] as a very pleasant home for the next year or two. [I was] indeed, sick and sorry enough, and heartily wish [myself] home."

How long is long?: The larger a vessel, the greater distances it could travel. The whaling schooner, the smallest whaler, generally undertook 6-month voyages, while brigs, barks, and ships might be at sea for three or four years. * The longest whaling voyage is believed to be that of the Ship Nile from 1858 to 1869 -- eleven years!

Men on board: The size of the crew depended on the size of the vessel and the number of whaleboats it carried – ranging from sixteen up to at least 36 on the largest ships.

These men were organized in a rigid hierarchy of Officers and crew: *The Captain was absolute master of this strange floating world; *The Officers – three or four Mates – were next in rank, each commanding a whaleboat. *The boatsteerers were the harpooneers and enjoyed more privileges than the rest of the crew; *The blacksmith, carpenter, cook, cooper (caskmaker), and steward also ranked higher than ordinary crewmen. When the crew chased a whale, these men remained behind as shipkeepers; *The foremast hands were the ordinary crewmen.

How they were paid: Each man received a "lay," or percentage of the profits, instead of wages, the size depending upon his status. The captain earned the largest share, perhaps 1/8th, and the green hand (inexperienced crewman) the least, as little as 1/350th. An ordinary crewman might earn only $25.00 for several years work.

Earning less than nothing: The crew might receive nothing on a voyage where profits were low. Even on a profitable trip, a whaleman might end up in debt to the shipowners. Cash advances for his family or to spend in ports of call, and any tobacco, boots, or clothes he purchased from the ship's store were charged against his lay. In debt as they sailed into home port, many men immediately signed on for another voyage.

Sleeping and eating: Meals and quarters reflected the ship's class structure:
- The Captain slept in a stateroom and enjoyed a cabin with a sofa and chairs in the stern (rear) of the ship. He ate the

best meals on shipboard. Ducks, pigs, and chickens were often carried in crates to provide meat for his table;

- The mates had smaller cabins in the stern and ate meals with the Captain in the main cabin;

- The boatsteerers (harpooneers) and the more skilled members of the crew, such as the blacksmith and cooper, had bunks in the steerage – an irregular-shaped compartment in the middle of the ship (midship). They ate in the main cabin after the captain and mates left, usually being served the same meals, except for butter and sugar. Like ordinary hands, they used molasses to sweeten their coffee or tea;

- The foremast hands – ordinary crewmen – slept in the forecastle, a narrow triangular-shaped room under the deck in the bow (front) of the ship, in narrow bunks that lined the walls. The only seats were the men's sea chests. In fair weather, the cook's helper carried tubs of food to the deck and the crewmen ate there, retreating below deck during foul weather.

An appetite for salt horse: Although the crew's rations ranged from unpleasant to revolting, hard work gave them good appetites, even for greasy pork, hard biscuits, and cockroach-laden molasses. Other fare included "salt horse" (heavily salted beef, pork, or horse), beans, rice, or potatoes. The chance to eat something fresh was a treat. At ports of call, fresh water, fruits, and vegetables were taken aboard. Cooks became used to preparing sea turtles, dolphins, sea birds, and fish. A ship cruising off the African coast once harpooned and ate a hippopotamus.

Living with accidents, vermin, and punishment: Apart from the dangers of the hunt, life on a whaleship could be unpleasant:

- Rats, cockroaches, bedbugs, and fleas were facts of life, perhaps because of the oil and blood that were not removed from the decks by scrubbing. The men endured these creatures in their food, in their bunks, and on their bodies – Sharp-edged tools, hostile natives, and shipboard arguments led to injuries. It was usually the captain who

dealt with illnesses, using limited knowledge and supplies
from the medicine chest. Occasionally, a Captain's wife on
board would nurse ailing crewmen

- Punishments included being "put in irons" and flogging
  (whipping). If a man disobeyed orders or otherwise
  displeased captain or mate, he suffered one or the other.
  The "cat-o'-nine-tails" (a whip of nine knotted lines)
  was often used. It was painful for the crewman who
  experienced it, and frightening for others to watch.

top

A Multi-Racial Enterprise

During most of the history of American whaling, ships drew their
crews from men of varied racial and ethnic backgrounds. The early
deep sea whalers usually carried crews of:

- Yankees from New England and Long Island;
- Gay Head Indians from Martha's Vineyard; and
- Negroes, as African-Americans were called at the time. On
  some ships, the men on board were all neighbors. It was
  possible in those days to begin as a foremast hand and work
  up to the position of Captain.

As the industry grew and New Bedford became its greatest center,
more men were needed for an increasing number of ships.
Although Yankees still went whaling, few shipped out as foremast
hands more than once. It was a cruel way to make a living and
the financial rewards were too few for all except the captain, the
Officers, and some of the more skilled members of the crew.

A League of Nations on board: Captains and ship owners picked
up hands wherever they could find them. Of a ship's crew, half
might be Americans, while the rest came from other nations. On
some vessels, the crew was entirely foreign-born. Racial and cultural
stereotypes persisted and three groups in particular experienced
limitations on advancement: African-Americans; Cape Verdeans;
Pacific Islanders (also known as "Kanakas," a term derived from
the Polynesian "Te Enata," which means "the men").

A kind of racial harmony: Genuine integration did not exist on most American whaleships, and violence sometimes flared. In general, however, men who were packed into tight quarters for years at a time and subject to the nearly unlimited power of the Captain and Officers, usually found it wise to tolerate each other.

Dealing with boredom: Whalemen devised ways of filling hours of inactivity: * Socializing In the late afternoon and early evening, most hands came on deck to socialize. They puffed on pipes, talked, read, mended clothes. They often broke into high-spirited singing and dancing. " *Scrimshaw is an art form developed by American whalemen, who used long hours of idleness and the availability of whale teeth and baleen (keratinous strips found in the mouths of baleen whales) to carve homecoming presents for loved ones. The most popular items were etched teeth and jagging wheels (pastry crimpers). The term "scrimshaw" also covers pieces whalemen created from sea shells, coconuts, tortoise shell, and other materials (Go to Scrimshaw: The Whaleman's Art for more information); Gams When whaleships met on the high seas, they usually held a "gam," an exchange of visits. This was a distinctive whaling custom. (Merchant ships, intent on getting cargoes to port quickly, exchanged only brief greetings.) The whaleboats ferried between the ships so that every crewman had a chance to exchange news and socialize. A gam might last a day or a week, but eventually the ships would separate and the crews would return to lonely hours of waiting for whales.

Logbooks: Logbooks were kept by the captain or first mate for all the ship's records. Routine entries recorded the ship's position (location), whales captured, the number of barrels of oil they yielded, wind direction, accidents and sicknesses on board, and anything else the logkeeper considered important. Private journals kept by crew members also recorded details of daily life on shipboard.

Chores: Days, weeks, sometimes months passed between whale sightings. Some time was filled with routine chores, such as washing the deck, setting sail (increasing or decreasing the number of sails on the masts), steering, or standing watch at night.

Routine days: The entire entry for November 18, 1858 for the Bark Ocean Bird records: "At daylight land in sight bearing E. by N. distant 50 miles -- wind light -- all hands variously employed -- ship steering E. by S. -- cook still off duty with the venerial."

And dramatic ones: A collection of logbooks analyzed by historian Stuart Sherman contains details of "castaways, mutinies, desertions, floggings, women stowaways, drunkenness, illicit shore leave experiences, scurvy, fever, collisions, fire at sea, stove boats, drownings, hurricanes, earthquakes, tidal waves, shipwrecks, ships struck by lightning, men falling from the masthead, hostile natives, barratry [fraud by a captain or crew at the expense of the shipowners], brutal Skippers, escape from Confederate raiders, hard luck voyages and ships crushed by ice."

Mutinies: Uprisings on whaleships were remarkably rare, considering the harsh conditions their crews suffered. Occasionally, however, a leader would rouse his fellow crewmen to action. On the New Bedford whaler Junior, mutineers killed all the Officers except the first mate one Christmas night. The crew, miserable over rotten meat they had been forced to eat, were led by Cyrus Plummer, who was angry about a flogging he had received. All the mutineers were eventually captured and punished.

Ports of Call: "In their search for oil," Richard Ellis writes in his book Men and Whales, "the roving whalers opened the world, much as the explorers of the 16th century had done in their quest for the wealth of the Indies."

Plum-pudding whaling: In the early years of American whaling, voyages were restricted to the Atlantic Ocean. A common route was to cruise south in Spring to the West Indies, then to the Azores, stopping at ports in these Portuguese islands, where whalers picked up fresh food,water, and additional crew. From there, the ships cruised past the Cape Verde Islands and the west coast of Africa, before recrossing the South Atlantic to the Brazil Banks or Falkland Islands. Returning to New England in July, the whalers refitted, then sailed for the Davis Straits between Greenland and

North America for the Summer. These relatively brief voyages were known as "plum-pudding whaling."

The vast expanse of the Pacific: The Rebecca of New Bedford sailed around the Horn (the southernmost tip of South America) in 1793, becoming one of the first whalers to enter the Pacific from an American port, launching the era of round-the-world- whaling.

Yankee whalers encountered scores of small islands and gave them Yankee names. They saw the mysterious stone faces of Easter Island, the lush isles of Hawaii, the frightening snowfields of the Antarctic. They sailed into Japanese waters and from there into the Arctic Ocean. After Captain Thomas W. Roys discovered bowhead whales in the Arctic in 1848, New Bedford ships soon followed. (See Arctic Whaling for more information.)

A unique way of life: Men – and sometimes families – on whaleships lived in a strange, floating world and experienced a way of life that was unlike any other. Its rigors repelled all but the hardiest and most adventurous, or those who were desperate for work or companionship. As Everett S. Allen wrote in Children of the Light, "Never, in all of man's history, has there been anything comparable to whaling in terms of what it demanded of those afloat who pursued it or of the vessels in which they sailed."

Appendix II

This section is my concise version of the inquiry into the loss of *Trident*.

The original report ran to 50 pages including several annotations from Mr MacWhirter.

MERCHANT SHIPPING ACT 1995
SECTION 269

REHEARING OF THE FORMAL INVESTIGATION
INTO THE LOSS OF THE
MOTOR FISHING VESSEL "TRIDENT"
REGISTERED AT PETERHEAD (OFFICIAL NUMBER
PD111)

REPORT BY
SIR STEPHEN S T YOUNG BT QC
SHERIFF PRINCIPAL OF GRAMPIAN, HIGHLAND
AND ISLANDS

MR F G NORMANDALE
MR N MACWHIRTER
ASSESSORS

To the Secretary of State for Transport

In pursuance of paragraph 12(b) of the Merchant Shipping (Formal Investigations) Rules 1985 I append my report on the rehearing of the formal investigation into the loss of the motor fishing vessel Trident registered at Peterhead (Official Number PD111).

Sir Stephen S T Young Bt QC

Sheriff Principal of Grampian, Highland and Islands

We concur in this report

Mr F G Normandale   Mr N MacWhirter

Assessor   Assessor

On 3 October 1974 the motor fishing vessel Trident and the seven members of her crew were lost at sea some distance to the south-east of Wick on the north-east coast of Scotland. Despite extensive searches, only a few items of wreckage were found, and of these only a lifebuoy and a liferaft were positively identified as having come from the Trident. There was no trace of the vessel or her crew, namely:

Position	Name	Age
Relief Skipper	Mr. Robert C. Cordiner.	36 yrs.
Engineer/Mate	Mr. Alexander Ritchie, Part Owner.	35 yrs.
Deckhand	Mr. George W. Nicol.	58 yrs.
Cook	Mr. Alexander Summers.	32 yrs.
Deck hand	Mr. James B. Tait.	32 yrs.
Deck hand	Mr. Thomas Thain.	32 yrs.
Deck hand	Mr. Alexander Mair.	30 yrs.

It had originally been indicated to the court that the RFI would last no more than three weeks. Regrettably, as all too often happens in cases such as this, this turned out to be a serious underestimate.

Ideally, I should have liked the inquiry to have been completed in one continuous session, however long this took. But for a variety of reasons which I need not elaborate upon here this was not possible. In the event four sessions were required and these took place between 19 October and 17 November 2009 inclusive, 22 February and 30 March 2010 inclusive, 25 May and 14 June 2010 inclusive and 12 to 14 July 2010 inclusive. In those four sessions the court sat to hear evidence and/or submissions on a total of fifty-five days.

I am persuaded that it would be helpful if I were to concentrate upon the questions which were stated by the Advocate General for Scotland, the first and last of which in particular seem to me to go to the heart of what this case is all about.

To make better sense of the story as a whole I shall take them in a rather different order from that in which they were stated by the Advocate General for Scotland.

6. In approximately what position is it now considered that the Trident was lost?

The wreck of the Trident was found lying on the seabed in position Latitude 58°20.24' N Longitude 002°40.09' W, and <u>it may be</u> <u>assumed therefore that this is where she was lost</u>. This position is approximately 11.9 nautical miles south east of the position (58°30' N 002°53' W) at which Mr. Lawrence Draper was asked to assess the wind and sea conditions for the purposes of the OFI.

7. What was the state of the weather, wind, sea state and visibility in the area traversed by the Trident leading up to and at the place and time when the Trident is considered to have been lost?

The Meteorological Office's summary of the weather conditions on 3 October, 1974 in the sea areas Cromarty and Fair Isle described the sea waves as having been "Rough (8 – 13 feet high) becoming very rough (13 – 20 feet) after midday". The wind was described as "NE to N Force 6 (25 knots) to gale 8 (35 knots) increasing to Force 9 (45 knots) in east of Cromarty during the late afternoon and evening" which compares well with AMI's estimate at the site of the sinking of Force 8 and Fugro GEOS' estimate of Force 7.

8(a) What was the condition of loading of the Trident at the time she was considered to have been lost?

Very many hours of court time were taken up during the RFI with an examination of the expert witness for the six families in regard to the lightweight and deadweight (and hence displacement) of the Trident at the time of her loss. I do not suppose that anyone who listened to all these hours of evidence could have been left in any doubt that the assessment of such matters is at best an inexact science, so that all that can realistically be hoped for are estimates that may be more or less reliable depending upon a variety of factors. This was rightly recognized by the members of the JPE. Thus, referring to their estimate of 150.59 tons for the Trident's lightship weight at the time of her loss.

The above TRIDENT Lightship figure is by no means certain. It is only as good as the limited documentary information available, and the best interpretation of the history and construction for both vessels, TRIDENT and SILVER LINING.

8(b) Were the intact statical stability characteristics of the Trident in substantial compliance with those recommended for fishing vessels by:

(i) the Department of Trade and Industry at the time of construction and completion of the vessel with regard to each of the standard loading conditions applicable to the vessel; and

(ii) the Department of Trade at the time of loss with regard to the estimated loss condition?

The intact statical stability characteristics recommended for fishing vessels both at the time of the construction and completion of the Trident and at the time of her loss were those contained in the IMCO 1968 Resolution A.168 (ES.IV).

8(c) What was the policy of the Department of Trade at the time of the loss of the Trident in relation to compliance with the statical stability criteria?

At the time of the loss of the Trident the Department of Trade did not insist upon full compliance with the IMCO recommended intact stability criteria. It was the policy of the Department to seek substantial compliance with these criteria, and it would have had regard to the extent to which a deficiency in one criterion could be compensated for by an excess in another.

8(d) Was the loss of the Trident caused or materially contributed to by any lack of statical stability?

No.

1.   Having regard to the evidence which is now available, what was or were the probable cause or causes of the loss of the Trident?

At the time of her loss the Trident was sailing at approximately 7 ¾ knots through the water. The wind and seas would have been on her port quarter. These conditions were modelled in the MARIN tank tests, and on many occasions in the course of the inquiry a DVD was played which showed the Trident capsizing on five occasions during test runs in the MARIN basin.

In a number of test runs, the model capsized suddenly in a manner that followed a consistent pattern. Typically, when the vessel encountered a deep trough followed by a large wave, she initially heeled to windward (port) in the trough.

The following large wave – generally near or at breaking – caught the stern causing her to yaw to port in combination with a fast roll to starboard. The bow of the vessel was thus held while the upward force of the wave action under the stern area further rolled her over beyond the point of vanishing stability.

The number of capsizes in the scale model tests was small and most large wave groups did not produce sinking (capsize) in the above manner, suggesting that position and movement relative to the wave were critical.

No statistical correlation was found between capsizes and any of the test variables – i.e. course, speed, wave height, wave steepness. This does not mean that such a relationship does not exist.

In layman's language I think three features of this capsizing mechanism stand out, namely (1) the absence of any warning (for example in the vessel's motions on the surface of the water) of what was about to happen, (2) the violence with which the vessel was thrown over onto her beam ends, and (3) the speed with which this happened. Thus the speed of the vessel's rotation about her longitudinal axis was very much faster than the speed of rotation which would have been implied by her normal rolling period in the sea conditions in which she then found herself.

9.   Was the loss of the Trident caused or materially contributed to by the wrongful act or default of any person or persons?

No. Various cases of fault were advanced against Mr. David Tait, the majority owner of the Trident, the White Fish Authority (now in the form of the Sea Fish Industry Authority) and, principally, Mr. Andrew Cumming, the designer of the Trident. There were various permutations to these cases of fault. For present purposes I do not think it is necessary to analyse all these permutations or express any opinion on them. At the end of the day they all appeared to depend upon the basic proposition that the Trident as built fell short of the IMCO recommended criteria in certain respects, that the extent of this should have been ascertained before her loss and that something should thereafter have been done to correct, or at least alleviate, this shortfall.

2.   Having regard to the evidence which is now available, what possible causes of the loss of the Trident can be eliminated?

I have already discussed the significance of the fact that, as designed and built, the Trident did not comply fully with the IMCO recommended criteria and have discounted this as a cause of her loss. In my opinion the following additional possible causes can also be eliminated:

(i)   fire and/or explosion in the engine room;

(ii)   critical machinery failure;

(iii)   propulsion failure;

(iv)   engine room flooding through internal mechanical failure;

(v)   loss of rudder and/or steering gear failure;

(vi)   taking aboard a sea or succession of seas;

(vii)   trapping of water on deck due to undersized freeing ports (but see the response to question 3 below);

(viii) down-flooding into engine room through external openings;

(ix)   down-flooding into the fish hold through the main hatch and ice scuttles;

(x)   down-flooding into other parts of the hull through doors, hatches and other external openings;

(xi)   shift of weight leading to severe list (but see again the response to question 3 below);

(xii)   flooding of wheelhouse leading to loss of control;

(xiii) ship manoeuvring for man-overboard;

(xiv)   collision with another vessel;

(xv)   collision with a submerged vessel or object;

(xvi)   snagging of towed gear leading to severe list;

(xvii) major structural failure;

(xviii) grounding of the Trident followed by sinking;

(xix)   capsizing when running before the wind and sea due to pure loss of stability when poised on the crest of a wave;

(xx)   synchronous rolling; and

(xxi)   parametric rolling.

3.   Having regard to the evidence which is now available, what other possible causes of the loss of the Trident remain open?

If the large pair trawl net was lashed on a pallet in front of the wheelhouse when the Trident set out on her last voyage, then the fact that there was no apparent sign of it during the underwater survey conducted in 2006 indicates that it must have broken free at some stage. Due to the overhang of the front wheelhouse windows it appears possible that this could have happened without those in the wheelhouse being aware of it. In this event it could have been washed to the starboard side of the vessel's main deck as she rolled violently, and in that position, it would have blocked some at least of the starboard freeing ports. It is true that the MARIN work suggests that no great quantities of water would been shipped onto the vessel's deck by the action of the quartering seas. But in some of the DVD clips a certain amount of water can be seen slopping over the bulwarks, and with the weight of the prevailing wind and the waves breaking it is possible that more water may have come on board than was apparent as a result of the MARIN work. Moreover, there was evidence that water was apt to flood through the freeing ports when the vessel rolled markedly, as she clearly would have been doing immediately before her loss. So one way or another I think that it is possible that there may have been more water on the deck than was allowed for by the JPE, and the free surface effect of this coupled with the movement of the large net could have had a significant impact on the vessel's stability, especially if the freeing ports on the starboard side had been blocked by the net washing out along the bulwarks on that side unobserved by the crew in the wheelhouse. Plainly it must remain a matter for speculation whether these events did occur and, if they did, precisely what effect they would have had on the stability of the Trident at the time of her loss. But I do consider that a loss of stability attributable to a combination of water being trapped on deck and the movement of the large net is one possibility that has not been eliminated by the evidence led at the RFI.

5. As at the commencement of her last voyage, was the Trident unseaworthy (as determined by the standards which applied in 1974) and, if so, did this make a material contribution to her loss?

What is meant by the word "unseaworthy?" In my opinion a vessel is unseaworthy if, when operated with the degree of care and competence to be expected of an ordinarily careful and competent crew, she is not reasonably fit to survive the ordinary perils of the sea such as she might reasonably be expected to encounter during her operational lifetime. Apart from the fact that two external openings had not been properly secured, there is no evidence in this case to suggest that the Trident was being operated by her crew in anything other than an ordinarily careful and competent manner. And, while the circumstances which had generated the wind and sea conditions which obtained at the time of her loss may have been unusual, there was certainly nothing so exceptional about these wind and sea conditions as to take them outwith the ambit of the ordinary perils of the sea that the Trident might reasonably have been expected to encounter during her operational lifetime. <u>Yet the simple fact is that she did not survive these conditions, and it follows in my opinion that she was unseaworthy</u>. In saying this, I recognize of course that she had been operated safely for the eighteen months or so preceding her loss. But this had been chiefly in the Firth of Clyde and the Irish Sea and off the west coast of Scotland, the waters of which are not necessarily comparable with those to be found in the North Sea.

4.   **Has any new evidence been discovered to bear on the issue of the seaworthiness of the Trident in any respect that made a material contribution to her loss?**

During the survey in the Summer of 2006 it was ascertained that the port side focs'le door and the fish hatch were not fully secured as they perhaps should have been when the vessel was at sea in conditions such as those prevailing at the time of her loss. It may therefore be said that the vessel was unseaworthy at that time by reason of these insecure openings. But it is clear that these did not make any material contribution to the vessel's loss.

10.   **What, if any, beneficial lessons can be learned from the loss incident and passed on to the current fishing industry?**

The JPE report stated,

In light of the passing of 35 years from the time of the loss to the finalisation of this report, and given the considerable changes to navigational, communication, life-saving and fire-fighting equipment, and the changes to the methods and testing of ship design, the JPE are of the view that any safety lessons that could have been learned have been superseded by the passage of time.

I confess that when I first read this paragraph, I was somewhat surprised to find that the JPE supposed that no safety lessons were to be learnt as a result of their extensive investigations into the loss of the Trident. Having now heard what some of their members had to say in evidence on this subject, I can understand why they expressed themselves as they did, having regard to their limited understanding of precisely what it was about the Trident that led to her capsize.

*Captain Barbara Campbell with voyage volunteers
in the Southern Ocean – Dave Mercer*

*Engineer Marco, Fred the Fish and Watch-leader Dave
on the stern platform – Colin Woodhead*

First of the Flood

Fred Normandale

Slack Water

Fred Normandale

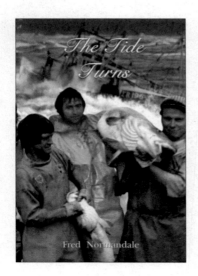

The Tide Turns

Fred Normandale

Ebbing Tide

Fred Normandale